Passage to the World

PASSAGE TO THE WORLD

The Emigrant Experience 1807–1940

KEVIN BROWN

Copyright © Kevin Brown 2013

First published in Great Britain in 2013 by
Seaforth Publishing,
Pen & Sword Books Ltd,
47 Church Street,
Barnsley S70 2AS

www.seaforthpublishing.com

British Library Cataloguing in Publication Data
A catalogue record for this book is available
from the British Library

ISBN 978 1 84832 136 6

Typeset and designed by M.A.T.S. Leigh-on-Sea, Essex
Printed and bound by CPI Antony Rowe, Great Britain

Contents

To Tommy and Lily Brown

Longa tibia exsilia et vastum maris aequor arandum
(Long-drawn-out is your exile
and boundless the oceans you must plough)

Publius Vergilius Maro, *Aeneid* II, 780

Preface

We are all migrants in some way, even if the journey is only from one street to the next or from one community to another, which is perhaps what makes us so interested in the story of those who embarked on a great adventure into the unknown, to a new and unfamiliar continent at a time when a journey by sea was hazardous and long. Shipwrecks and disease were only two of the perils to be faced and to embark on the journey demanded great courage. Just moving house can be stressful enough, without being completely uprooted and having to face unknown seas.

This book is about a journey of discovery, a rite of passage as the emigrant travelled between the old and new worlds, separated by the vast ocean. It is but a short incident in the journey to a new life. That journey began with the decision to seek out new shores, and perhaps only ended when the emigrant had established a new life, for better or for worse. Yet, for most migrants in the great age of emigration in the nineteenth and early twentieth centuries, that journey by ship was life-changing and an unforgettable experience at a time when travel was not easy and the sea held the terror of the unknown. Each emigrant had his or her own tale and unique experience, but it is the sum of those individual stories that helps us understand the experience of what it was like to travel on an emigrant ship.

The stories of those emigrants who sailed from Europe to the Americas, Australia and New Zealand, and on the coolie ships from India and China to the West Indies, Mauritius and South America, are all diverse. The length of the journey and the social and ethnic origins of the emigrants all made for differences. However, a major influence on all of these emigrant ships, for good or ill, was the abolition of the slave trade and the need for alternative uses for ships that had previously carried slaves, the need for a new form of human cargo, and for alternative sources of labour for the colonies and the new United States. The end of the transportation of convicts to Australia had a similar impact, while the standards laid down on the convict ships offered a model for emigrant ships which has benefited passengers ever since, including those on the luxury liners. Attempts to reform the iniquities of steerage and to learn the lessons from disasters striking emigrant ships also contributed to the improvement of maritime conditions from which the modern passenger and crew have profited – from medical care to lifeboats.

Although the common impression of emigrant ships is of the miseries of steerage, many emigrants travelled in more luxury, and considered themselves superior to those in steerage. They would probably have agreed with the Belgian legislation of 1876 which denied emigrant status to anyone on an emigrant ship taking their meals at the captain's or an officer's table, though it should not be forgotten that even a magnificent liner like the *Titanic* was officially classed as an emigrant ship. Inevitably, many of the memoirs of voyages on emigrant ships come from these better-off and more educated emigrants, but are still a marvellous source for understanding what it was like to be on those ships. Occasionally there is a voice from the humbler emigrant in the official record, however rare, which summons up their world as seen from below.

While the abolition of the slave trade, and then the boost to the emigrant business given by the end of the French Wars, makes a defined starting point for this book, the end date was always going to be more elastic. The First World War marked a watershed in the history of migration to the United States, when, following the peak of immigration from Europe, the war slowed it all down and in the early 1920s restrictions were put in place. Emigration to Australia, however, continued. The Second World War again brought a halt to the shipping of emigrants other than for the deportation to the dominions of enemy aliens. After the war, emigration continued but the story of the so-called 'ten-pound Poms' is another story, as is that of emigration in the reverse direction, the influx from the former colonies of immigrants to Britain beginning with the much-told voyage of the *Windrush*. In the post-war years too, emigration by air became more significant than by sea.

Research and writing inevitably involve ploughing a lone furrow through an ocean of source material and information, rather than being in the crowded huddle of steerage – yet none of it would be possible without the support and help of many people. The staffs of the various archives, libraries and museums that I have visited in the course of research for this book are all under pressure, as budgets and staffing levels are slashed as a result of the economic crisis, but they continue to give a service which is often undervalued. All of them are contributing to preserving and making available those original sources which make it possible to study and understand the past. I wish to thank them for carrying on with that essential work against the tide of sometimes unrelenting, woeful philistinism.

In Trieste, I am very grateful to Lorenzo Glavici for sharing with me his love of his native city and for giving me a tour of the city with an emphasis on Trieste's maritime and emigrant history, adding a personal dimension with his own family's story and experiences. David Evison of the Gibraltar History Society showed me Gibraltar's naval hospitals which gave me an insight into the places involved in the care for the survivors from the sinking of the *Utopia*. I also wish to thank for their help and support: Tudor Allen, Gale Lewis, Ron Dixon, Giuseppe Conti (Sindaco of Bardi), Denis Beiso of Gibraltar Archives, Lorna Swift of the Garrison Library in Gibraltar, and Robert Gardiner and his colleagues at Seaforth Publishing. I must also mention the late Duncan MacLeod of the University of Oxford, whose stimulating tutorials when I was studying a further subject on nineteenth-century American history, albeit at an undergraduate level, saw my first delving into the history of immigration, and reinforced in an inspiring way the view that history should be fun as well as intellectually demanding. There are also the people who, on learning of my latest project, have shown interest and made suggestions about avenues that may or may not be worth investigating, including members of the audience for the lectures I gave on the *Independence of the Seas* earlier this year, and an attendee at my lecture in Menorca in aid of the world's first permanent naval hospital in June 2011. Everyone who has helped or made suggestions for this book has shared that simple joy and enjoyment in studying history, which brings the past back to life and helps inspire the writer with the knowledge that there will be an appreciative and informed audience for another reconstruction of the past.

Indeed, so many people have expressed a personal interest in the emigrant story, shown by the large number of visitors I have seen on my visits to such emigration museums as Ellis Island, the Ballinstadt at Hamburg, the German National Emigration Museum at Bremen, the Museo del Mare in Genoa, the SS *Great Britain,* the Merseyside Maritime Museum, the Museum of London in Docklands, and the new Sea City Museum at Southampton, among many such museums, all of which I recommend to the interested reader. In 2013 a major new emigration museum, the Red Star Line Museum, opens at Antwerp. This suggests that emigration is a subject that continues to touch us all in this multicultural society. The emigrant ships helped to make the modern world, and it is their exciting, if sometimes monotonous, unfamiliar, and life-changing world we are about to explore.

London
21 September 2012

I

Seafaring Adventurers

Emigrant ships were a useful means of getting rid of inconvenient people. They were also as much melting points as the new countries and colonies to which they were carrying their human cargoes, all with their own reasons for uprooting themselves, their own hopes and dreams of a better future. The novelist Charles Dickens found the gloom of steerage a strange but positive world when he evoked it in 1850:

> I seemed to stand in a picture by Ostade. Among the great beams, bulks and ringbolts of the ship, and the emigrant-berths and chests, and bundles, and barrels, and heaps of miscellaneous baggage – lighted up, here and there, by dangling lanterns; and elsewhere by the yellow daylight straying down a windsail or a hatchway – were crowded groups of people making new friendships, taking leave of one another, talking, laughing, crying, eating and drinking; some already settled down with their households arranged, and tiny children established on stools or dwarf elbow-chairs; others despairing of a resting-place and wandering disconsolately. From babies who had but a week or two of life behind them, to crooked old men and women who seemed to have but a week or two of life before them; and from ploughmen bodily carrying out soil of England on their boots, to smiths taking away samples of its soot and smoke upon their skins; every age and occupation seemed to be crammed into the narrow compass of the 'tween decks.[1]

Just as aristocratic families sent off bothersome younger sons to the colonies, nineteenth-century novelists also found emigration useful for dispatching troublesome characters to a better future and to find a happy ending. At the end of *David Copperfield*, Charles Dickens optimistically depicted emigration to Australia as the answer to most problems. David Copperfield sees his friends sail off from Gravesend and considers that 'a sight at once so beautiful, so mournful, and so hopeful, as the glorious ship, lying still on the flushed water, with all the life on board her crowded at the bulwarks and there clustering, for a moment, bareheaded and silent, I never saw.'[2] The honest fisherman Peggotty recovers his pride and dignity after seeing his family torn apart by a philanderer; Little Emily, the deceived and fallen woman, finds redemption through caring for the sick and looking after children both on the voyage and in her future home; her equally morally frail friend Martha marries a farmer; and even that 'lone, lorn creature' Mrs Gummidge is more cheerful in a new country. The irrepressible and improvident Mr Micawber uncharacteristically manages to make a success of his life and ends up a magistrate, rather than the inmate of a debtor's prison which was his invariable lot in England. Yet in many ways, emigration is almost too convenient a literary device to tie up the untidy loose ends of existence and leave the hero with a perfect life at home. G K Chesterton purported to 'have a horrible feeling that David Copperfield will send even his aunt to Australia if she worries him too much about the donkeys', against which she waged ceaseless war when they trespassed on the grass in front of her cottage.[3]

It was not only in his fiction that Dickens as a reformer looked upon emigration as a solution to social problems. Together with his friend, the wealthy philanthropist Angela Burdett-Coutts, he was the founder of Urania Cottage, a home in Lime Grove, Shepherds Bush, for destitute young women, most of them rescued from prostitution. These real life equivalents of Little Emily and Martha in his autobiographical novel were trained as seamstresses and then sent to build new lives for themselves in Australia. In 1853, six years after setting up the home for the redemption of fallen women, Dickens reflected in his periodical *Household Words* on its success and on the salutary effects of beginning again in a new world:

Of these fifty-six cases, seven went away by their own desire during their probation; ten were sent away for misconduct in the home; seven ran away; three emigrated and relapsed on the passage out;

thirty (of whom seven are now married) on their arrival in Australia or elsewhere, entered into good service, acquired a good character and have done so well ever since as to establish a strong pre-possession in favour of others sent out from the same quarter.[4]

In his novel *The New Magdalen*, Dickens's friend Wilkie Collins also depicted emigration to the colonies as an answer for the fallen woman seeking to redeem herself, though with a twist to the usual tale. Collins's heroine, Mercy Merrick, is saved from prostitution by a young clergyman, Julian Gray, who not only rescues her from a life of sin but falls in love with her and marries her. Both of them now being beyond the social and ecclesiastical pale, the only solution is a new life in another country, and 'we shall find five hundred adventurers like ourselves when we join the emigrant ship, for whom their native land has no occupation and no home. Gentlemen of the Statistical Department, add two more to the number of social failures produced by England in the year of our Lord eighteen hundred and seventy-one – Julian Gray and Mercy Merrick.[5]

Dickens, more than Collins, shared an optimistic and constructive vision of emigration to the colonies with many of his contemporaries and depicted the voyage out as an exciting adventure, but many later writers have seen it as a much less positive experience for the emigrant. Perhaps the classic expression of this is the lyrical description of the horrors of steerage by the historian Oscar Handlin, which is an imaginative reworking of many first-hand descriptions, and heavily coloured by his own family legends of the trauma of being uprooted from a familiar homeland to find refuge on an unfamiliar continent. For Handlin, the emigrant ships were filled with 'seafaring adventurers out to discover new continents, amidst the retching noisome stench, the stomach-turning filth of hundreds of bodies confined in close quarters.'[6]

Whether optimistic or pessimistic, excited or apprehensive, the decision to emigrate was never taken lightly. Often it was the result of economic changes. Between the end of the French Wars in 1815 and the onset of the American Civil War in 1860, the main areas of Europe from which emigrants set out were the British Isles, Germany and Scandinavia, all of which had seen agrarian economies give way to industrial ones. Alongside a movement from countryside to town in search of new livelihoods went a movement to other countries and continents which seemed to offer greater opportunities. A second wave of emigration, reaching its peak at the end of the nineteenth century, originated in southern and eastern Europe. From Italy and Greece came unskilled labourers uprooted by the breakdown of traditional peasant economies. Emigrants from the Austro-Hungarian and Russian empires were also in search of shelter from religious and political persecution. Always there was a sense that things would be better in an unfamiliar country.

Such fallible hopes were often encouraged by official government-sponsored schemes which saw emigration as way of cleansing a state of its social problems. The British government in particular saw the value of emigration as a remedy for social distress, and as a safety-valve for economic discontent, when it encouraged its Irish subjects to seek refuge from the potato famine of the 1840s in far-off continents rather than see them flock to England, although for many Irish peasants expensive fares made it impossible for them to afford to go any further afield than the British mainland. The Irish Poor Law Act of 1838 had permitted the Irish poor law authorities to encourage emigration financially, powers extended in 1849 in the face of the famine.[7] Although it was only a small proportion of the total number of emigrants, the Irish Boards of Guardians assisted 45,000 emigrants between 1849 and 1906.[8]

Similarly, the 1834 Poor Law Amendment Act had allowed Boards of Guardians to borrow money to provide assisted passages for paupers.[9] Since the late eighteenth century Australia had been seen first as a dumping ground for convicts, and then as an economic resource calling out for colonisation. From 1831 the British government sponsored emigration to Australia that would come to define standards on commercial emigrant ships. It also encouraged settlers to move to Upper Canada and the Cape through appointing local recruiting agents, advertising assisted passages, and offering free land. Over 10,500 emigrants took advantage of these opportunities in South Africa and Canada between 1815 and 1825.[10]

Not all of the emigrants were paupers. Even with government subsidies, an emigrant still needed some means to move overseas.

Although 'it has been generally supposed that the free emigrants are all paupers, glad to escape from the thraldom and confinement of a union workhouse', it was more the case that:

> the chief portion are cottagers, most of whom have never received parish relief—families struggling with numerous difficulties to gain a precarious livelihood, and enduring severe privations and hardships in the inclement season of winter; and some few are persons who have been better off in the world, but, reduced by unforeseen events, are desirous of speculating with their little remnant of property, under a hope of retrieving their circumstances, and amongst these may be found individuals whose wounded pride cannot bear the thoughts of their old associates and friends witnessing their descent to poverty.[11]

For such people clinging to status and respectability, the opportunity to emigrate offered a way forward. Elizabeth Gaskell, like her friend Charles Dickens, saw government-sponsored emigration as a means of improvement for the disgraced but respectable poor when she sent the eponymous heroine of *Mary Barton* and her husband-to-be Jem Wilson off on an emigrant ship to a happy ending, after Jem's former master had 'been written to by Government to recommend an intelligent man, well acquainted with mechanics, as instrument-maker to the Agricultural College they are establishing at Toronto, in Canada. It is a comfortable appointment, house, land, and a good percentage on the instruments made.'[12]

The sale of Crown lands in the British colonies helped to provide the funds for the encouragement of emigration from the mother country, not so much for the relief of domestic problems as for the development of the colonies themselves, although the imperial government was always pleased when these two motives coincided. A short-lived Emigration Commission was established in 1831, followed by the Colonial Land and Emigration Commission in 1840, to provide information on opportunities in the colonies, and the sale of Crown lands in the colonies. Pamphlets, handbills and press releases were circulated with information for would-be emigrants. Agents throughout the country recruited and vetted candidates for assisted or free passages, and arranged for their voyages to the colonies, mainly Australia.[13] This governmental agency was closed in 1878 after complaints from the colonial governments about the quality and quantity of the migrants it sent out, and in 1886 the Colonial Office set up the Emigrants' Information Office, which confined itself to providing newspapers, co-operative societies, libraries and country clergymen with circulars, handbooks and posters on the opportunities available overseas to working men and women. It stressed that it was 'no part of the duties of the Emigrants' Information Office either to encourage or discourage emigration', in contrast to earlier initiatives.[14]

It was not until the beginning of the twentieth century that the British government again became actively involved in sponsoring emigration. The problem of cyclical depression and the resultant higher costs of poor relief once more suggested that the state should involve itself in emigration. Under the 1905 Unemployed Workmen Act, committees were set up to foster the emigration of the unemployed and their families. By the outbreak of the First World War, 26,430 emigrants had left Britain to go to Australia and Canada at a cost of less than £10 a head.[15] After the war, emigration was once more seen as a way of dealing with the perennial problem of unemployment. In 1919 free passages to the empire were offered to demobilised servicemen. This was regularised with the Empire Settlement Act of 1922 which provided free passage for ex-servicemen, and assisted passages for others, until it lapsed in 1972.

The governments of the dominions and colonies helped to fund such assisted passages but after the Second World War, when skill shortages and a declining birth rate made Britain less willing to lose skilled workers at a time when the dominions, especially Australia, were still calling for migrants, there was competition between the mother country and the former colonies for labour in an era when the austerities of life in post-war Britain made an escape abroad seem especially desirable.[16] In the 1949 film *The Huggetts Abroad*, emigration to South Africa seems the answer for a London family, when Jack Warner's Joe Huggett loses his job and his wife Ethel, played by Kathleen Harrison, has had enough of ration queues and make-do and mend, but homesickness, and a suspicion of anything that seems 'foreign', attracts them back home even before they reach their destination, a message that the British government would have found welcome in days of labour shortages.[17]

Colonial governments, keen to develop their economies and societies faster than any natural rate of increase dependent on birth rates would allow, were themselves active in recruiting immigrants of the desirable type. Official recruitment agents were appointed by the governments of New Zealand, Australia and Canada to encourage migrants to sail to their own countries from the 1850s onwards. Queensland was especially active, partly because it needed to try hard to attract people to a distant colony tainted in the popular mind with convict transportation. In 1860, a year after Queensland separated from New South Wales, Henry Jordan was appointed as the new colony's agent and spent the next five years lecturing on and advertising the advantages of moving to Queensland, as well as offering land grants to full-paying migrants and free passages to poorer emigrants. He arranged for the local passenger agents of the shipping company J Baines and Co, whose Black Ball line carried the migrants to Australia, to recruit and screen potential migrants in return for payment of a 5 per cent commission. These agents were often shopkeepers, 'well and respectably known in their different localities', who could call upon their local connections to select the right recruits.[18] Such respectable shopkeepers formed a contrast to some less reputable agents, such as the 'recruiting sergeants for emigration', Archibald MacLean and Roderick McLellan, who had been sent to Inverness gaol in 1802 for trying to lure emigrants from the Hebrides through parades of flags and bagpipes, the reading out of forged emigrant letters to raise expectations, and by getting their recruits drunk on 'vast quantities of spirits' before signing them up for emigration.[19]

Later, the dominions depended upon their high commissions to be responsible for advertising, recruiting and dispatching British emigrants to a 'Better Britain', where the ethos of the new country would reflect the old, but life would be very much better. Lectures, exhibitions, shopping days, advertisements and, once moving pictures had become popular, promotional films were all used to attract migrants. It was claimed that one poster campaign featured the biggest wall advertisement in London next to the site of Australia House in the Strand.[20]

It was not only colonial governments who were actively recruiting migrants, but also chartered land companies that had been granted or had purchased tracts of land they now wished to develop. The New Zealand Land Company, established in 1839 after claiming to have purchased two million acres from the Maoris for £9,000, hired agents to attract the labourers and craftsmen they needed to settle what was effectively virgin territory. These agents, who used pamphlets, prospectuses and handbills to publicise the attractions of New Zealand, made some attempt to vet the suitability of the settlers they had recruited, but such screening was often more perfunctory than it might have been, simply because of the need to fill the emigrant ships that had been chartered. The Otago and Canterbury Associations even sent pioneer settlers back home to sell the benefits and blessings of emigration to their family, friends and neighbours. It was a variation on the custom of publicising the real and manufactured letters home of migrants detailing their wonderful new lives in order to encourage others to follow their example.[21]

Many of the migrants attracted to move out to the colonies by emigrant agents were disillusioned by what they found in trying to build new lives on arrival. John Hillary, a shopkeeper from Tow Law, County Durham, had been persuaded to sell up and emigrate with his family to New Zealand in 1879 after hearing a lecture by the Reverend James Berry, an agent for the New Zealand government, and after reading the pamphlets Berry had distributed. However, arriving in New Zealand in the middle of a trade depression, Hillary had been unable to find work in Canterbury and was bitter about what he saw as 'the inconsistency of inveigling people away from their comfortable English homes by means of exaggerated and one-sided lectures and pamphlets, to sorrow, untold suffering, disappointment and almost despair.'[22] Hillary's ire against the agent who had tempted him to seek the 'promised land' in New Zealand was shared by other migrants, including Mr Howard from Consett, who had only managed to find twelve days' work in an office, and Mr Richards, casually employed, whose 'blood boiled when speaking of the Rev J Berry who had by letter advised him out, as he also did me.' Hillary, who returned home to England after six months, was 'sorry to have thus to speak of ministers, but what respect can we have for men who will so disgrace the sacred office as to stoop for money to such disreputable work.'[23]

Commercial companies followed colonial governments in recruiting both for industrial workers and also for professional and management staff. The 'Appointments Vacant' columns of such quality newspapers as *The Times* were filled with opportunities in the colonies for well-educated young men from middle-class backgrounds. In 1847 a free passage was offered to 'any qualified gentleman' surgeons wishing to go to Adelaide.[24] *The Times* in September 1889 had advertisements for an assistant engineer to work on a tea plantation in Assam, who should be aged about twenty-five, 'a thoroughly practical engineer of good education and social standing ... with experience in the control of labour', and who should be prepared to pay for his own passage out. The same issue of the newspaper also advertised on behalf of 'a young lady, well-educated, partly on Continent, domesticated and used to and very clever with children, would give services on voyage and afterwards, in return for passage out' to New Zealand.[25]

Meanwhile, other young professional men were using the 'Situations Wanted' columns to find jobs in the colonies before emigrating, as in 1848 where 'a gentleman of scientific attainments, who has had extensive and varied managerial experience with unexceptional references in the mining district of Wales and Cornwall, is desirous of a similar colonial engagement' in South Australia.[26] Another advertisement was addressed 'to families going to the Cape or Australia', who might wish to engage and offer a privately assisted passage to 'a steady healthy man aged 27, as a draper exclusively or to a general store', an employee who 'can keep books or act as corresponding agent, and willing to make himself useful'.[27] Such emigrants were highly desirable in the colonies, but equally might be considered a loss to the mother country that could not offer them the opportunities they sought overseas.

Not all states were so keen on encouraging emigration. Within the Russian and Austro-Hungarian empires there were mazes of restrictions on internal travel which added to the emigrant's difficulties. Not until 1857 did the Habsburgs recognise freedom of movement within their domains, but even then placed restrictions on travel abroad. Any emigrant, defined under a letter patent of Joseph II in

1784 as 'any person who moves from Our Hereditary Lands abroad with the intention of staying there', was deemed to have lost all his civil rights and could have his property confiscated. After 1834, 'legal emigration' without any loss of property rights was given official recognition, although the emigrant was still stripped of his citizenship. The laws were further liberalised after 1867 with penalties for emigration only applying to conscripts, though the avoidance of military service was often a prime motive for emigration.

Although the number of emigrants from central Europe continued to rise through the nineteenth century, it was officially discouraged. Brochures, fliers and newspaper advertisements encouraging emigration were banned, and in 1895 travel agents were forbidden to encourage emigration or even sell cargo hold tickets for the transoceanic ships of foreign shippers. After 1897 anyone encouraging emigration could be imprisoned.[28] Yet, despite the opposition of industrialists concerned about the loss of labour and the imperial armed forces fearing a reduction in the number of conscripts, emigration from Austro-Hungarian provinces continued, encouraged by such vested interests as shipping and railway companies. Critics of emigration such as the Austrian Alexander Löffler called for strong government action to make an exodus from the empire less attractive: 'Our government must pass economic, social and political measures to ensure the loyalty of the labour force of the homeland ... but the state cannot achieve that if it continues to run along with a truncheon like a policeman shouting "you must love me."'[29]

Most of the European empires were particularly concerned about maintaining the supply of conscripts and reservists for their armed forces, and forbade the emigration of anyone considered vital to the defence capabilities of the state. The German empire forbade any young man aged between seventeen and twenty-five from emigrating unless he had been granted special leave, had been freed from his obligation to do military service, or had provided a substitute in the army. In the realms of the Austro-Hungarian emperor, there were similar regulations forbidding anyone over seventeen from emigrating until military service had been completed, though permission might be granted to leave the country to any young man wealthy enough to deposit sums ranging from 100 to 1,000 crowns, as a guarantee that he would return to do his military service when his passport expired; defaulters forfeited their bail. Although emigration was very much regarded as a personal matter in Italy, permission to emigrate was refused if there were any suspicion that the emigrant was trying to evade his military obligations. This could be hard on eighteen-year-olds who, if considered to be good cannon fodder, might have to wait another ten years to the age of twenty-eight before they again had a right to emigrate. Even such small, ostensibly pacific, countries as Norway and Sweden limited the right of emigration of healthy young men who might be needed for national defence.[30]

The state might have a role in discouraging and encouraging migration according to its own needs and the economic and social problems it had to deal with, but philanthropy also had a part to play in encouraging men and women to seek a better life overseas. Stephen Vere Forster, a wealthy Anglo-Irish landowner, wrote a popular guide for emigrants[31] and spent over £55,000 of his own money in helping 22,615 Irish peasants to emigrate between 1849 and 1889.[32] In 1880 he wrote to the nationalist politician and proponent of Home Rule for Ireland, Charles Stewart Parnell, advocating 'assisted emigration as the most practicable and certain mode of, not only temporarily but permanently, relieving the present poverty and ever-recurring distress in the West of Ireland', since 'it is as natural and prudent for young people to emigrate from over-peopled countries to new regions as it is for young bees to swarm'. He himself was prepared to subsidise such emigrants leaving the distressed parts of western Ireland for the United States of America, at the rate of £2 per person up to a total of £15,000, as he considered that 'these persons have no reasonable expectation of improvement in their condition here, but they might, under your auspices, migrate to happier homes in a magnificent country which has an ever-increasing glorious future before it, and where there is already a greater number of inhabitants of Irish extraction than there is even in Ireland itself.'[33]

Local emigration societies were also established to encourage the migration of paupers. The Highland and Island Emigration Society was founded in 1852 under the patronage of Prince Albert, to alleviate distress among Scottish shepherds and farm workers. It was stressed that the aid given would not be 'gratuitous', but that 'the emigrants are required to pay, within a specified time, the sums advanced to them; and as the sum is repaid it will be employed in making advances to other needy persons desirous to emigrate; the emigrant repaying an advance will have the privilege of naming a person at home who will have a preferable claim to assistance.'[34] It was believed that these migrants were surplus to domestic labour needs, and that emigration could offer a speedy and cheap solution to the problem of rural poverty. The Wiltshire Emigration Society was formed in 1850 by the local landowners Earl Bruce and Sidney Herbert, and ensured that selected emigrants left on time, even paying the train fares of agricultural workers from Chippenham to Plymouth where they could embark on their voyages, equipped with a Bible and Prayer Book supplied by the Emigrants' Employment Society. Bruce, who took a keen personal interest in the Society and his charges, actually paid some of the deposits for the migrants himself and travelled with one of the largest groups of sponsored emigrants to inspect for himself the ships, *John Knox* and *Marion*, on which his people were to sail.[35]

Some trades unions also encouraged emigration by their members during the nineteenth century, and even acted as emigration agents. In 1873 the New Zealand authorities hired Henry Taylor and Christopher Holloway of the National Agricultural Labourers' Union to act as agents to select suitable migrants and accompany them all the way to New Zealand. They received twice the rates of pay of an average farm worker and their expenses for undertaking this role, using their standing among the agricultural communities of Warwickshire and Oxfordshire to attract migrants. The contingent set off from Leamington on 13 December 1873, picking up a further group from the village of Tysoe at Banbury, and yet more emigrants at Oxford, including villagers from Wootton. By the time they reached Plymouth, where wagons collected their baggage to take it to the depot, there were seven hundred men, women and children in the party. They set sail in two vessels of the New Zealand Shipping Company, the steamer *Mongol* and the sailing ship *Scimitar* on 23 and 24 December. Only once the entire group had arrived in New Zealand by early March 1874 and left quarantine was the job of Taylor and Holloway complete.[36]

Emigration was not only portrayed as a solution to rural poverty but also to urban deprivation. Such organisations as the East End

Emigration Society and the Church Emigration Society were responses to concerns about unemployment, low wages, poor prospects, and the perception of the permanent degeneration of the urban racial stock. The Salvation Army in particular saw emigration and the establishment of special labour colonies overseas as the way to redemption for the ex-alcoholic, the former prostitute, and other once disreputable members of the 'submerged tenth' of 'Darkest England'. In 1890 William Booth, founder of the Salvation Army, depicted transplanting social problems overseas as an easier matter than it would have been in an earlier age:

> A journey over sea is a very different thing now to what it was when a voyage to Australia consumed more than six months, when emigrants were crowded by hundreds into sailing ships, and scenes of abominable sin and brutality were the normal incidents of the passage. The world has grown much smaller since the electric telegraph was discovered and side by side with the shrinkage of this planet under the influence of steam and electricity there has come a sense of brotherhood and a consciousness of community of interest and of nationality on the part of the English-speaking people throughout the world. To change from Devon to Australia is not such a change in many respects as merely to cross over from Devon to Normandy.[37]

Although it never proved possible for the Salvation Army to establish the colonies for social and moral redemption envisaged by General Booth, it did play an active part in encouraging working-class emigration through offering advice to would-be emigrants, offering loans, supervising passages, writing letters of recommendation to employers in the colonies and opening hostels for the migrants selected for assistance. At first these arrangements were ad hoc, but in 1903 were formalised in the Migration and Settlement Department, which after 1905 even charted its own emigrant ships.[38] By 1937, it had sent out over 200,000 migrants, mainly to Canada and Australia, and claimed a high success rate. The majority of these, mainly young men, came from British towns and were sent to work on farms. Single young women were normally found positions in domestic service.

Unemployed youths with no prospects were given three months' basic training in farm work at a Salvation Army training centre at Hadleigh in Essex, before being shipped out to the farm labouring jobs that had been arranged for them in advance.[39]

Following the example of the Salvation Army, the Boy Scouts Association also dabbled with emigration as a form of adventurous self-improvement. It opened its own Migration Department in 1922 which encouraged its young men to seek exciting new opportunities in the dominions, especially the white colonies, and even offered scholarships to colleges in Australia, Canada and Southern Rhodesia.[40] These young men, aged between fifteen and nineteen, were recommended by their local commissioners to the Boy Scout movement in their destinations, and were given help and support at every stage of their journey, though their sponsors overseas were warned 'don't coddle the boys, but ensure that the Boy Scout in his new home overseas shall know that he has friends within reach who are in touch with the Headquarters of your Movement here at home, and with his own people'.[41] Self-reliance and solidarity were the hallmarks of the Boy Scout at home and abroad.

Less happy than that of these young knights of empire was the experience of children forced into involuntary migration by churches and orphanages. Unlike the God-fearing paragons of the Boy Scout movement, the children in the care of poor law authorities and charities were seen as a social problem to be solved by sending them to the far-flung corners of the empire. Thomas Barnardo saw emigration as a means 'to relieve the population pressure in our congested cities', which he saw as 'the moral cesspools I and others are continually engaged in deodorising'. He argued in 1889 that the solution was not to return the children he had rescued from the slums they had come from, as that would simply make it harder to help others, since their training in a Dr Barnardo's Home would have given them an advantage in getting ahead which would keep others back.

What avails it to take the weakest out of the struggle, to train them into robustness, and then to throw them back with their new accession of vital force into the crowd who are already engaged in snatching the morsels from each other's mouths? The miseries of those yet unhelped would only be aggravated and intensified by such a process.[42]

The argument owed much to Darwinian ideas of natural selection, but a deciding factor was that it was much cheaper to send children overseas than it was to maintain them in an orphanage in Britain: a one-off payment of £15, rather than the £12 a year it would have cost to keep a child in an orphanage at home. The first party of fifty boys was sent from Dr Barnardo's to Canada in 1882, and the first group of girls, the youngest of them aged only four, in 1883.

In selecting children for emigration, Barnardo was concerned that the children 'should be thoroughly sound and healthy in body and without predisposition to disease, having besides no disablement in limb and no failure of intellect that would interfere with their progress in life.' All children were given a medical examination before leaving England and another inspection on arrival in Canada. It was essential that 'only the flower of our stock are to be sent to Canada', and 'that upon reaching Canada, all children are to come under the care of properly qualified persons connected with our institutions on the Canadian side, by whom they are to be distributed carefully into well-selected homes.'[43] Barnardo publicised the successes of his scheme, telling such stories as that of fourteen-year-old Louisa, whose mother 'has been one of the vilest characters of the streets of East London', but who, with her sister, had been 'veritably saved so as by fire', and had thrived when placed with the family of a Methodist minister.[44]

However, the actual experience of many children sent overseas by Dr Barnardo's Homes was not always as positive as the published propaganda suggested. Some of the children sent overseas had been the victims of 'philanthropic abduction'. Barnardo admitted that he had sent forty-seven children to Canada, without their parents' consent, to save them from neglect. The Roman Catholic Church accused him of 'spiriting' children away to convert them to Protestantism, though he later agreed to refer any Catholic child to a Roman Catholic care agency.[45] Although the emigration scheme was partly intended to ensure that good racial stock was sent out to the colonies, some of the children sent out did not live up to this ideal and suffered accordingly. George Everitt Green was simple-minded and had poor eyesight. The first Canadian farmer with whom he was placed sent him back because he was unable to see well enough for farm work. Sent to work for Helen Findlay on her farmstead, he was abused and neglected, dying emaciated and covered in welts in 1895. The newspapers and trades unions did not protest about the abuses of the child emigrant scheme, but used the case to protest against the way in which philanthropists such as Barnardo had made 'Canada a common dumping ground for large numbers of the vicious, the lame, the halt and the blind.'[46]

The Big Brother Movement, launched in 1925, aimed to attract a better class of young emigrant to Australia from the middle classes, rather than rescuing children who were sliding into delinquency. The idea was that moral guidance would be provided to young men emigrating to Australia by 'Big Brothers', usually recruited from service organisations such as the Royal Agricultural Societies, the Rotary Clubs, the Chambers of Commerce, and predominantly city business and professional men of the same religion as the 'Little Brother' whom they promised to assist. In turn the Little Brother was intended to be a physically fit, upright, clean-cut, well-mannered British young man who was determined to work hard on the land in Australia. The leaders of the Big Brother Movement wished to recruit immigrants from a social class which did not usually migrate, and were partially successful. Of the first 1,515 Little Brothers brought to Australia between 1926 and 1929, 121 had attended a public school and 914 of the others had enjoyed some secondary education. However, the support received by many of the young immigrants was limited by the fact that many of their mentors were based in the cities, whereas they were sent to isolated farms. The Great Depression also meant that Australian businessmen were preoccupied with more personal and pressing matters than the fortunes of their Little Brothers.[47]

Young middle-class immigrants were not the only people needing to be nurtured in the dominions and colonies. In 1849 Edward Gibbon Wakefield declared that 'a colony that is not attractive to women is an unattractive colony.'[48] More men were emigrating to the colonies than women, resulting in an imbalance of the sexes which did not bode well for the future of the new countries. In 1872 twice as many young single men were leaving Great Britain as young unattached women, 110,765 men and only 50,277 women.[49] There was a need to encourage the emigration of suitable brides for the young settlers, to save them from the vices of alcoholism, frequenting brothels, catching venereal diseases, weakening the racial stock by miscegenation and 'unnatural vices'. For this a better class of woman was needed than the fallen women sent for redemption by the Salvation Army or Charles Dickens and Angela Burdett-Coutts.

Various philanthropic organisations acted as glorified colonial marriage bureaux. In New South Wales in 1849, Caroline Chisholm founded the Family Colonisation Loan Society to encourage British families to settle in the colony, and the British Ladies Female Emigration Society to encourage the migration of single women and protect them on their voyages out to Australia. Sidney Herbert, one of the members of the committee of the Family Colonisation Loan Society, also sponsored the emigration of 1,300 impoverished London needle-women to Australia between 1850 and 1854 until his Fund for Promoting Female Emigration ran out of money. Meanwhile the Columbia Emigration Society sent over one hundred women to Vancouver Island in the 1860s to take up domestic service with a view to marrying businessmen and gold miners. The Female Middle Class Emigration Society, founded by the feminist Maria Rye in 1862, loaned passage money to teachers and governesses.[50]

William Thackeray was not altogether impressed when he saw some of the young women being sent out to Australia in 1869, waiting for the train at Fenchurch Street Station to take them to their boat at Gravesend. He thought that they would hold no appeal for a fashionably suited dandy whose 'handkerchief smells of Bond Street musk and mille fleur', but would be good enough for 'a sun burnt settler out of the Bush', whose sensibilities would not be upset by the coarseness of the girls, and 'won't feel any of these exquisite tortures, or understand this kind of laughter, or object to Molly because her hands are coarse and her ankles thick, but he will take her back to his farm where she will nurse his children, bake his dough, milk his cows and cook his kangaroo for him.'[51] Yet Thackeray, almost anticipating later stereotypes of the democratic Australian, presciently acknowledged that things would be different in Australia where old class differences would no longer matter:

They will know nothing of that Gothic society, with its ranks and hierarchies, its cumbrous ceremonies, its glittering antique paraphernalia in which we have been educated, in which rich and poor still acquiesce, and which multitudes of us both still admire; far removed from these old world traditions, they will be bred up in the midst of plenty, freedom, manly brotherhood. Do you think if your worship's grandson goes into the Australian woods or meets the grandchild of one of yonder women by the banks of the Warrawarra, the Australian will take a hat off, or bob a curtsy, to the new comer? He will hold out his hand and say, 'Stranger, come into my house, and take a shakedown, and have a share of our supper. You come out of the old country, do you? There was some people were kind to my grandmother there and sent her out to Melbourne. Times are changed since then, come in and welcome.'[52]

It was felt that, whereas men could be left to organise their own emigration, women needed more protection. Joseph Chamberlain argued in 1901 that 'women alone and unprotected cannot safely be sent great distances across the seas, to arrive in strange lands where they have no friends and relatives to look after them, and where they do not know how to act until employment comes to them.'[53] Nevertheless, men also needed guidance if they were to move to another country. However, in the majority of cases this did not come from voluntary agencies, or indeed governments, but from more commercial sources. Emigration was a business as much as it was an emotional decision by individuals. Without emigration agencies, it would have been much more difficult for families and individual travellers to decide where to go in search of a better life and to get to their port of departure. Ticket agents played a decisive role in organising travel to the ports of departure, in arranging shipboard passages and onward travel in the new country.

Shipping companies and their agents encouraged emigration through a network of emigration agencies in the ports and major cities, posters and advertisement extolling the attractions of the new country, and recruitment campaigns in person and in newspapers. Relying on commission and accordingly biased, they did not always offer the best advice. In the United Kingdom such passage brokers were meant to be licensed, but in practice many of them were not bothered about legal registration. For such a ticket agent 'his business is to sell tickets', and 'he will sell a ticket to a man who is going, in his opinion, to prove an absolute failure, just as quickly as he will sell a ticket to a man whom he thinks is going to be a marked success.'[54] As a result of these 'unchecked activities of shipping agents who know very little of the needs of the Dominions and really care less', undesirable immigrants were arriving in Canada and Australia.[55] Some passenger brokers were guilty of 'extortion on every hand, in the shape of charges for making out entries, taking charge of luggage', or even arranging passage for a party of husbandmen to Virginia when they were actually making for Boston, with the result that 'the emigrant in reality often pays more for his passage than he would, were he to make his arrangements with the merchant, independent of these men.'[56] Some Dutch brokers in 1818 did not even take the German emigrants they had duped to the right continent, for 'cargoes of emigrants, who had wholly or partially paid their passage to the United States, after suffering almost starvation on shipboard, have, on various pretexts, been landed at Lisbon or the western islands, and left to perish in strange countries, unless saved by the already over-burthened demands on the few that are able to assist them'. The British passengers on the *Mary Ann* in 1818, however, took matters into their own hand when the ship was bound for St John, but they 'not wishing to go there, rose upon the crew and brought the vessel into Boston.'[57] Nonetheless, not all these brokers were criminals or incompetents and 'the English Government has taken what pains it could, by a system of licensing, to keep in order the passenger brokers; but the great competition leads to frauds, practiced by their runners, if not by them.'[58] Attempts during the First World War to introduce a more stringent regulation and licensing of passage brokers and their agents by a centralised emigration authority came to nothing when the 1918 Emigration Bill was not passed into law, but eventually many of these passenger agents evolved into modern travel agents.

Although emigrant agents were rampant, personal ties were the most powerful forces in encouraging migration. Chain emigration started once one set of emigrants had become established in a particular place and had written home in glowing terms about their new lives. Andrew Morris, a Lancashire weaver who had emigrated to Philadelphia in

1831, wrote to his family that his new home would 'do for every person that is willing to work for a living as there is plenty of work and good wages'. He was keen for his brother William 'to come as he is young and if Father and Mother and him was here and living together they would do very well.'[59] Others like Wilhelm Stille from Westphalia warned his family in 1836 that 'I wouldn't tell any family to come here ... except young people, for it is hard to travel as a family and it costs quite a lot, and when you first come to this country you don't know the language and face an uphill climb', but told them that life in Ohio was worth the effort of adjusting to the new language as 'when they've been here for a while and get a taste for freedom, and see the good crops growing here and all without manure, and that the land is so easy to work, then ... they feel sorry for their friends who are still in Germany.'[60] William Smyth, living in Philadelphia in 1837, was even more upbeat when he told his nephew Robert in County Antrim, Ireland, that 'you are not coming to strangers ... you will come to the best home you ever had and if you are coming I wish you to come on the first vessel that will sail from Londonderry belonging to James Corscadden as I have paid your passage and sent you two pounds for pocket money which James Corscadden will pay you.'[61]

As well as sending money for tickets and travel costs home for their families and friends to join them, migrants also sent financial assistance to those still in the old country. Between 1900 and 1906 the New York post office sent 12,304,485 money orders worth $239,367,047.56 overseas on behalf of migrants, mainly to the Austro-Hungarian empire, Russia and Italy.[62] Such largesse confirmed the impression that the new country was a land of plenty given by emigration magazines and letters to newspapers intended to encourage emigration. Such a letter in a Norwegian emigrant magazine in 1845 compared the lot of an emigrant to the American West who 'at the end of two years ... has become an independent man and is in a position to marry without having to worry for himself or his family, and in all probability he may look forward to a pleasant and carefree future', with his situation 'if this young man had stayed in Norway', and 'at the end of two years he would have been in about the same position as he was at the beginning.'[63]

Handbooks offered advice for intending emigrants with recommendations on where to settle, how to get there, what to take and what to expect on the journey. They influenced settlement patterns among different emigrant groups. Ole Rynning, for example, wrote a pamphlet in 1838 advising prospective Norwegian emigrants, emphasising those aspects of American society that would appeal to peasants and artisans, including the availability of land, freedom of religion, the possibility of forming a communal society with fellow countrymen and better wages. This book continued to be popular in Norway for many years after Rynning's death.[64] Gottfried Duden's 1829 book about Missouri, depicted as a new Rhineland along the Missouri River, induced many Germans not only to emigrate but to settle in Missouri.[65] British publishers gave advice on settlement in Australia aimed at encouraging a better class of emigrant to set out for the 'Australian dependencies', where 'emigration, no longer confined to the compelled and necessitous, has become almost a fashion; and thousands in the middle ranks of life are now making the most remote colonies their home, and forgetting the dangers of the voyage, and the 15,000 miles of water that separate them from the antipodes, cheerfully embark their families and fortunes in the hope of realizing, in a new clime, those promises of wealth and independence so glowingly held out to the intended emigrant in those favoured lands.'[66] But advice from friends and relations remained more potent than the printed word.

Italian emigration came largely from the south of the country and was regulated by personal connections and the padrone system prevalent there. Padroni based in the United States would recruit casual labourers for construction and railway work, organise everything for them, and control them through their own knowledge of the local job market and of English. Many of these Italian economic migrants, even the more highly skilled and better educated among them, were unable to get any better job than wielding a pick and shovel, not only because of the language barrier or lack of skills, but because of 'the racial prejudice which is intense among the native population'. Such migrants rarely intended to stay long and often returned home after a few years. The same prejudice was also shown towards Italians from northern Italy, who themselves looked down on their southern countrymen.[67] They too looked to padroni to make arrangements for them and hoped to return home once they had made their fortunes. As early as 1874 there were complaints that 'thousands of Italians go in search of work abroad, then come back within a couple of years, bringing with them a small amount of savings, along with some bad habits.'[68]

Many migrants to North America never intended to remain permanently. These 'birds of passage' wanted to earn money overseas in order to enjoy a better life in their homelands. As transatlantic crossings became shorter and safer, it became easier for a migrant to return home when there were economic downturns in the United States or improved opportunities at home. Others returned home to see their families and then returned to the New World. Italians, Hungarians, Croatians, Slovenes and Slovaks were most likely to be only temporary emigrants but even migrants from northern and western Europe made more frequent journeys back to their original homes.

Many of them were motivated by homesickness. The miner John Wilson had emigrated from the Great Northern Coalfield to the coalmines of Pennsylvania in 1864, but after a few years 'was strongly imbued with the desire to return to Durham', though he could not explain even to himself why he felt so strongly about going home despite enjoying higher wages, better housing, and generally enjoying a better life in America. His wife would have preferred to stay where they were, but could not dissuade him from returning.[69] Another miner, Peter Lee, was less settled during his year in the United States in 1886, moving restlessly from one pit job to another and from state to state, until he realised that it was vain to 'see if I could do better in America' than he had done in England.[70] Lee had left his sweetheart behind in England. A subsequent attempt to move to South Africa some ten years later also failed because he missed the wife and children left behind at home while he attempted to establish himself in a new country.

For all emigrants, whether they intended to leave forever or only for a short period, the first stage of their new life was the journey to the port. Before leaving home, Irish emigrants would have a blessing from the parish priest to give them spiritual strength. They would also be sent off with an American Wake, modelled after the traditional wake for the dead, mourning the loss of family and friends but also celebrating the new life ahead of them.[71] English emigrants set off more soberly. Two groups in 1844 from separate parishes in Bucking-hamshire and Northamptonshire joined up on the road and travelled to Deptford together. Both parties were travelling in hay wagons, carrying the luggage, women and children, with the men walking alongside, 'the younger men trudging it with seeming glee'. Indeed, all these emigrants 'seemed to be cheerful; and their clean and decent appearance bore witness to the propriety of their general habits.'[72] These particular English emigrants had a shorter journey than most emigrants, whereas for the Irish travelling to Liverpool on the open decks of cattle ships, crossing the Irish Sea could be a worse ordeal than the Atlantic voyage.

Emigrants from landlocked parts of continental Europe also faced obstacles to their journeys. In 1823 it took Johann Jacob Rütlinger a month to travel to the Zuider Zee from Switzerland by barge, raft, wagon, coach and on foot. As he travelled up the Rhine, he was confronted by extortionate demands at each river toll station and attempts at cheating him from innkeepers and boatmen. At the Dutch frontier there was another set of freight, customs and passport duties. Even when he finally reached Amsterdam he was beset by cheats and prostitutes:

> Everywhere the whores stood at the door, gaily dressed and called out to us, 'Come on in, farmer.' Or sometimes they even pulled us by the sleeve. When you come across parts of the city like this, you begin to think that there is not one decent house to be found.[73]

It was not an experience that would leave behind a fond last memory of Europe.

The journey became easier as the European railway network became more comprehensive and complete. Journeys that would once have taken several weeks now took only a few days. They were also less expensive as emigrants could save on the costs of lodging and food as well as take advantage of the reduced ticket prices and discounts for luggage offered by many railway companies. Special emigrant trains were also provided. At first these were little better than cattle trucks but by the 1880s the French Compagnie Générale Transatlantique was providing special emigrant carriages fitted with bunks and adequate luggage space. Food and drink were included in the price. Yet as late as 1908 the Italian Inspector of Emigrants Teodorico Rosati could complain about the Italian railway companies which 'granted emigrants a fifty per cent discount on standard rates and packed them into fourth class carriages which then travelled slower than goods trains and even had to give way to cattle trains.'[74]

For emigrants from the Russian empire, there was still the hurdle of having to be medically examined at one of the thirteen control stations on the German borders with Austria and Russia, established after a cholera epidemic in 1892 to control emigration from areas considered prone to infection, both physical and political. In the immediate aftermath of the 1892 Hamburg cholera epidemic, troops had been stationed on the German frontier to prevent Russian emigrants passing through the country. The Hamburg–Amerika and Norddeutscher Lloyd shipping companies had lost profits through this ban on emigrants from Russia, so had agreed to erect and maintain control stations at the frontier railway towns to screen out undesirables. In 1906–7, 455,916 intended immigrants were examined at these control stations, of whom 11,814 were rejected. In 1911 at the control station at Myslowitz the walls were 'alive with vermin', and it was 'not only difficult, but practically impossible to get any food while beer and whisky tempted the hungry and the thirsty.' The medical examination itself was often perfunctory, but 'the clothing and baggage of some of the Russian Jews was disinfected.' Then travel tickets were returned to those who had passed the inspection and they could continue their journey.[75]

Thirteen-year-old Mary Antin found her experience of the central control station in Ruhleben near Berlin to be a confusing experience when she passed through it on her journey from Lithuania to Boston via Hamburg, during which 'we emigrants were herded at the stations, packed in the cars, and driven from place to place like cattle'.[76] After having had their luggage taken from them by the porters, the transit emigrants were led into a small room where 'we were undressed and a slippery substance, that could have been anything, was rubbed on our bodies', before the shock when 'without warning, a warm shower sprinkled down on us.' While the emigrants were being disinfected, their clothes were given a similar treatment and then returned to them and 'we had to find our clothing from this huge heap of clothes, almost blinded with the steam.' The attendants rushed them to find their own clothes and get dressed in case they missed their train. Mary Antin was relieved that 'we were just being prepared for the onward journey, cleansed of all imaginable germs.'[77]

There was more of such frightening and humiliating treatment awaiting at other stages of the journey to the ports. In 1907 metal worker Fritz Kummel was shocked at Bremen main train station that 'from time to time ... people came out of a side building screaming, sometimes also with their chests bared. Anyone who wanted to know what had happened was told in sign language that they had been inoculated', and 'small bloody scratches could be seen on the upper arms.' As many of the immigrants did not understand what was happening to them because they were not German speakers, the experience must have been both frightening and, as Kummel observed, 'humiliating for many.'[78]

Albin Kunc from Llubljana emigrated to the United States in 1903 after having worked for several months for the Rommel emigration agency in Basle. When the train carrying a group of emigrants from Ljubljana reached Basle by train, they were greeted by agents of the emigration company, and 'each passenger had a badge affixed to his chest, so that each agent could recognise his people.' For the agents, the emigrants were regarded as 'just livestock' and treated with very little courtesy, although they were fed and guided to the train for the next stage of their journey to Paris, where a Compagnie Générale Trans-atlantique agent transferred them to another station for the train for Le Havre, where, after an overnight journey, the train took them straight to the dock where they would board the steamship for America. When 'the sea air became apparent ... some emigrants began to feel a little strange and many were afraid of the sea.' Every stage of the route to the port had been handled with efficiency, and such through ticketing made the journey easier for the emigrant. It didn't prevent apprehension about what was to come, and 'a lot of the women began reciting the rosary.'[79]

Ultimately, the decision to emigrate was always a personal one, albeit that it might have been dictated by economic or political necessity. Governments, philanthropists and shipping companies could point out the advantages of emigration, but in the end persuasion had its limits, and every man, woman and family made a choice according to personal priorities and financial circumstances. Emigration was a business with profits for all those engaged in furthering it, and for the countries, dominions and colonies that would benefit from it. However, the choice of whether to go and where to go was that of the emigrant, who on reaching the port of departure stood on the verge of the new life that he or she had chosen to pursue. It was only the beginning of the journey that would take them far across the oceans.

2

Farewell to the Old World

For many a weary emigrant, the port was a bewildering pandemonium of more or less organised plunder, where he was the prey of passenger brokers, provision dealers, lodging-house keepers and petty criminals, all of them with the one object of fleecing the innocent traveller as soon as he set foot on the quay. Tickets were sold for non-existent ships, shopkeepers overcharged for provisions, money changers cheated on the transaction and innkeepers offered poor service for high prices. Runners picked up the luggage of emigrants and took it off to either a particular lodging house or passage broker's office, forcing the gullible to follow them and be tricked into parting with money for a poor deal. At St Katherine's Dock in the Port of London in 1848, 'for days, hired vagabonds had been touting at every wharf and public house in the neighbourhood; and the call, although not so openly made as that of an omnibus conductor, only varied inasmuch as "America" was sub-stituted for "Charing Cross" or "Paddington".' These fraudsters 'took passengers for almost whatever they could get, paying no regard as to whether or not they had stores to last the voyage, or would starve before they were halfway across the Atlantic'.[1] Pickpockets and conmen were everywhere and prostitutes preyed on the innocent and not so innocent. In Liverpool in 1852 many of the streetwalkers had arrived 'with unspotted characters and innocent hearts', until, robbed of their passage money, they had been 'driven to a life of infamy by the demands of hunger.'[2]

Even for those emigrants who had escaped being fleeced on the quay, the scene they found themselves in was a strange, unfriendly world. In 1855 passengers in Liverpool boarding a packet for Boston found everything around them bewildering and alien:

Unlettered and inexperienced, everything seemed dreamlike to their senses – the hauling of blocks and ropes, the cries of busy seamen as they heave around the capstan, the hoarse cries of officers, the strange bustle below and aloft, the rise and expansion of the huge masses of canvas that wing their floating home, and will soon cover it with piled up clouds. Here are women with swollen eyes, who have just parted with near and dear ones, perhaps never to meet again, and mothers seeking to hush their wailing babies. In one place sits an aged woman ... listless and sad, scarcely conscious of the bustle and confusion around her ... The voyage across the Atlantic is another dreary chapter in an existence made up of periods of strife with hard adversities.[3]

First of all there was a passage to be arranged. Dealing with the emigrant agents was daunting enough before the journey could begin. These men were not employed by shipowners but were working for brokers who bought space in many different ships. Often this was the unused space of a cargo ship. Sometimes the agents did not have enough capacity to accommodate everyone who had been sold a passage, and some of the emigrants had no choice but to wait several weeks for another ship. Other agents packed all the waiting emigrants into any available ship, even if it meant gross overcrowding. Canny emigrants were advised not to accept the first suggestion made by the agent, but to try to inspect the various ships in port to see which were seaworthy and properly managed. The cheapest ships were rarely the best, the Canadian timber ships being notoriously cheap and unsafe. The emigrants haggled for 'the best bargain they can with the passenger-brokers' for 'the competition in this trade is very great, and fares, accordingly, vary from day to day, and even from hour to hour, being sometimes as high as £5 per passenger in the steerage, and sometimes as low as £3 10s.'[4]

Having negotiated a passage and bought a ticket, the emigrant needed to be fitted out for the journey at a chandler's shop. Handbooks for emigrants advised them on what they should equip themselves with, both for life overseas and on the voyage. In 1828 A C Buchanan advised emigrants sailing to America to provide themselves with provisions for a twelve-week voyage, including potatoes, carrots, turnips, onions, cured pork and beef, dried peas, dried fish, ship's biscuits, flour, rice, coffee, tea, sugar and medications, including wine and brandy. A very basic diet for a family of five would cost £7, although it would have been very easy to have spent three times that amount.[5] Even on government-assisted passages to Australia where food was supplied, emigrants were advised to take supplements for their diet.

Essential purchases, 'which every emigrant must possess on a voyage, whether aided by the Government bounty, or not', included a knife and fork, tea- and tablespoon, pewter plate, tin mug, meat dish, water can, wash basin, scrubbing brush, cabbage nets for attaching to the rigging and drying small items of clothing in, a bath brick, sandpaper, a hammer and nails, a long leather strap and buckles for securing a bed on deck when twice a week it would be exposed to the sun and air for purification, and at least three pounds of marine soap.[6] Mattresses, bought by the emigrants, would be thrown overboard at the end of the voyage, soiled, sometimes verminous, and unfit for the new life ahead.

Advice was also given on suitable clothing, where 'what is chiefly required is a couple of suits of common strong slops, with a sufficiency of linen, worsted and cotton stockings, and a few handkerchiefs.' Guidebooks warned the emigrant 'not to fall into the error of thinking that old clothes are good enough for the rough duty of a sea voyage, that very roughness requiring them to be both new and strong; if otherwise, the constant repairing which will be necessary with both male and female apparel will become an incessant tax on the emigrant's time and patience.' At the same time 'to take out a redundancy of clothing is especially impolitic, as all such articles can be obtained as abundantly and cheaply there as in England, besides, by so doing, adding materially to the bulk of his luggage, which in every case should be condensed into as small a compass as possible.'[7] Even when sailing conditions had improved on the shorter voyages being undertaken in the early twentieth century, a young emigrant already in America, Konstanty Butkowski, sent advice home on what his brother Antoni should bring with him on the voyage, 'as to clothes, bring the worst you have, about three old shirts, so that you can get changed on the ship. And when you have happily crossed the water, throw away these rags. Don't bring anything else with you, only what you're wearing.'[8]

With all these preparations to be made at the port and also while waiting for a ship, the emigrants needed somewhere to stay, and were once more at the mercy of unscrupulous lodging-house keepers. At Bremen in 1868, 150–60 emigrants were packed into the house of Frau Segelke, where there were no more than twenty beds, and 'the lounge was packed full of people, not on beds or mattresses, but on tables, chairs and on the bare floors ... male and female persons were lying in a jumble, entirely obscuring the floor, on straw sacks'. These emigrants were perhaps luckier than those accommodated in lofts, byres, barns and barges at Bremerhaven in 1847, or camped in tents at the dockside and along the roads leading to Le Havre.[9] It was no wonder that Georg Brandt, embarking at Bremerhaven in 1841 on his way from Hanover to New Orleans, should consider that 'fraud is customary trade here; anyone who does not have his wits about him is likely to be conned'.[10]

Equally notorious was Liverpool, which by the 1840s had become the leading European emigrant port. As a centre of the slave trade until abolition in 1807, the port had developed a new role in the transportation of emigrants after the end of the French wars. In 1818 a regular scheduled packet boat service was started to New York, originally intended for business travel and freight. The ships bringing bulky raw materials from North America, such as timber, cotton, flax, wool, tobacco and wheat, had spare capacity available on the return journey from Liverpool, as their cargo of manufactured goods, including textiles, was less bulky. Space in steerage could be used for transporting emigrants. As the emigrant trade increased, Liverpool thrived and by 1845 there were 20,521 ships trading through the port.[11]

Liverpool was chosen by emigrants from all over Europe as their departure point. It was cheaper for most travellers from northern Europe to emigrate indirectly from Liverpool than directly from a more convenient European port. Feeder ships carried the emigrants from ports in Germany, Russia, Finland, Norway and Denmark to the British east coast ports of Hull, Leith or London, from where they would transfer to a train to take them to Liverpool, Glasgow or Southampton for the ships that would finally take them on to the United States, Canada and Australia. The crossing from Oslo to Hull took three days and from Trondheim four, followed by a seven-hour railway journey to

Liverpool. Southampton was also favoured by emigrants arriving in Hull, Le Havre and Cherbourg as it was more convenient than Liverpool. Irish emigrants also took feeder ships for the shorter North Sea crossing to Liverpool, a pattern not significantly challenged by the opening of a port at Queenstown (Cobh) by the Cunard and Inman Lines in 1857, where some Irish emigrants could board near Dublin.[12]

Paul Knaplund left his family's farm in Norway in 1906 and had to take two steamers through the fjords to get to Trondheim, where rival agents of the steamship companies pounced on emigrants at the quayside. Knaplund, off to America to improve his education, 'felt that he was either just carrion for others to batten on or a sheep to be herded and pushed into the proper enclosure'.[13] He himself boarded the *Tasso*, a cargo liner belonging to the Wilson Line which dominated the transit emigrant trade between Scandinavia and Hull. The floor was covered with a layer of sawdust to absorb vomit. The bunks lacked mattresses and sheets, but had blankets, which had been recently laundered yet contained the carcases of rats. Most of the departing migrants were celebrating with heavy drinking and singing, and 'everyone seemed to have a host of friends, all were jolly and certain of finding at least one gold mine in America'. As the ship set sail, 'pledges of eternal friendship rang across the water', but Knaplund, travelling without companions, 'seemed utterly alone'.[14] Hull too overwhelmed him with 'the heavy horses with big fetlocks, the large wagons, the drivers' shouts in an unfamiliar tongue, the street signs, and the foreign-looking houses which made everything seem so alien.' Travelling in a train for the first time in his life, en route to Liverpool he thought 'the pall of smoke over English cities dreadful; the countryside, on the other hand, was green and altogether charming'.[15]

The main shipping companies in Liverpool, Cunard, White Star, Inman and Guion, were quick to involve themselves in the emigrant trade once they realised that this could be lucrative. Cunard, founded in 1839, and the New York and Liverpool United States Mail Steamship Company, generally known as the Collins Line, originally competed for the mail contracts, but soon became involved in the transport of emigrants. The Inman Line concentrated on emigrant passengers from its early days. Meanwhile, the Liverpool and Great Western Steamship Company Limited, popularly known as the Guion

Line, which began transatlantic crossings in 1866, was one of the first to develop strong links with other companies to bring emigrants to Liverpool, including the Wilson Line and North Eastern Railway. These companies were responsive to change and when in the late nineteenth century there was a drop in emigration from Ireland and a rise in emigration from central and eastern Europe, they adapted to the increased competition from the German ports, closer to the homes of the new emigrants, by calling at Southampton, Genoa and Naples. Indeed, in 1907 the White Star Line moved the focus of its operations to Southampton, which since 1858 had been used by British shipping companies and their major continental rivals, acting as a convenient British port of call for Norddeutscher Lloyd from 1858 and Hamburg–Amerika from 1883.

For many French and German emigrants the ports at Le Havre, Cherbourg, Antwerp, Rotterdam and Amsterdam acted as stopping points on their way to Liverpool as well as for ships sailing directly to North America. In the 1840s an American shipbroker, Washington Finlay, set up in business at Mainz to promote passages from Antwerp and Le Havre, both of which were easily and cheaply reached from the interior of Germany. Using a network of agents spread across southern Germany, Finlay was able to broker 12,743 passages to New York and 2,682 to New Orleans in 1849. Political refugees in the aftermath of the 1848 revolutions and young men dodging their military obligations especially liked Le Havre and Antwerp because few questions were asked of them, unlike at those ports in the German states.[16]

The main German emigrant port of Bremerhaven at the mouth of the River Weser had been founded in 1827 in an attempt to maintain the trading importance of the old Hanseatic city of Bremen, whose harbour had been silting up since the sixteenth century. By the early nineteenth century the larger ships could no longer dock in the port at Bremen but it was important for the burghers to maintain trade with North America, particularly the import of tobacco and flour from Baltimore and cotton and sugar from New Orleans. In return for these commodities, Bremen exported emigrants. The only solution to maintaining the prosperity of the city state was to establish a new port at the mouth of the Weser under the control of Bremen, on land purchased from the king of Hanover, the neighbouring state.

The city of Bremen wanted to keep control over its new port and conducted all the business of emigration in the old city itself. In 1840 the Senate of Bremen passed a resolution that any merchant or businessman making a profit from emigration at Bremerhaven must actually remain resident in Bremen so that 'the colony of Bremerhaven did not come to own a line of business that by rights belonged to Bremen.' Bremen was even entered as the place of departure on the passenger manifestos for ships sailing from Bremerhaven.[17]

Emigrants, having completed all their business in Bremen, would then board overcrowded river barges organised by the city government to take them down the Weser to Bremerhaven, a journey that could take three days. Exposed to the elements and uncomfortable, these barges were perhaps the least efficient part of the process of emigrating via Bremen and Bremerhaven. It was only at ebb tide that these barges could make the final stretch of this river journey and reach the ships. Water transport from Bremen to Bremerhaven was improved in the 1840s and the journey shortened by one day when the connected barges began to be towed to the mouth of the Weser by a steam-powered tugboat. Only after the completion of a railway line from Bremen to Bremerhaven in 1862 did getting to the port become easier.

Bremen, however, was the first major port city to attempt to improve the quality of life for emigrants, during their stay there and onboard ships departing from her port. The Bremen Senate, hoping to encourage emigration, passed legislation in 1832 requiring emigrant ships to be seaworthy, to maintain accurate passenger lists of everyone on board, and to have minimum standards of space for each passenger as well as keeping provisions for ninety days at sea.[18] The formation of the Norddeutscher Lloyd Bremen line by Bremen merchant Hermann Heinrich Meier in 1857 helped to cement Bremerhaven's importance as the main emigrant port in North Germany. From the first, Norddeutscher Lloyd only used steamships, starting up a scheduled service to New York in 1863. Bremerhaven very much became a company town with the majority of its inhabitants employed in the emigrant agency, in the clearance halls, at the docks or on board Lloyd ships. Its main agent, Friedrich Miíler, developed a network of emigration agents that reached into Poland and Hungary.[19]

Hamburg was later than Bremen in seeking a share of the profits that came from the emigrant trade. Indeed, after the end of the French Revolutionary and Napoleonic Wars, Hamburg City Council had discouraged emigration to avoid beggars filling the streets and dishonest emigration agents preying upon them, as had happened in the older emigrant ports of northern Europe such as Antwerp, Le Havre, Rotterdam and Amsterdam. However, the success of Bremen in controlling and regulating emigration prompted the City Council to pass its own regulations for emigrant ships in 1837, which laid down that the height of steerage was to be 5 feet 6 inches and that each bunk should have minimum dimensions of 74 inches by 25 inches.[20]

Some emigrants were discouraged from travelling through Hamburg because of its poor reputation for exploiting travellers. Hotels and shopkeepers sent runners to the railway station to meet emigrants and offer them hotel rooms and provisions for the ship at inflated prices for poor quality so that, as in so many ports, 'the beer they drink and the food they buy, the necessary and unnecessary things which they are urged to purchase, are excessively dear, by virtue of the fact that a double profit is made for the benefit of the officials or the company which they represent.'[21] The government of Bavaria in reaction to this even prohibited its citizens from leaving through Hamburg and recommended Bremen as a better and safer alternative. In an attempt to stamp out abuses and improve the reputation of Hamburg, an Association for the Protection of Emigrants was set up in 1850, which provided information on exchange rates for money, the average price of hotel rooms, and recommendations on equipment.

Generally, emigrants from the Austro-Hungarian empire emigrated from the north German ports and it was only after 1903 that attempts were made to establish Trieste as an emigrant port for the Dual Monarchy. An earlier attempt to transport emigrants to Brazil on three steamships rented from the Austria Lloyd company by the banker brothers Isacco and Giuseppe Morpurgo in 1888 had come to nothing. In November 1903 the Cunard steamship *Aurania* began an emigrant service to New York with stops in Fiume (Rijeka), Venice, Palermo, Naples, Algiers and Gibraltar. In June 1904 the newly founded Unione Austriaca di Navigazione, also known as the Austro Americana e Fratelli Cosulich, began its own service to New York, using the steamships *Gertu*, *Giulia* and *Freda* on a route calling at

Messina, Naples and Palermo. Soon Trieste was a leading emigration centre for people from Galicia, Dalmatia, Carniola (Slovenia), Bukovina, Croatia and Bosnia–Herzegovina going to the United States, Canada and South America. Significantly, ethnically Italian emigrants from Trieste's natural hinterland of the Austrian Littoral, which comprised the Triestine hinterlands, Istria and the Kvarner islands, preferred to emigrate through western ports.[22] Trieste was also notable for the number of returnees who used it as a port of re-entry for returning emigrants, not only local seasonal labourers but also penniless Hungarians who became a burden on the Triestine hospital and social services.[23]

Genoa, Naples and Palermo were the only emigration ports officially recognised by the Italian government, which was praised because it 'safeguards its emigrants admirably at Naples and Genoa; but other governments are seemingly unconcerned.'[24] The Italian Emigration Act of 1888 restricted the role of the state in regulating emigration to the elimination of abuses by agents and shipowners, ensuring that contracts were fair and conditions on the ship were adequate. A further Emigration Act in 1901 abolished the role of emigration agents and made the shipping companies responsible at all stages of the emigration process. It also established the role of the Italian state in the protection of emigrants. In 1902 the Prinetti Decree banned subsidised emigration to Brazil, and in 1911 emigration to Argentina was suspended for thirteen months to prevent the exploitation of emigrants.[25]

The cry of preventing the exploitation of emigrants on the ships of foreign companies could be used to cripple foreign competition for the emigrant trade. In 1906 the Italian government issued a circular 'limiting maritime services in Italian waters to the Italian flag' in an attempt to restrict Italian emigration to Italian registered vessels. The Navigazione Generale Italiana, otherwise known as the Florio–Rubattino Line, had recently expanded its fleet and was trying to attract passengers sailing to both North and South America. The company received a state subsidy for carrying the mail and 'enjoys powerful political influence' which adopted 'the governing principle' of 'the protection of the native as against the foreign shipping interest.' As the Italian line had newer and faster ships than its competitors, a prudent move was to make it financially more advantageous for ships offering shorter voyages and to exclude all the older single-screw ships from the trade.[26] The press was also mobilised to campaign against non-Italian shipping companies carrying Italian emigrants. The *Ora*, a Palermo newspaper, advised emigrants to 'prefer our ships to foreign vessels because experience shows that the treatment and humanity on board our ships is invariably beyond comparison with those of other nations and that besides on an Italian ship the same language is spoken and friends are found amongst the crew to alleviate the evils and sufferings of long passage.' The newspaper cited the case of three Spanish ships purporting to be Italian ones which had landed 1,047 returning Italian migrants at Genoa, who had been 'collected by fraud and deception in the Argentine metropolis', and had then been given insufficient rations on a thirty-four-day voyage on ships with poor sanitary arrangements, prompting the newspaper to express its outrage at the 'swindling and brigandage in the hands of thieves and rascals who so cruelly deceive poor Italians.'[27]

Other states were passing legislation to give their own ports a commercial advantage. In 1886 the Hamburg Senate passed regulations intended to stop ships from transporting emigrants to other ports for the passage across the oceans, by extending the laws applicable to voyages directly from Hamburg to also cover indirect emigration, since 'this system is contrary to the real interest of the emigrants who not only have to submit themselves to the troublesome disembarkation in an intermediate port (mostly an English one) and to undergo an overland transport to the port of embarkation ... but the emigrants are also deprived of the possibility to form a judgment as to the way and manner in which the transport during the greater part of the voyage, the passage across the ocean, will take place.' Now, the guarantees given by the 'Emigration Acts in force at this City as regards practicability and fitness of the means of transport until the end of their sea voyage ... and safeguarding of their interests in every respect' were extended to cover indirect emigration.[28] The British Consul General in Hamburg was convinced that the effect of these new regulations would be that the business of 'British vessels engaged in the indirect transport of emigrants ... will be seriously if not entirely crippled'.[29]

The German empire introduced further regulations in 1898 to protect the German shipping companies, making it compulsory for steam companies carrying emigrants from Germany to have licences from the imperial government so that 'foreign ships are allowed under the Act and regulations to carry German emigrants, but only by permission of the central authority which can be refused at discretion.'[30] The Castle Line complained that the Bundesrat was proposing to refuse licences for the traffic between Europe and North America to all British steam companies other than the Cunard and White Star Lines, and to exclude the British companies from the German emigration traffic to South Africa in favour of Lloyd Norddeutscher and Hamburg–Amerika. The Castle Line had carried emigrants from Germany for many years but was refused a licence and was informed that this was because 'the British Government does not recognize the German emigration certificate for German ships but only those of the British Board of Trade'.[31]

The shipping companies themselves realised that to be competitive they needed to provide better facilities in the ports for the emigrants. Bremen led the way in 1850 with the opening of the Auswandererhaus, the Emigrants' House, funded by the merchants of Bremen. Despite opposition from local innkeepers and a high price of 66 pfennigs a day, it proved popular with emigrants and was effective in curtailing the activities of the runners. An impressive building with an almost 'palatial character' in its heyday and still imposing in what still survives of it today, the Auswandererhaus had a kitchen which could cater for 3,500 diners in its dining hall with the 'most splendid' food that most of the emigrants were unlikely to have enjoyed at home, such as 'robust soup, good vegetables, fat meat and thick bacon.' There were dormitories for more than two thousand emigrants, storage rooms for their luggage and, for their spiritual needs, a chapel, offering daily services for Protestants, but masses for Catholics only on sailing days. There were three sick bays containing thirty-five beds, and regular visits from doctors. The writer Hermann Allmers averred that 'no other port of emigration, be it Hamburg, Antwerp, Ostend or Le Havre, is lucky enough to have a similar or even slightly similar institution.'[32]

The Auswandererhaus at Bremerhaven was soon rendered redundant when the railway link from Bremen made it possible for emigrants to transfer directly from the train to ship and no longer needed to be lodged in Bremerhaven. It was not until 1907 that Lloyd

Norddeutscher and its general agent Friedrich Missler built emigrant halls for 3,500 in Bremen close to the railway station, for migrants from Russia, Poland, Galicia, Slovakia, Slovenia, Romania and Croatia. Such halls were intended as a means of controlling emigrants from other countries who might be carrying infections. Until then, inns had provided all that the emigrants passing through Bremen needed, offering 'good lodging and working flawlessly.'[33]

It was certainly in the interest of the shipping lines to ensure that their passengers were healthy and free of any infectious diseases before they boarded ship, if only because any emigrants refused entry into the United States had to be returned to the port of embarkation at the expense of the shipping company. Safeguards were necessary in port before embarkation. Such screening also meant more control and supervision over the emigrants than had once been necessary. At Liverpool in 1911 an Armenian girl was detained for six months on account of trachoma. Even after she had been discharged as cured by her doctor, she was rejected twice by the White Star Line and the Cunard Company as being likely to be turned back on reaching America, and 'the fact that the steamship companies are required to bring back all rejected passengers and are penalized for taking them over to America is ... a most efficient safeguard.'[34] American doctors were also employed to carry out health checks as the emigrants boarded their ship, but 'this medical watchdog' was feared and resented by most emigrants as he stood 'between two policemen, chewing on a cigar and taking some snuff', while he 'watches, touches, pushes and rejects the emigrants parading in front of him', and 'one by one he turns eyelids inside out, there in the open among the dust, alternating this finger-eye exercise and the squeezing of his cigar, which draws badly.'[35]

In Britain there had long been depots for emigrants on government-assisted passages to Australia and New Zealand. Facilities in such depots were basic, but made a good impression on agents for the colonies and medical inspectors. In 1883, Mr Deering, the Assistant Agent-General for South Australia, impressed by the cleanliness of the beds and walls at the Plymouth Emigrant Depot, 'had no idea that emigrants were so well-treated.'[36] Ellen Joyce conceded that 'of course you have to rough it at the Depot', because 'in providing for so many, everything must be simple and plain, and only what is necessary; but everything is scrupulously clean and sweet.' The mattresses were stuffed with cocoa fibre, considered to be vermin-proof, and the sheets and blankets supplied to emigrants for their two nights in the depot were regularly washed. Mrs Joyce was suitably appreciative that 'when you hear that all the walls are lime-washed after the departure of every ship, and the floors and berths scrubbed with carbolic soap, you will see how carefully all matters of health are attended to.'[37]

However, many emigrants complained of the 'dirty state of the Establishment and the want of such ordinary comforts as the severity of the weather would render essential.' They also criticised the smallness of the berths and found 'the filthy condition of the bedding almost incredible. Vermin appears to have abounded.'[38] The complaints of emigrants actually staying in the Plymouth Depot were supported by the Port Sanitary Officer, Francis Fox, who criticised the sanitary arrangements, whereby sewage was discharged immediately under the platform on which all the emigrants exercised and amused themselves. This sewage was left exposed at low tide, which 'must of necessity affect the atmosphere breathed by those on the platform above'.[39] At that time miasma, or bad smells, was generally thought to be responsible for infections. Yet, despite the defects in cleanliness and facilities, 'good health prevailed amongst its inmates'.[40] The different perceptions of emigrants and visitors may be down to all defects being concealed during official inspections, and to the fear that 'if a general impression were to get abroad in England, among the people who are going out, that the Depot was a filthy place, not fit for the reception of decent and modest people of the working class, it would be bad enough; but it would be much more serious if such an impression should prevail among the large number of colonists in Australia and New Zealand who are sending home for their friends.'[41]

John Hillary and his family had found the same Plymouth Depot to be relatively clean in 1879, but thought that many of the emigrants there were dirty and diseased. They were disturbed by having to mix with people 'of the lowest type', and later suspected that it was mixing with a lower class of person that resulted in their children falling sick on the voyage, and the whole family being quarantined when they arrived in New Zealand. Most of these social inferiors were Irish and Scottish, but the depot officials made no distinction between them and what the Hillarys considered to be 'a number of respectable people who turn from such treatment with tears in their eyes, or looks which say "is Thy servant a dog?"' John Hillary considered himself, as a Wesleyan Methodist preacher and shopkeeper, to be socially superior to the general run of emigrants, who were 'of low class and need strict discipline'. For him, sitting in the mess hall 'amidst concertina playing, singing, shouting, whistling, stamping, screaming babies and all the hideous noises by which people could disturb each other' was enough to 'make the place more like hell'.[42]

Attempts were made to reassure people both at home and in the colonies that emigrants, especially young women, passing through the depots were well looked after. Ellen Joyce was impressed by the services held for young women going to Queensland by the sub-matron of the Plymouth Depot, and the singing of an appropriate hymn, 'Go Forward Christian Emigrant Beneath His Banner True'. These young women had surrendered their embarkation orders to the Master on arrival at the depot and had then been given tea in a large hall in the women's quarters of the depot. Travelling as a group, they had been allowed to form their own mess and choose a mess captain from amongst themselves. Medical inspections, 'passing the doctor', had been suitably decorous.[43] Mrs Joyce, as a supporter of female emigration, was keen to reassure the families of the young women emigrants that they would be well looked after, physically, morally and spiritually.

Conditions in hostels organised by shipping companies were often no better than in state-sponsored emigration depots. Austro-Americana bought a large house at Servola, a suburb of Trieste, to house 1,000 emigrants passing through Trieste, but this proved grossly inadequate to the demands on it.[44] The building had formerly been used as a sanatorium for consumptive children who might benefit from sea bathing. The Trieste sanitary authorities thought that the facility was overcrowded and should only house seven hundred if there were to be any hope of carrying out any form of adequate disinfection regularly. The beds were too close together, there was 'an unbearable stench in the dormitories', and 'waste is just piled up in the courtyard, where it remains for days, and then it is given to the farmers.' Smallpox and typhoid broke out in 1913 and Austro-Americana was forced to use 'even its own ships, functioning as temporary hotels at sea; a floating hotel prevented the city from being overwhelmed with emigrants lodging in the centre, which would endanger our public health.' After the epidemics had been contained, the company began to expand and upgrade the hostel at Servola and construct adjacent quarantine facilities, though the heyday of migration from the Austro-Hungarian lands was to end with the outbreak of war. Following the war, Trieste itself was to become part of the Kingdom of Italy with its own more centrally located and established emigrant ports.[45]

At Liverpool, Cunard provided free accommodation for emigrants awaiting embarkation in what amounted to 'a village by itself in the centre of Liverpool, and consists of several buildings, holding over 2,000 guests if need be'. Since many of the guests, mainly transit emigrants, were not native English speakers, attempts were made to place them into hotels according to their original nationality, with separate Swedish and German hotels, and 'mostly all the hotel employees were Britonized foreigners, so as to be able to understand the foreign-speaking guests.' Guests were greeted on arrival by a matron and hotel keeper in Cunard uniform, who offered refreshments and showed guests to their quarters. Men and women were strictly segregated and accommodated in dormitories sleeping no more than fifteen people, which were 'well-ventilated and provided with steam heat and electric light.' Wholesome food was offered in the dining rooms. The 'Cunard Hotel system' was visited daily by a company doctor to carry out medical examinations to identify any ill or diseased passengers who might be rejected on reaching America.[46]

Similarly, at Rotterdam, the Holland–America Line opened a comfortable emigrant hotel but, before they could be admitted to it, newly arrived intending emigrants had to undergo the humiliation of medical examination and disinfection in an observation shed. While they took an antiseptic bath and had their hair shampooed with a mixture of soft soap, carbolic acid, creolin and petroleum, their clothes were disinfected. The hair of all the men and boys was close cropped with clippers as a precaution against hair lice, though women and girls were spared this particular indignity. Even so, they were required to use a fine tooth comb attached by a brass chain in each bathroom.[47]

Compulsory bathing and fumigation also faced travellers arriving at the Auswandererhallen built in 1900 by the Hamburg–Amerika Line on the island of Veddel near Hamburg, where 'they are required to take baths and their clothing is disinfected; after which they constantly emit the delicious odours of hot steam and carbolic acid.'[48] Only once the passengers and their luggage had both been thoroughly disinfected were they allowed to pass to the 'clean side' of the emigrant depot, with its dormitories, hotels, shops, restaurants and churches.

In Germany such strict sanitary and medical supervision of the emigrants was a response to the 1892 cholera epidemic in Hamburg which had been blamed on Russian emigrants passing through the port. The water supply was infected and over the course of six weeks in November and December 1892 nearly ten thousand people died. Bremen, where the public health authorities had followed the advice of the bacteriologist Robert Koch in safeguarding its water supplies from contamination, only had six deaths from cholera in that period.[49] Emigrant traffic was disrupted as the German government prohibited all eastern Europeans from crossing the border into East Prussia. Hamburg also banned emigrants from entering the city. The very existence of the Hamburg–Amerika line, and its Bremen competitor Norddeutscher Lloyd, was threatened. Albert Ballin, director of the Hamburg–Amerika Line, declared that 'without 'tween deck passengers I would be bankrupt within a few weeks.'[50] The Senate in Hamburg soon allowed emigrants to enter the city and on its orders Ballin had a barracks for them built on the Amerikakai. Meanwhile the imperial government had allowed intending emigrants to pass through Germany to the ports, but only after the shipping companies financed the setting up of tight emigrant border controls with medical checks at the main border crossings, transit railway stations and in the ports. A cordon sanitaire was intended to protect Germany from infections brought by migrants in transit.

In Hamburg, too, a cordon sanitaire was also planned to segregate the emigrants from the city. In 1900 the City of Hamburg gave Hamburg–Amerika the island of Veddel in the Elbe to build accommodation for emigrants in Auswandererhallen, emigrants' halls, that were more appealing than the old insanitary barracks on the Amerikakai previously used for Russian emigrants. There 'spacious buildings stand grouped around a church with a handsome tower like a small town surrounded by a high palisade.' It was a town, though, that was 'located so that emigrants arrive there from a special railway station facility and are taken on board without coming into contact with the city.'[51] Many of the emigrants quartered there had bought all-inclusive tickets which covered travel to Hamburg, accommodation in the Auswandererhallen and passage by ship to the New World. As a result they had no contact with the cities they passed through or with Hamburg itself. Until 1908 the Russian emigrants were not allowed to leave Veddel Island.

Transit passengers from other countries were not obliged to stay in the Auswandererhallen, but many chose to do so because it was cheap and safe, representing a loss of custom for the shops and hotels of Hamburg. Hotels were set up for wealthier emigrants and there were many distractions for them while waiting for their ship, including regular brass band concerts, Protestant and Catholic churches, a synagogue, separate dining halls for Christians and Jews, a barber shop, bureau de change, and shops 'selling clothes, hats, musical instruments, suitcases, brandy bottles, cheap jewellery', labelled in different languages. It was a world in limbo, in which segregation not only kept Hamburg free from infection but gave the emigrants security where 'five thousand people a day and two million a year rove back and forth here, each locked within the small circle of his trembling desires, all together a mass of migration of peoples, disquiet, disappointment, hope.'[52]

Each morning trumpets heralded the beginning of the doctors' rounds and all residents were expected to undergo repeated medical checks until the final medical inspection shortly before embarkation. The disinfection facilities and sewage system were built to the latest technical standards, though allowance had to be made for those of the emigrants, 'some of them from rather uncultivated regions', a euphemism for Russians and Poles, who 'don't know how to use water closets'.[53] Doctors ensured that public health was maintained in these transient communities deliberately isolated from the world around them. These repeated medical inspections were resented and 'May the Lord protect you from the bath' was said by the Zionist economist Georg Halpern of Munich to be the parting good luck wish of many a Jewish emigrant from Russia, which could be interpreted as 'May the Lord protect you from Ballin and his hygienic checkpoints.'[54]

Having passed the medical inspections and reached their embarkation day, emigrants from the Ballinstadt on Veddel Island near Hamburg were marched off to the tenders that would take them down the Elbe to the steamships anchored in the river outside the port of Hamburg. A brass band played to speed them on their way and impart a sense of occasion. By the early twentieth century, most steamships were berthed at the port of Cuxhaven, which had been developed in 1896 for the bigger ships too big for the port facilities at Hamburg. Trains took the emigrants to the redbrick HAPAG–Hallen passenger halls, today still impressive even in a semi-derelict state, where they would board their ships.[55]

In some ports watching the departure of emigrants almost became a tourist attraction. At Fiume, where Cunard had begun a regular passenger service to New York in 1903, the Archduchess Maria Josefa paid a visit to watch the screening of emigrants boarding the *Pannonia*. Fiorello La Guardia, later to become mayor of New York, was a United States official overseeing the medical inspection of the emigrants at Fiume, and was not impressed that 'big shots would obtain permits from Hungarian officials to watch the scene' and recalled seeing thirty or forty visitors standing 'on the first-class deck where they would get a gallery view of the entire procedure'.[56] At Naples there was a similar interest in passengers boarding the *Prinzessin Irene* in 1903, some of whom 'staggered under the weight of great cloth wrapped bundles, others lugged huge valises by the grass ropes which kept them from bursting open because of their flimsy construction; and even the tots carried fibre baskets of fruit, straw-cased flasks of wine, cheese forms looped with string and small rush-bottomed chairs for deck sitting.'[57] One first-class passenger, the daughter of a Philadelphia clergyman, was surprised to see an emigrant family in tears as they said goodbye to an old man and conceded that 'these dirty repulsive creatures really seem to show traces of finer feelings.'[58]

As a pilot guided the ship out of the harbour, two important ceremonies took place, searching for stowaways and the roll call of passengers. Stowaways might have been brought onboard concealed in trunks or chests, with air-holes to prevent them from suffocating, or even in barrels, 'packed up to their chins in salt, or biscuits, or other provisions, to the imminent hazard of their lives.'[59] They would then hope to emerge once all the tickets had been inspected and collected. The crew would search the ship thoroughly, so that any unwanted passengers could be returned to shore by the tugboat where they would be brought before a magistrate. Any stowaway not discovered in time was made to work his or her passage and given the most unpleasant and disagreeable jobs. Once this search had been completed, the steerage passengers were brought out on deck and asked to show their tickets so that a check could be made against the passenger manifest, and for the ship's doctor to give the emigrants another cursory medical inspection.

The scene as the ship set sail is vividly evoked by the artist Henry O'Neil in his 1861 painting *The Parting Cheer*.[60] The artist concentrated on the emotions of those left behind as an emigrant ship leaves from an undefined location along the Thames. Red- and blue-shirted sailors cheer from the deck of the ship and the sides of the rigging, emigrants are partly in shadow on the deck below, but the viewer's attention is drawn to the people on land of all social classes and age. In the foreground a widow dressed in mourning, weeping into a lace handkerchief, is comforted by a fashionably dressed girl in a purple shawl, a small boy in a belted tunic and tam-o'-shanter hat, and a cairn terrier. Behind this affluent-looking family group is a bare-headed woman in a plain grey dress being comforted by a young man, interpreted at the time as a brother looking after his sister whose lover is sailing away from her. A working-class woman wipes away her tears using her apron. On the far left of the painting a mournful-faced woman holds two small children, one of them asleep. Towards the back of the crowd a father holds a chubby, wholesome-looking infant waving a union flag. Throughout the crowd scene, people are waving flags, handkerchiefs and walking sticks in a gesture of farewell. Among them is a black man waving his hat, perhaps included to show O'Neil's support for the anti-slavery movement in the year in which the American Civil War began. All the men show British stoicism in supporting the weeping women. The *Saturday Review* wrote of the painting that 'never, perhaps, do Englishmen so thoroughly throw off their reserve as on the occasion of such a parting, and we doubt whether the varied forms of demonstrative grief here expressed are at all exaggerated'.[61]

Similar emotions were also evoked on board the ship as the crowds waved farewell with raised hats and flapping handkerchiefs at Liverpool in 1850:

It is then, if at any time, that the eyes of the emigrants begin to moisten with regret at the thought that they are looking for the last time at the old country – that country which, although, in all probability, associated principally with the remembrance of sorrow and suffering, of semi-starvation, and a constant battle for the merest crust necessary to support existence is, nevertheless, the country of their fathers, the country of their childhood, and consecrated to their hearts by many a token. The last look, if known to be the last, is always sorrowful, and refuses, in most instances, to see the wrong and the suffering, the error and the misery, which may have impelled the one who takes it, to venture from the old into the new, from the tried to the untried path, and to recommence existence under new auspices, and with new and totally different prospects. 'Farewell, England! Blessings on thee – stern and niggard as thou art. Harshly, mother, thou hast used me, And my bread thou hast refused me: But 'tis agony to part' is doubtless the feeling uppermost in the mind of many thousands of the poorer class of English emigrants at the moment when the cheers of the spectators and of their friends on shore proclaim the instant of departure from the land of their birth.[62]

There was no going back from this point. As Paul Knaplund leaving his native Norway in 1906 reflected, 'with grim resolve he was cutting loose from the past, closing a chapter of his life ... Like the ship on the fjord he had cast off, broken the mooring; leaving a snug harbour he was hoisting sail and heading for the trackless sea.'[63] The passage to a new life had begun.

3

Human Freight

There was a sense of excitement when a ship set sail for the New World, mingled with apprehension and a great deal of confusion. Even as the *Star of the West* left the dock at Liverpool on its maiden voyage to New York in December 1850, crammed with 385, mainly Irish, passengers, latecomers were still arriving and had to toss their chests and bundles of luggage on board from the quay. The men among them found it comparatively easy to clamber aboard by the rigging but it was not so easy for the women, at least one of whom became entangled and with 'her drapery sadly discomposed, and her legs still more sadly exposed to the loiterers on shore, might be heard imploring aid from the sailors or passengers above.' Packages which fell into the dock were retrieved by the crew of a small boat following the ship and handed up to the men on deck. When the ship had cleared the dock and begun its course down the River Mersey, 'the spectators on shore took off their hats and cheered lustily, and the cheer was repeated by the whole body of emigrants on deck, who raised a shout that must have been heard at the distance of a mile even in the noisy and busy thoroughfares of Liverpool'.[1]

Such stirring send-offs were common in many European ports in the heyday of the emigrant ships. They were but a prelude to the very real horrors of steerage, with hundreds of people crowded together in squalid, cramped, poorly-lit compartments for journeys that could take about six weeks to North America in the days of sail, and considerably longer with adverse winds and bad weather. Many of the ships had actually been built for the carriage of cargo, but the cargoes of textiles and iron being carried westwards to North America took up much less space than the cotton and tobacco brought back to Europe on the eastward journey. Human freight was a way of making a trading voyage across the Atlantic more economical. Canny shipowners, especially those who had been involved in the slave trade until its abolition in 1807, realised that emigrants could make up a lucrative form of freight. In the days of the slave trade there had been a 'triangular trade' system, with manufactured goods being transported to West Africa and exchanged for slaves, who in turn were shipped across the Atlantic on the so-called 'Middle Passage' and sold to Caribbean sugar planters or American cotton and tobacco plantations, whose products were brought back to Europe. Now the trade was two-way. However, although not packed in as tightly as slaves in the hold of a slave ship, and not shackled, many of the emigrants who made up the new live freight felt as if they had been condemned to the horrors of another Middle Passage.

The emigrants were accommodated more as freight than like human beings. Temporary decks were laid out over the cargo in the lower hold, and fitted out with rough pine berths, and stocked with sufficient provisions and water for the voyage. British vessels engaged in the timber trade with Canada were considered to be the worst ones to travel on, though often the cheapest. In the 1820s and 1830s the cheapest fares from Ireland to Quebec cost as little as 30 shillings, half the fare from Liverpool to New York. These timber ships may have been cheap, but had a bad reputation as 'some of the worst kind of ships afloat.' A survey of twenty-five emigrant ships in the port of Liverpool in April 1846 revealed that nine of them had defective timbers, while a further eight had had their defects repaired; only six were wholly 'in an efficient condition.'[2] American packet ships of the Black Ball and Red Swallowtail lines were considered the best, though even these, designed for carrying cargo rather than passengers, offered little comfort or even decency. American emigrant ships were notorious for the way in which they 'leave the whole deck on which emigrants were berthed undivided in any way', so that there was no segregation of male and female passengers.[3] Moreover, the berths were only separated from each other by a 9-inch plank so that when the berths were filled with bedding there was no division at all, with the result that men, women and children all lay in 'one promiscuous heap' stretching the entire length of the ship.[4]

On the *Thomas Gelstone,* sailing from Londonderry to Montreal in 1834, there was a passage of no more than three feet between the side and centre berths, each of which contained more than five people who had no option but to eat in their berths for the nine weeks of their passage because of the lack of room. One berth was occupied by a man, his wife, his sister and five children. Another accommodated six young women with five men in the berth above them and eight men in the next one.[5] Such overcrowding had changed little from the 1750s when passengers on ships from the Netherlands were 'packed densely, like herrings so to say, in the large sea vessels'[6] and many of them cried out in their misery, 'Oh, that I were home again, and if I had to lie in my pig-sty!'[7] Almost a hundred years later, in 1848 Robert Whyte, travelling from Ireland to Quebec, despaired that 'the Black Hole of Calcutta was a mercy compared to the holds of these vessels. Yet simultaneously foreigners, Germans from Hamburg and Bremen are arriving, all healthy, robust and cheerful.'[8]

Moralists urged that the sexes in steerage should be segregated into three separate compartments. Single men would go forwards, single women aft and married couples amidships, similar to the arrangements on board British government-sponsored ships to Australia. Preferring to be berthed with people they knew and to keep extended family units together, the passengers themselves opposed such arrangements. Parents, in particular, were afraid of 'the contamination of their daughters, if removed from under their own eye, by improper characters among the single women who might be on board.'[9] Nevertheless, when the 1852 British Passenger Act stipulated that single men should be separated from the other passengers, it had little effect on maintaining public decency in steerage. A cabin passenger William Hancock observed that love-making was the principal activity in steerage, 'most of the arrangements, or lack of such, being such as to permit of the most unrestricted intercourse and placing modesty and decency at a discount.'[10]

Shipowners had themselves opposed proposals for dividing up steerage on the grounds that it would impede the flow of air and make the already serious problem of providing adequate ventilation even worse. Until the late 1840s the only way of ventilating steerage was through the hatches, which had to be kept closed in rough seas. On the six-week voyage of the *Thomas Gelstone* from Londonderry to

Montreal in 1834, the passengers were relieved that 'fortunately a succession of fine weather enabled them to keep the hatches open; in a storm they would have smothered.'[11] It was not surprising that the stench of steerage should be commented on by such observers as Joseph Morin, a quarantine station inspector on the St Lawrence, who remarked in 1830 that 'the harbour master's boatmen had no difficulty at the distance of gunshot, either when the wind was favourable or in a dead calm, in distinguishing by the odour alone a crowded ship.'[12]

Unseaworthy vessels did not always reach their destinations. The *Robert Isaac,* built at Baltimore in 1831, 'had the character of being a good staunch seaworthy vessel' when in September 1845 she was chartered 'in the usual manner to carry a number of emigrants to New York', and there was 'no suspicion that she was in every respect suitable for the voyage.' The ship set sail from Liverpool, fully stocked with 'a full quantity of provisions and water'.[13] But after six weeks at sea, the *Robert Isaac* 'was obliged to put back to the Azores where she was condemned as unseaworthy.' The unfortunate passengers were brought back to England by the *Forth* West India mail steamer, but were landed at Southampton rather than Liverpool from which they had departed. Most of them were destitute and needed assistance. The Colonial Land and Emigration Office sent an officer to enquire into the circumstances of the case, but he found that he did not need to afford any aid to the passengers since 'he was anticipated by the benevolence of the inhabitants of Southampton, and nothing was more gratifying than the prompt and efficient charity displayed by them.' The people of Southampton offered them accommodation and clothing, while the various railway companies took them to their original 'place of departure' free of charge and arranged lodging for them on their 'transit through London.'[14] Eighty of the emigrants continued with their journey to the United States, but others preferred to be 'forwarded to their homes' and abandon their plans of a new life in a new country.[15]

Concern in the United States over the ventilation and overcrowding of sailing packets led to the passing of the 1848 American Passenger Act, which laid down a legal minimum of space for each passenger and imposed requirements for ensuring the adequate circulation of air. Paradoxically, the results of this Act were worse conditions and yet more inadequate ventilation in steerage. With fewer steerage passengers allowed in the available space and a shortage of storage, the only way of maintaining profits was to build larger ships. After 1850 most American packet ships were three-decker with two steerage compartments, one above the other. With three decks, instead of two as before, they towered forty feet above the waterline. Every steerage compartment was required to have at least two ventilators and also hatchways designed so that they could be left open permanently. However, it was difficult to ventilate effectively the lower of the two steerage decks, which were darker and airless compared with the one steerage compartment of older ships, whilst the passengers in the upper steerage were assailed by the stench and effluvia from below.[16] The lower steerage on the orlop deck of the *Leibnitz*, accommodating 150 passengers for seventy days in 1868, was considered by the New York Commissioners of Emigration to be 'a perfect pest-hole, calculated to kill the healthiest man.' The planks making up its floor were so flimsy and so little supported that 'they shook when walking on them.' It was lit only by some lanterns 'that on account of the foulness of the air ... could scarcely burn.'[17]

Conditions on these new ships were exposed by the Irish land reformer and philanthropist Stephen Vere Forster, sailing in steerage on the newly built Black Star liner *Washington* in October 1850. He described the ship, carrying nine hundred steerage passengers, as 'a magnificent vessel of 1600 tons register burthen ... very strong and dry, and probably as well furnished as the best of the emigrant ships between Liverpool and New York.' He even praised the 'two lofty and well-ventilated passenger decks' with their 'high bulwarks, over six feet, to protect the decks from the spray of the sea.' However, he was more critical of the brutality of the ship's officers and their refusal to issue the passengers with the food supplies of oatmeal, rice, flour and biscuits to which they were entitled, having 'paid for and secured our passages ... in the confident expectation that the allowance of provisions promised in our contract tickets would be faithfully delivered to us.' Only water was doled out to the passengers in the first four days of the voyage. When food was issued on a more regular basis, the correct rations were rarely distributed and the distribution of provisions was invariably accompanied by ill-treatment, with passengers being 'cursed and abused, and cuffed and kicked' by the mates, while a sailor stood alongside with a rope's end to lay about him. Twice the mates, 'having served out water to about 30 persons … said they would give no more water out till the next morning, and kept their word.' When one passenger tried to hand a letter of complaint to the captain, he was knocked down by the first mate. The cook showed favouritism to passengers who plied him with bribes of money or whisky, cooking five or six meals for them daily, while passengers who did not pay a bribe were lucky to get one cooked meal a day, and often only got a hot meal on alternate days. Twelve children died of dysentery 'brought on by want of nourishing food.'[18] Vere Forster drew up a memorial of complaint, signed by 128 of his fellow passengers, but with no positive results at a time when extortion was common on other ships, such as the *Blanche* sailing from Liverpool to New Orleans in 1850, whose master practised 'a most disgraceful system of extortion', charging grossly inflated prices for necessities.[19]

Such brutality from the crew was especially feared by women passengers. The captain of the *Bache McEver*, which arrived in New Orleans from Cork in 1849, was accused of having 'conducted himself harshly and in a most improper manner to some of the female passengers', through 'having held out the inducement of better rations to two who were almost starving in the hope that they would accede to his infamous designs.'[20] The New York Commissioners of Emigration complained in 1860 of the way in which 'after reaching the high seas … the captain frequently selects some unprotected female from among the passengers, induces her to visit his cabin, and when there, abusing his power as commander, partly by threats, and partly by promises of marriage, accomplishes her ruin, and retains her in his quarters for the rest of the journey, for the indulgence of his vicious passions and the purposes of prostitution.' Other ship's officers followed the example of their captain in preying upon single young women, only to abandon them as soon as they reached shore, 'without any remedy for the past wrong which has been done upon them.'[21]

Hunger and control over provisions by the crew created the conditions in which captain and crew could abuse their positions. Until 1815 there was no requirement for a ship to carry provisions for its passengers. Whether they did or not, or whether passengers had to depend on what supplies they brought with them, depended on their contracts with the shipowner, though unscrupulous captains could ignore such agreements. Poor and inadequate supplies could cause misery on an emigrant ship as Gottlieb Mittelberger had recorded in 1750:

> But during the voyage there is on board these ships terrible misery, stench, fumes, horror, many kinds of sickness, fever, dysentery, headache, heat, constipation, boils, scurvy, cancer, mouth-rot, and the like, all of which come from old and sharply salted food and meat, also from very bad and foul water, so that many die miserably.[22]

German passengers on *General Wayne* in 1805 were denied provisions by the captain, despite having agreed that they would be allowed a certain quantity of meat, bread, peas, fish, vinegar, butter, potatoes and tobacco, and a dram of whisky every morning. After fourteen days at sea they were rationed to two biscuits, a pint of water, and two ounces of meat a day. After two or three weeks, some of the men, desperate to feed their families, broke into the stores for bread. The culprits were tied down and lashed. The rest of the passengers were also punished, with the men being denied any bread and the women only given one biscuit instead of two. Twenty-five men, women and children starved to death and 'the hunger was so great on board that all the bones about the ship were hunted up by them, pounded with a hammer and eaten.' Appeals to Captain Conklin were in vain, even when, 'what is more lamentable, some of the deceased persons, not many hours before their death, crawled on their hands and feet to the captain, and begged him, for God's sake, to give them a mouthful of bread or a drop of water to keep them from perishing.'[23]

After 1805 an official scale of victuals for emigrant ships was laid down for British ships. It was increasingly recognised in Parliament that 'it was the duty of government towards emigrants to see that they were not shipped in any case without a competent supply of food and water'. It was accepted that 'the food might be of the very commonest description, but a proper quantity of it they should have', and 'the water should be of a drinkable quality, shipped in a condition fit for human creatures; and not in old casks which had recently contained molasses or salt hides'.[24] In practice, though, emigrants from Great Britain and Ireland continued to be allowed to bring their own provisions. For many emigrants this was indeed a matter of personal choice. Irish emigrants preferred to bring with them a bag of potatoes, some oatmeal, and a few dried herrings, since they 'were made sick by a diet of beef and pudding.' The Scots considered that 'oatmeal and water was all that was necessary'. Hard ship's biscuits were popular with few travellers.[25] Inevitably, many emigrants arrived at the sea ports with insufficient supplies to last for their whole journey. In order to avoid being stopped from embarking, 'the same bag of meal or other provisions was shown as belonging to several persons in succession.'[26] When provisions inevitably ran low, passengers often stole from each other.

Many of the more unscrupulous captains, however, saw this as an opportunity to make a profit for themselves, and took little trouble to make sure that all passengers were adequately supplied. Moreover, having encouraged the unwitting emigrants to believe that their passages would be shorter than they would actually be, often no more than three weeks, they would wait until the emigrants had exhausted their stores and then sell them provisions at inflated price, often as much as 400 per cent of the actual cost price. Parish emigrants from England, who were entitled to receive rations of biscuit and beef or pork, paid for by the parish authorities funding their emigration, were also cheated by being given short measures and poor quality meat. This diet was not considered especially suitable, anyway, since 'they are incapable from seasickness of using this solid food at the beginning of the passage, when for want of small stores such as tea, sugar, coffee, oatmeal and flour, they fall into a state of debility and low spirits, by which they are incapacitated from the exertions required for cleanliness and exercise, and also indisposed to solid food, more particularly the women and children.'[27]

It was not until 1842 that the British government finally adopted proper regulations for the issue of provisions by the ship in a futile attempt to curb these abuses. In order to keep costs down, the far from generous scale only provided for 7 lbs of food for each person a week, with half of it being in bread or biscuit, and the rest in potatoes.

Gradually, the scale was extended to include flour, rice, molasses, tea, sugar, beef and pork, but no control over quality was maintained and much of what was supplied was inedible. William Mure, the British consul at New Orleans, complained to the Colonial Office that on most ships coming from Liverpool 'the bread is mostly condemned bread, ground over with a little fresh flour, sugar and saleratus[28] and re-baked. It would kill a horse.'[29] He actually blamed the poor quality of the pork for an outbreak of fever on the *Blanche* in 1850.

Yet even when passengers in steerage received regular, adequate and edible provisions, they were often too ill with seasickness to cook it for themselves. After 1852 all emigrant ships departing from United Kingdom ports were required to carry cooked rather than raw food. Already ships carrying over a hundred passengers were required to carry 'a seafaring person to act as passengers' cook, and also with a proper cooking apparatus.' After its adoption by the American Passenger Act of 1855, this regulation became standard on all emigrant ships. Legislation, however, could not improve the quality of the food available or the environment in which it was eaten. On the *Prinzessin Irene* in 1903, emigrants from Naples were fed macaroni, beef, boiled potatoes and red wine, each ladled out from a separate 25-gallon mess tin. It was inevitably cold before everyone could be served. The biscuits served at breakfast were 'as hard as a landlord's heart, and as tasteless as a bit of rag carpet'.[30] Some cooks and stewards made a profit by selling the leftovers from the first- and second-class dining rooms to the steerage passengers.[31] As late as 1908 emigrants on some Italian vessels, 'squatting on the decks near the stairs, with a plate between the legs and a piece of bread between the feet, ate their pasta like beggars at the doors of convents.'[32]

Water was another problem aboard the sailing ships. Stored in wooden casks that had formerly held oil, vinegar, turpentine or wine, it was often undrinkable except in extremity. The Reverend William Bell, travelling on the *Rothiemurchus* from Leith to Quebec in 1817 complained that:

Our water has for some time been very bad. When it was drawn out of the casks it was no cleaner than that of a dirty kennel after a shower of rain, so that its appearance alone was sufficient to sicken one. But its dirty appearance was not its worst quality. It had such a rancid smell that to be in the same neighbourhood was enough to turn the stomach.[33]

The casks themselves were often in poor condition, 'very many of them old oak casks, made up with pine heads, which therefore leak, if they do not fall to pieces, which often happens.'[34] This situation was slow to change and in 1848 such a 'want of pure water was sensibly felt by the afflicted creatures' on stricken ships, who not only lacked adequate drinking water but also clean water for washing themselves and their clothes. Hygiene inevitably took a second place to thirst-quenching.[35]

What was to solve the problem of contaminated water was the use of iron tanks for the storage of water. With the water so unpleasant to drink, alcohol was an attractive alternative for passengers and crew. Stephen Vere Forster believed that on many ships 'drunkenness, with its consequent train of ruffianly debasement, is not discouraged, because it is profitable to the captain, who traffics in grog'; he further claimed that 'once or twice a week ardent spirits were sold indiscriminately to the passengers, producing scenes of unchecked blackguardism beyond description.'[36]

Inevitably, the abiding memories of most emigrants of their experience in steerage on the sailing ships was of seasickness, foul odours, and the monotony of the sea. On well-run ships, especially those sailing from Bremen, discipline was tight and the emigrants were kept busy. British and American ships were less well regulated although they followed a similar regime. All steerage passengers were required to rise from their berths at six in the morning in summer and seven in winter. After dressing, and washing themselves, when water was available for that purpose, the passengers were set to work by the second mate to clean steerage while those designated as cooks for mess groups of eight or twelve passengers would be sent on deck to prepare breakfast under the overall supervision of the ship's cook, a member of the crew. In fine weather all the steerage passengers would eat on deck, but had to stay in steerage in stormy weather, when sometimes it was impossible for them to have their three cooked meals a day, which were normally at eight, one and six o'clock. Smoking was only allowed on deck and candles could not be lit for fear of fire.[37] That did not stop many of the emigrants from breaking the rules against smoking, swearing, card playing and fighting to break the monotony of a long voyage.

It was a technological revolution that changed the conditions in which emigrants crossed the Atlantic and reduced the number of days of monotony. Steamships offered faster journeys but at first were far too expensive for the majority of emigrants even to consider. Cabin fares on the new Cunard and Collins mail steamships cost eight times as much as the cost of passage in steerage on a sailing ship, which was typically between £3 10s and £5. Samuel Cunard, founder of the Cunard Lines, told the British Parliament considering the plight of victims of the Irish potato famine in 1847 that 'you could not possibly, I think, send them by steamer; it is so very expensive.'[38] Yet, as the financier Melmotte recognised in Anthony Trollope's *The Way We Live Now* of 1875, there was money to be made from shipping emigrants, and so 'he had a fleet – or soon would have a fleet of emigrant ships – ready to carry every discontented Irishman out of Ireland.'[39]

But it was during the dark years of the Irish famine that mass emigration by steamship really became a possibility with the launch in 1850 of the Inman Lines screw ship *City of Glasgow*, which had space for fifty-two first-class passengers, fifty-eight passengers in second class and four hundred in steerage. Although fitted with a bathroom, the ship was functional rather than luxurious with its 'internal fittings ... tasteful and genteel, and got up with a view to comfort and pleasantness, rather than to dazzle with unprofitable brilliancy'.[40] With an improved engine and boiler, a more efficient hull design and an improved propeller, this iron screw steamship could keep costs down, allowing for cheaper fares. The boilers consumed no more than twenty tons of coal a day compared with the sixty tons burned on Cunard's *America*, although it was slower than the sleeker mail liners. It was possible to keep fares down to £21 in first class and £12 12s in second. Although the first newspaper advertisements firmly stated 'no steerage passengers taken', it was hailed as 'an effort to combine a reasonable degree of speed with certainty and cheapness.'[41]

The decision to carry emigrants in steerage on the *City of Glasgow* and subsequent Inman Line steamships was a direct response to the famine caused by the Irish potato blight. The senior partner in the Inman Line, John Grubb Richardson, was a Quaker with a strong social conscience, who had in 1847 built a model industrial village at Bessbrook in County Armagh, which had the dual advantage of 'enabling us to control our people and do them good in every sense.'[42] Encouraging the emigration of labourers who wished to flee Ireland in the hunger years, by offering fares in steerage at only £6 6s, was another opportunity for him to combine social concern with sound commercial sense. Richardson's junior partner William Inman was less easily convinced of the business benefits of carrying steerage passengers, but soon changed his mind after he and his wife sailed to Philadelphia aboard the *City of Glasgow* with four hundred emigrants in steerage. He 'learned to look upon them as the safest cargo', since 'they made the ship buoyant and fire could not break out without some living person on board immediately noticing it.' Inman ensured that the steerage passengers were efficiently stowed, with single men and women at each end, separated by married couples. They took up less space than cabin passengers and did not expect the same level of steward service. For the emigrants themselves, the attraction was that the cost of their passage was not much more than on the sailing ships, but the journey only took about two weeks, with less discomfort and less risk of epidemics breaking out. Humanitarian and business interests were at one.[43]

Steerage on the *City of Glasgow* soon became popular, but the ship was not to remain long in the emigrant trade. The flagship of the Inman Line, it set sail 'in a state of perfect efficiency' from Liverpool for Philadelphia on 1 March 1854 with 111 cabin passengers, 293 people in steerage, and seventy-six crew. It was the last that was heard of the ship.[44] When the ship had still not reached Philadelphia after five and a half weeks at sea, the shipowners acknowledged that there was 'some anxiety being felt for her safety' among the families and friends of its passengers and crew, but declared that 'we ourselves feel no anxiety for her safety.' There was enough meat aboard for forty-six days at the rate of a pound for each person each day, fifty-four days of bread and flour, 6 tons of potatoes and fresh water for fifty-four days. There was only enough coal aboard to last for twenty-four days, but the ship could use its sails. The owners believed 'the vessel to be detained in the ice on the banks of Newfoundland and unable to make her way out of it.'[45] By May, after various false sightings, there was no doubt that the ship was lost, or that 'the most painful apprehensions are entertained as to her fate.'[46]

Concern about the safety of iron screw ships in the North Atlantic was again raised when the Inman Line lost a further ship a few months after the never to be resolved disappearance of the *City of Glasgow*. In September 1854 the *City of Philadelphia* ran aground on its maiden voyage, because none of the compasses on board were giving the same reading, thought to be the result of magnetic distortion by the iron hull, and star navigation was impossible in dense fog and driving rain. Fortunately, no lives were lost in this latest disaster for the Inman Line, but business inevitably suffered and the company only survived because its ships were needed to carry troops and supplies for the British forces during the Crimean War, a period of which William Inman acknowledged that 'we made our chief profits in the war.' By the time that Inman passenger services to North America were resumed in spring 1856, passengers, no longer mindful of the disasters of 1854, flocked back to the cheap fares and shorter voyages on offer.[47]

As the Quaker John Richardson had dissolved his partnership with William Inman at the beginning of the Crimean War, rather than be involved in servicing the sinews of war, the connections with Quaker business interests in Philadelphia were dropped, and the ships now sailed to New York, which brought the Inman Line into direct competition with Cunard.[48] Samuel Cunard was most interested in maintaining his contracts for carrying the mail and averred that 'for long voyages paddles unquestionably are the best', and that 'the screw propeller is an excellent auxiliary to a sailing ship, but to carry mails with regulated time you must have paddle wheels.'[49] He was adamant that 'generally through the year we have found that the paddle is more regular than the screw', which he ascribed to the way that 'the shaft frequently gets out of order, and the fans are frequently broken off.'[50] He also considered that the Inman Line screw ships with their emigrants were unsafe. Cunard, unlike Inman, prided himself that no lives had yet been lost on his ships, because of his continued reliance on the older but supposedly safer technology of paddle steamers, and claimed that 'we should not after twenty years' experience, continue to build paddle ships if we had not some good reason derived from our experience.'[51] He also believed that his mail ships with only cabin passengers were safer for carrying the mail because in an emergency good order could be more easily maintained:

> I have always considered it inconsistent with the safety of the mails to carry emigrants, and have never, during the twenty years we have been engaged in this service carried any ... Our ships are provided with boats sufficient to secure the safety of the crew and passengers in case of accident from fire, or any other cause; and generally we have enough to do to take care of them and the mails. But if we had 400 or 500 emigrants, the emigrants will cause the immediate loss of the whole, for they rush to the boats, and we have no control over them ... If you carry emigrants, you run the risk of losing the mails.[52]

Cunard's business partners were less conservative in their views of screw steamers and less prejudiced in seeing the commercial value of emigrants. They, together with the other prestigious lines, such as the National and Collins Lines, soon followed the Inman Line in profiting from the large numbers of emigrants leaving Europe for North America. In 1862 the Cunard Line launched its first screw ship intended for the emigrant trade. The *China* carried 160 passengers in first class and 770 in steerage. It was also more economical in its fuel consumption than the faster ships intended for the transport of mail, burning a mere 82 tons of coal each day. So profitable was this new venture that a second emigrant steamship, the *Cuba*, was launched in 1864, plying the route from Liverpool to New York with a stop at Queenstown to pick up Irish emigrants. There still remained a prejudice amongst paying passengers towards the screw ships, seen as 'the dernier resort of poor people who could afford nothing better',[53] although some passengers saw them in a more romantic light as being 'like a revolving auger, boring an endless gimlet hole in the eastern horizon', and gliding 'through the water like a bird through the air, without jerk and without pause.'[54] *The Lancet* reported that now for the vast majority of emigrants 'the middle passage has very few horrors.'[55]

However, when Samuel Amos travelled in steerage on the *City of New York* in 1865 his first impression, standing on deck in the Mersey, 'strewn with freight and baggage of every imaginable description', was that 'you would have thought that chaos had come again'. Around him was 'the turmoil' of 'emigrants laden with trunks, bedding, cooking utensils ... stumbling confusedly about', where 'the men are cursing, the women taking frantic leave of their friends, children crying, agents and officials with throats of brass shouting and endeavouring in vain to drive the emigrants below as they come on board from the tug, while loud above all is heard the deafening noise of the steam as the engines are preparing for their long haul.'[56] Escaping in search of his berth, Amos found 'confusion worse confounded':

> Follow me now into the compartment in which I have discovered 'Berth No 25'. It is a space two yards long by one broad, and to the left and right of this rise three tiers of bunks. Imagine the drawer frame of a chemist's shop destitute of its drawers and you will form a good idea of these same bunks. There are twenty of them in the compartment and into each one the future occupant is busy putting what bedding he has provided himself with as the company provides nothing excepting space and victuals.[57]

The taller occupants of these cramped bunks had no option but to sleep with their legs hanging over the ends. Apprehensive about the weight of the Frenchman who had the bunk above his, Amos offered to swap places with him. Amos's nineteen berth mates were indeed from all parts of Europe: two United States sailors returning from China, two Englishmen, four Frenchmen, four Irishmen who boarded at Queenstown, two Germans, two Swedes, a Dutchman, a Spaniard, and a Polish priest on his way to Mexico, whose ways of passing the tedium of the passage all confirmed Amos in his prejudices about their national stereotypes:

> The Yankees are chewing and talking politics. The Englishmen are walking backwards and forward in the corridor. The French are playing cards and chattering gaily the while. The Germans are lying in bed smoking. Of course the Spaniard is sleeping; while the Swede is reading the history of Charles the Twelfth, and the Dutchman cleaning his tin plates.[58]

The Irish were happy so long as they had a bottle of whisky for solace, but once that had gone became argumentative since 'now his whisky is done, he has nothing to fall back on', and 'he becomes quite gloomy and low-spirited, and is just about to take to his bed when, in sheer desperation, he makes a vigorous onslaught on the taller of the two Yankees', only to be restrained by his fellow passengers and taken away by the steward and his boys to sober up.[59]

The Italian medical inspector Teodorico Rosati considered that the dormitories in steerage, with their straw mattresses provided by the emigrants themselves and thrown overboard at the end of the voyage, were soon 'reduced, one way or another, to the condition of a dog kennel'.[60] On one British ship in 1888 there were sixteen people in one cabin which was so narrow that there was no room 'for a stout man to pass', and the cabins were soon 'fouled with vomit.'[61] The Board of Trade was aware that steerage conditions for poorly-clad and rough-mannered passengers in 1888 were bad enough to evoke 'feelings both of pity and disgust', but admitted that they were no worse than 'the crowded cottage of an English labourer, the close, narrow garret of the workman, or the cabin of the Connemara peasant.'[62] However, any attempts to improve conditions would mean such a steep rise in fares as to make them unaffordable for most emigrants.

Despite the crowding, the steamships did represent a great improvement over the conditions on the sailing ships, and it was the behaviour of many of the emigrants themselves that tended to make life in steerage difficult. As there was little room for luggage and all but the essentials went into the hold, many passengers had no choice but to wear the same clothes for the entire voyage. Some men wore their one suit of clothing throughout the passage, however much it might be stained by rain, seawater, food, urine and vomit, with little opportunity to clean either themselves or their filthy garments.[63] Many of the 'younger passengers of the better class at the commencement of their voyage endeavoured to keep up appearances in spite of all difficulties, and to present themselves on deck fresh from a careful toilette and in all the neatness of clean linen', but as the journey went on they no longer bothered to keep themselves looking neat, and 'languid and weary, they crowded on deck, unwashed and uncombed ... and they thought no more of struggling against adverse circumstances and were content to "peg along" until their feminine instincts revived at the welcome sight of the wished for land.'[64]

Emigrants from poorer backgrounds were even blamed for any squalor found in steerage:

> Another fact that the sentimental humanitarian, in his efforts at reformation, often loses sight of, or does not know, is that the large majority of these people are of the lowest order of humanity. They are filthy in their habits, coarse in manner and often low in their instincts ... A great amount of discomfort among these emigrants arises from their own ignorance and life-long habits. Many of them have lived in hovels to which the steerage of a steamship, in comparison, is a palace.[65]

For such people, in the eyes of their more affluent critics, by 1873 'the treatment of steerage passengers on the responsible and respectable English and German lines is generally good, judged by the popular standard of what is due the poor and ignorant classes in return for value given by them.'[66]

Middle-class moralists were concerned about the conditions in which young women were travelling, especially single, unaccompanied young women. There was outrage when in 1881 the Irish writer Charlotte O'Brien alleged in a letter in the *Pall Mall Gazette* revealing the 'Horrors of an Emigrant Ship', that single women and married couples were berthed in the same compartments of steerage on White Star ships amidst scenes of 'sin, full of ravening wickedness and all manner of uncleanness.'[67] However, after she was invited to inspect the ship in question, the *Germanic*, she wrote to the Secretary of State for Ireland to say that 'as it is at present, nothing can exceed the beauty and perfection of the arrangements. I can in no way reconcile my former impressions with what was to-day shown us' on *Germanic*, yet refused to concede that her charges against the emigrant ships might be sensationalist and overdrawn.[68] Joseph Chamberlain at the Board of Trade was keen not only that single men, women, and married couples should be separately accommodated for the sake of decency, but also that every emigrant ship carrying a significant number of single women should have 'a woman of character and experience in the position of a matron.'[69]

The women passengers were objects of lust not just to their fellow male passengers, but also to the crew. In the evenings some of the

sailors, cooks, engineers and firemen would go on the upper deck to
flirt with them, occasionally becoming obscene in their language and
threatening the men from steerage who tried to defend their
womenfolk. Under the influence of alcohol, 'one young mariner put
his arm around the waist of a very handsome young Englishwoman,
whose lady-like dress and appearance had so far prevented her from
being molested' in this way. When her husband went to her defence, the
sailor had to be held back from starting a fight. The ship's master told
the aggrieved husband that the delinquent would be handed over to
the authorities for punishment when the ship reached New York, but
the sailor was later seen by some of the emigrants on shore 'in a state
of great hilarity and beer', and he told them 'with much blasphemy
that he had cut his connection with the ship' to escape any punishment.
As a result, many of the women chose to remain below deck to avoid
any harassment. A middle-class Roman Catholic London clerk, who
had fallen into poverty and found himself in steerage on a White Star
ship in 1872, thus witnessing this harassment of women emigrants,
considered that 'most of our troubles arose from the crew and
attendants rather than the arrangements of the ship itself.'[70]

On the Guion Line's *Alaska* in 1884, the bakers, stewards and sailors
were almost always drunk on porter, though only one of them, the
bartender, was unpleasant to the steerage passengers. It was even
possible for the crew and passengers to become friends. Thomas I
Wharton, a twenty-five-year-old Philadelphia lawyer, had on a whim
decided to travel in steerage, having previously made a voyage to
Europe in the luxury of first class. Considering that the fare in steerage
from New York to Liverpool on the Cunarder *Oregon* was only 15
dollars, and was 4 guineas, then the equivalent of 21 dollars, for the
return journey from Liverpool on the *Alaska*, he decided that 'it must
be more profitable to travel than stay at home.' He was not unhappy
with his berth, made of canvas on an iron frame, and commented that
'none of us were really uncomfortable at all, except for the
grumblers.'[71] He also made firm friends with the sailor Ned Kennedy
after sharing his flask with him one day, and regretted that he might
never again meet the 'good soul he was', with his 'brown beard,
oilskins and bare feet', and with whom he discussed books they had
both read.[72] Wharton considered that life in steerage allowed a

passenger greater freedom to make friends with the crew, and find out what was going on throughout the ship, than travelling in the greater luxury and formality of cabin class:

> The steerage passenger, in spite of ropes and placards, is really free of the ship. What cabin grandee is invited into the forecastle, or walks welcome into the quartermaster's room? Has the warm friendship of the baker, or is even on speaking terms with the firemen? Knows when the watches relieve each other, or what his dinner is going to be before he gets it? Sees the ice dragged up from the ice-house, and the beef hauled into the galley? Hears what is going on up on the bridge, in the engine room, in the second cabin, down in the stoke-room? ... For my own part, I am ashamed of the airs I have given myself in the days when I was a first-class passenger, and the next time I travel first-class I shall be less proud.[73]

Inevitably, the food in steerage was not as good as in cabin class, but Wharton considered that 'really it is good fare', though he did think, even though 'I do not wish to be unjust to the Guion victuals', that 'I was treated better by the Cunard company.'[74] Salt cod served on Fridays was not to his taste, but he found the simple, hurriedly served, bread and meat to be excellent, unlike the unbaked bread, lack of fresh meat and inedible potatoes served to the more than a thousand steerage passengers on the *City of Paris* in 1868.[75] Samuel Amos, travelling in 1865 on another Inman ship *City of New York*, had considered the food 'good and abundant', but admitted that 'the only thing one craves is a little more variety.'[76] The hot rolls, butter and coffee served to steerage passengers for breakfast was a contrast to the breakfasts for cabin passengers on the *City of Boston*, for which 'England and America seem to be alternately ransacked for the juiciest hams and the most succulent beef and mutton', leading Henry Morford to declare that 'I have never breakfasted and dined so well elsewhere as during that period.'[77] In steerage, meals were served from large buckets and eaten at tables, where available, or at the emigrant's berth. Breakfast in 1872 on White Star ships was little more than watery coffee, bread, biscuits and potatoes. Dinner at noon would begin with soup, often 'a hot compound with a faint reminiscence of gravy and mutton bones', followed by invariably inedible meat or salt fish, steamed potatoes and boiled rice. Tea at five o'clock was served with biscuits and butter. Sundays might be marked by a treat of plum duff pudding with raisins. Such 'victuals seemed generally to be of good quality and, except in the case of the fresh bread and sugar, were provided with lavish if not wasteful abundance.'[78]

With some passengers eating at their berths in bad weather, or because they did not wish to eat on deck, where there were no separate dining rooms keeping steerage clean was difficult. The sleeping compartments would be cleaned every day after breakfast. Thomas Wharton was impressed that 'this was always fairly well done, as far as I could tell', and that 'the floor was well swept and scrubbed, and the steerage generally smelt sweet enough by the time we returned to it.'[79] The United States Congress enquiry into steerage conditions in 1873 found that the newer ships were better ventilated and cleaner, with the stewards sweeping the floors and sprinkling sand and sawdust on them every day, so that 'much of the cruelty, ill-usage and general discomfort of the steerage passage belong to the history of the past.'[80] Wharton would have agreed with that assessment with the rider that 'in certain particulars, the sanitary conditions were not the best possible', though that 'is, of course, in great part the fault of the emigrants.'[81] Some of them even had to be taught how to use the lavatories.

Effluence remained a perennial problem on the ships. The better class of steamer had separate lavatories for men and women, fitted with washbasins and provided with hot and cold water deemed 'essential to the comfort of the passengers and conducive to health'.[82] On the White Star ships to New York in 1872, the lavatory for the forward steerage had a tile floor, eight water closets, four hand basins and four sinks. One passenger considered that 'putting aside the absence of any privacy, the arrangements were suitable and the fittings generally clean.'[83] Generally, however, there were never enough water closets for the large number of passengers carried. The *Angelo*, employed in 1881 to carry emigrants from Sweden to Liverpool where they would take ship for America, only had small and cramped lavatories, lacking water for flushing, which were condemned as 'more evil-smelling, unsatisfactory places it is difficult to imagine.'[84] Another ship in 1888 had its toilets located on the same deck as the ship's hospital; these consisted of five seats over a trough, without any partitions to afford even the most minimal of privacy. On that ship there were no toilets below deck, so that desperate 'passengers sometimes make use of the alleyway which forms a sort of gutter around the ship.' The result of this was that the bilge became fouled and putrescent, producing noxious gases which travelled upwards 'compromising the health not merely of steerage but also the first class passengers.' It did not escape the public health officials that 'there is no such thing as steerage bilge. Class distinctions cannot be maintained in what is practically the ship's sewer.' E de Amicis, sailing on an Italian vessel in the same year, complained that 'the place that should have been the cleanest was a horror, with only one bath for 1,500 third class passengers.'[85]

As the nineteenth century continued, the improvement of steerage conditions slowed and then reversed. The 1908 United States Immigration Committee found that conditions in steerage had deteriorated since the 1880s. The number of water closets and wash basins installed were still too few considering the number of passengers involved, and 'the floors of both wash rooms and water closets are damp and often filthy until the last day of the voyage, when they are cleaned in preparation for the inspection at the port of entry.'[86] Indeed, general standards of hygiene were more than inadequate:

Sweeping is the only form of cleaning done. No sick cans are furnished, and not even large receptacles for waste. The vomitings of the sick are often permitted to remain a long time before being removed. The floors, when iron, are continually damp, and when of wood, they reek with foul odour because they are not washed.[87]

This decline in standards was partly due to the greater number of emigrants now coming from southern and eastern Europe, which reached almost 1,300,000 in 1907. Older ships were being used and there was much overcrowding. In 1904 the *Celtic* arrived in New York with 283 more passengers than it had berths for,[88] and in 1906 women on the same ship had to be put into the men's quarters.[89] There was also a vague feeling that the growing number of immigrants from Italy, Poland, Russia and the Austro-Hungarian empire were of an inferior racial stock who would not appreciate better conditions. A Cunard official in 1888 considered it a sign of the superiority of Cunard ships that they mainly carried respectable British and Scandinavian emigrants, and hardly any Italians or Slavs.[90]

Edward Steiner, a frequent traveller on emigrant ships, thought that 'steerage ought to be and could be abolished by law', and that while 'it is true that the Italian and Polish peasant may not be accustomed to better things at home and might not be happier in better surroundings nor know how to use them ... it is a bad introduction to our life to treat him like an animal when he is coming to us.'[91] Even on an elegant and spacious ship like *Kaiser Wilhelm II* of the North German Line, the emigrants were housed in 1906 in the hold, and 'packed like cattle, making a walk on deck when the weather is good, absolutely impossible, while to breathe clean air below in rough weather, when the hatches are down is an equal impossibility.'[92] In that, it differed little from the emigrant ships of 1864 when the former sailor John Wilson and his wife 'suffered for ten nights with the companionways fastened down ... to keep the water from flooding down below, and to keep the fear-stricken passengers out of the way of the sailors.' Wilson was not worried when 'the water could be heard rushing about on deck', but as someone who had been to sea in his youth, as one of his friends pointed out, 'it's nowt to thou; thou's used tid.'[93]

For a woman investigator for the 1911 United States Emigration Commission, travelling in disguise as a Bohemian peasant, 'during those twelve days in the steerage, I lived in a disorder and in surroundings that offended every sense', where she had to contend with the dirt where 'everything was dirty, sticky and disagreeable to the touch', and the noise from 'the vile language of the men, the screams of the women defending themselves, the crying of children ... and practically every sound that reached the ear irritated beyond endurance.' What she found most repugnant was 'the general air of immorality', and 'the improper, indecent and forced mingling of men and women, who were strangers and often did not understand one word of the same language.'[94]

Steerage on such ships reflected the melting pot of the new world to which the passengers were heading. It also marked a midway point between the old and new worlds. Edward Steiner noted that the position of the average steerage passenger was 'part of his lot in life; the ship is just like Russia, Austria, Poland or Italy. The cabin passengers are the lords and ladies, the sailors and officers are the police and the army, while the captain is the king or czar.'[95] It was also an opportunity to meet the other nationalities he would be living and working amongst in the new country.

Charles Dickens evoked the mixture and companionship of people travelling in steerage in the 1840s when he sent the eponymous hero of his novel *Martin Chuzzlewit* to North America:

There were English people, Irish people, Welsh people, and Scotch people there; all with their little store of coarse food and shabby clothes; and nearly all with their families of children. There were children of all ages; from the baby at the breast, to the slattern-girl who was as much a grown woman as her mother. Every kind of domestic suffering that is born in poverty, illness, banishment, sorrow, and long travel in bad weather, was crammed into the little space; and yet there was infinitely less of complaint and querulousness, and infinitely more of mutual assistance and general kindness to be found in that unwholesome ark, than in many brilliant ballrooms.[96]

Whilst Martin Chuzzlewit was ashamed to be travelling in such low company in steerage, and hid in his berth so as not to be recognised, or to have to mingle with his perceived social inferiors, his manservant Mark Tapley was happy to help his fellow travellers to overcome the difficulties of the voyage by assisting them with any chores needed and, through little acts of human kindness, kept spirits up. Dickens's picture of the atmosphere in steerage could have applied throughout the nineteenth century, but with a greater mixture of nationalities and tongues to add to the confusion.

The journalist Stephen Graham, having decided in March 1912 to 'follow up the movements of the people out of the depths of Europe into America', found himself in 'a strange gathering of seekers, despairers, wanderers, pioneers, criminals, scapegoats', amongst whom 'no one ever saw a greater miscellaneity and promiscuity of peoples brought together by accident.'[97] Among them were dandified Spaniards, homely Italian families, a Danish engineer, cowboys returning to the American West, boisterous Flemings, 'gentle youths in shirts which womenfolk had embroidered in Little Russia', Jewish patriarchs in gabardines, Norwegians in knitted jackets, Italian men 'resting their elbows on the table as if they'd just come into a public house in their native land', smart Americans in spruce suits, and Russian peasants. As well as farm labourers there were coal miners, weavers, spinners, tailors, clerks, shop keepers, musicians, and even music hall artistes.[98] As the journey progressed, these very different people began to mix with each other. When 'two dreamy Norwegians' began to play their concertinas, 'rough men danced with one another, and the more fortunate danced with the girls, dance after dance endlessly.'[99] A homesick young Englishman, forced into emigration by unemployment and the feeling that 'England's pretty well played out', soon forgot the sweetheart he had left behind, to dance with a pretty Russian girl. Young men flirted with new-found girlfriends and an Irishman tossed his girl in a blanket in a bout of high spirits. Drinkers and gamblers found like-minded companions among other nationalities. By contrast, the loner Paul Knaplund on the *Caronia* in 1906 found that, because 'the Cunarder's passengers were a microcosm of Europe with its babel of tongues and its class distinctions', it was very obvious that many emigrants in steerage did not much socialise beyond their immediate families, friends or fellow countrymen, and that 'the third-class passengers who divided into national groups never mingled with either those from the steerage or those from second'.[100] The more gregarious Graham passed the time by teaching English to some of the Russian emigrants who, together with Jewish passengers, had been allocated 'the dirtiest cabins in the ship', where each night 'the Slavs were saying their prayers whilst just above them we British were singing comic songs or listening to them'.[101]

Yet amongst all the frantic socialising, there was still a sense of 'how lonely it is on the steerage deck in the crowd of a thousand strangers, hearing a score of unknown tongues about your ears, hearing your own language so pronounced you scarce recognise it.'[102] The emigrant ship could indeed be a lonely place of passage to the unknown.

4

Once a Convict ...

Not all emigrants were voluntarily seeking a better life, but were being sent to the colonies in the hope that starting again would help them to expiate the crimes they had committed in the past from which they were escaping, and to remove a source of delinquency from the home country. The emigrants on government-assisted passages to Australia owed a great deal to the ordeals of the convicts, whose transportation had begun the European settlement of Australia and whose shipboard experience laid down the standards for all emigrant ships. The first convict ships were sent out to Botany Bay in 1787 under the command of Captain Arthur Phillip, who had protested when presented with 568 male and 191 female convicts, dirty and naked from the gaols in which they had been confined. Sixteen of them died from gaol fever, as typhus was then known, even before the six transport ships sailed. Many of the women were so ferocious that every night they had to be battened down in the hold because 'the hatches over the place where they were confined could not be suffered to be laid off, during the night, without a promiscuous intercourse immediately taking place between them and the seamen and marines'.[1] Arthur Bowes, surgeon on the *Lady Penrhyn*, which only carried women convicts, considered that 'there was never a more abandoned set of wretches collected in any place at any period than are now to be met with in this ship.' The voyage lasted 250 days before the Royal Navy Captain Phillip brought his fleet into Port Jackson, effectively founding Australia on the shores of Sydney Harbour.

Only twenty of the convicts had died during that voyage, partly because of the £2,000 worth of drugs provided for the convict fleet, and the supplies of fresh fruit and vegetables taken on board at Rio de Janeiro. Bowes believed that not only were the officers well-fed, and

'I may venture to say our table on board ship will yield the palm to few tables on shore', but also believed that the convicts were given better treatment than they deserved:

> During a long and tedious voyage, when they have been under the necessity of stowing them very close together, it is rather extra-ordinary how very healthy the convicts on board this ship in particular, and the fleet in general, have been ... But this pheno-menon will not appear so strange when I inform my readers how well the Government provided for the convicts. I believe I may venture to say few marines going out of England upon service were ever better provided for than these convicts are, and, to the credit of the officers and surgeons of the different ships, the greatest attention is paid to making them keep themselves and their berths well aired and perfectly clean; which together with the remarkably fine weather ... has not a little conduced to their health.[2]

The early convict ships were under the control of the Royal Navy, but after 1795 transportation was left in the hands of private contractors, who were paid £18 for each convict they carried, whether dead or alive. It was possibly more commercially profitable if some of the men, women and children on board were to die, since the contractor could sell their victuals at inflated prices in the new colony of Botany Bay. In the hope of ensuring that more care would be taken of the convicts during the voyage, the British Government began to pay a bonus of £4 10s 6d for each convict landed in good health. Notwithstanding such a generous financial incentive, the more unscrupulous masters of ships carried so much private cargo for sale in Australia that on the *Atlas* the scuttles could not be opened, and the atmosphere below deck became so foul that candles were extinguished by it.[3] Moreover, once embarked on a convict ship, the prisoners were subject to beatings and floggings to keep them in order. On the *Britannia* in 1797, floggings of two hundred and three hundred lashes were common; not surprisingly the death rate was one in seventeen. Of the 6,634 convicts transported between 1787 and 1800, one in 8.57 of the men and one in 28.2 of the women died.[4]

The scandal of the convict ships was brought to public attention in 1814 when fifty-four men, including the master, the two mates and the surgeon, as well as convicts and crew, died of typhus on the *Surrey*. The disease had appeared within a fortnight of the ship sailing and the ship had been fumigated. However, only twenty convicts had been allowed on deck to exercise at any one time. Soap was not issued, so that it could be held back for sale on arrival, and the convicts' wine ration had been withheld. The surviving crew members were in such a poor condition that they could not bring the ship into harbour. William Redfern, an assistant colonial surgeon appointed to enquire into what had happened, remarked that it was 'only to be wondered at that so few died', but that the voyage of the *Surrey* offered 'an awful and useful lesson.' He recommended a more generous allowance of wine and lemon juice to prevent scurvy, better and cleaner clothing for the convicts, regular exercise, and 'an effusion of cold water over the body' to prevent the spread of the 'most subtle poison' of typhus. More importantly, he recommended that the surgeon on a convict ship should be given complete authority to challenge brutal, incompetent or drunken captains, and to enforce strict standards of sanitation and hygiene. Redfern was well-placed to make such recommendations. He had been a naval surgeon until he himself had been transported in 1801 for taking part in the Nore naval mutiny of 1797. After working as an assistant surgeon at the Norfolk Island penal settlement, he was pardoned in 1803, but continued to work as a surgeon in the new colony before joining the Colonial Medical Establishment at Sydney in 1808. The construction of a new general hospital at Sydney was one of his most lauded achievements, but perhaps even more important was the acceptance of his recommendations about the role of the surgeon on convict ships.[5]

As a result of Redfern's recommendations, the surgeon super-intendent was to play an important role on the convict ships until the end of transportation in 1868, and also on the emigrant ships which were to become even more important than the convict ships for the settlement of Australia. Appointed by the Admiralty and with a naval background, the surgeon superintendent had powers over the unfettering of the convicts, the time for exercise and fresh air on deck, the issue of rations, the administration of punishments, and even the placing of guards. Medical examinations were held before boarding and anyone suffering from an infectious disease was not allowed to embark. Clean uniforms were given to the newly washed and shaved convicts, whose quarters were regularly fumigated. The decks were frequently holystoned to keep them clean. The surgeon was even charged with ensuring that religious services were held and that something was done to educate the children on board. It was all designed to maintain the health and morale of the ships and was based on the role played by surgeons on the ships of the Royal Navy, which in this, as in other areas, offered a model for the improvement in standards of health and hygiene outside the naval forces.[6]

Discipline was strict but the convicts could not always be kept under firm control. After a mutiny on the *Chapman* had been suppressed, the surgeon was terrified of going below deck to tend the wounds inflicted on the prisoners by the guards, because of the vicious character of the mutineers.[7] In 1823 Surgeon Hall was threatened when 'six women conspired to murder me', encouraged by a bottle of rum from the mate, 'and did actually form a mutiny of an alarming nature, in which I was knocked down in the prison, beaten and kicked.'[8] Despite attempts to improve their lot through better conditions, an adequate diet, exercise, dancing, boxing, classes in tailoring and handicrafts, and religious instruction, the convicts often remained recalcitrant.

John Campbell, an ex-naval surgeon who had also sailed on a Greenland whaling vessel, was appointed as superintendent surgeon on the *William Jardine* in 1850, a time when 'the service had for a long time carried on very successfully and the arrangements made to ensure the health and safety of the convicts left little to be desired.' He had sole charge of the arrangements for the 261 convicts aboard this former slave ship, and was responsible for organising the convicts into messes, allocating them work, supervising the work of the religious instructor in educating the children, and punishing anyone who disobeyed the hygiene regulations. It was his responsibility to issue regulations for the conduct of the prisoners, with punishments for 'swearing, insolence and dirty habits', as well as for 'profanation of the Sabbath day'. Faces and hands were to be washed daily and a bath taken once a week, while prisoners were also forbidden to have any personal possessions. Under his regime, 'the greatest order and regularity prevails, and the prison deck is so clean that it would be difficult to detect a dirty spot.' It was little wonder that Campbell was later appointed senior medical officer at Dartmoor prison.[9]

By this time free emigrants were also being carried on convict ships, so it was even more important that discipline was effective. Not everyone approved of this mix. Surgeon Thomas Keown on the *Hyderabad,* which carried 287 convicts, thirty-eight guards and seventy-five emigrant women and children in 1850, complained that this 'recent plan of making the ship half-emigrant, half prison, is an additional charge and service of anxiety, and taken in all its features by no means to be applauded.' He felt strongly that 'the ship should be one thing or the other' and that 'nowhere is strict discipline so much required, but when the quarter deck is crowded with women and children, it is impossible to feel quite safe, were the prisoners disposed to mutiny.'[10] There was an additional concern in the days of the Australian gold rush that crews would often behave so badly during the voyage that they were dismissed on arrival, condemned to three months on the treadmill in prison for their offences, and then released to make their way to the gold fields.[11]

Paying passengers were just as opposed as Keown to the transport of criminals and juvenile delinquents aboard the same ships they were travelling on. When a group of boys from Parkhurst prison was sent to New Zealand on the *Mandarin* in 1843, 'the passengers were not prepared till after they had engaged their cabins to proceed to Hobart Town, as to expect boys of the description of these from Parkhurst but their good order and conduct appear to neutralise the prejudice which one might expect, and the annoyance consequent on the fact of their coming on board having been concealed.'[12] At first the junior ship's officers, 'who on trifling or no grounds whatever are ready to kick and cuff the boys', were most antagonistic towards these unwelcome passengers, while Mr Innes, the superintendent of emigrants in charge of the boys, was worried about 'too great familiarity arising between the boys and the seamen which I discourage by every means in my power'.[13] He was also conscious that there was confusion between his own remit as superintendent of the boys and that of the surgeon superintendent, and complained that 'the captain does not appear to conceive that I had anything to do in respect to the diet, and his consultations on this point were confined to the surgeon and himself.'[14] Very soon the other passengers, captain and crew were united in condemnation of the 'convicts' and of Innes' failure to keep them 'in a proper state of subordination'. The boys were accused of theft, of stealing liquor from the hold and getting drunk on it, of opening the scuttles and 'thereby endangering the cargo', and of unsocial habits when they 'encumber the deck with their filth thereby rendering it as a common sink much to the annoyance of everyone and to the obstruction of the crew in the working of the ship.'[15] Innes naively believed that his boys were innocent and found 'great pleasure in continuing to observe the good feeling towards each other which subsists among them.'[16] It was the other passengers who were provoking them to bad behaviour, including one man who tried to get one of the boys 'to strike him by standing upon his toes, calling him a d[amne]d convict'.[17] Indeed the boys 'cannot be engaged in the most harmless amusements without a collection of cabin passengers being found gazing at them from the poop end and indulging their offensive remarks.'[18] The behaviour of the cabin passengers themselves was of more concern to Innes who commented that 'the drunkenness on the part of the passengers in the cabin appears to be uncontrolled and I much regret the example, as well in that as in cursing and the profanation of God's name, which is offered to the boys', and felt strongly that it was 'injudicious to send such boys in a vessel in which there are any passengers.'[19] His only ally on a ship which 'consistently maintains the character of a low pot house'[20] was the surgeon, who himself inadvertently 'spoke of some articles for the use of the "convicts" which he instantly corrected by using the word "emigrants"'.[21]

Steerage passengers enjoying government-assisted passages, tightly regulated by the Colonial Land and Emigration Commission, were under the control of the surgeon superintendent, whose responsibilities went beyond the medical to cover the entire welfare of these passengers. Responsible to him were a superintendent, 'appointed to report to the former any complaint, or any improper conduct that may be going on, and to see that every person has his due allowance of food served out to him by the steward', and a schoolmaster.[22] In the absence of a clergyman on board, the surgeon superintendent was also expected to officiate at the church services held on deck every Sunday. He additionally had to ensure that there was no 'gambling, rioting and quarrelsome behaviour', that there was no smoking below deck and that there was no 'swearing or profane language'.[23]

Even when matrons were appointed to supervise the women passengers, the surgeon superintendent was not absolved of responsibility for their moral and physical welfare. On the *Oxford* travelling to New Zealand in 1883, 'the matron, who is doubtless a worthy and conscientious person, proved to be quite unfitted both physically and mentally for the task of maintaining discipline on board ship', with the result that 'the services of the surgeon superintendent were constantly called upon for the preservation of order amongst those under her charge.'[24] It was a heavy responsibility for one man, who also had medical care of all the passengers in an environment where disease could quickly spread. John Hood, a passenger on the *Lady Kennaway* in 1841, thought that one surgeon was not enough on emigrant ships, as 'were the one medical man to be taken ill whilst disease was on board, fearful indeed would be the state of the helpless passengers.'[25]

Despite their importance for the welfare and supervision of the emigrants, the standard of the surgeon superintendents could be variable. At first, preference had been given to the employment of retired naval surgeons, many of them with experience of service on the convict ships, but who had had little contact previously with pregnant mothers, small children and babies. After 1840 the Emigration Commission began to favour the employment of civilian doctors, who might be more sympathetic to the needs of the emigrants. Yet it was a role which many civilian doctors were not keen to pursue because it was seen as low status and as offering neither prestige nor good conditions. Many medical men would have agreed with Charles Dickens's unflattering portrayal of Dr Haggage, doctor at the Marshalsea debtor's prison in *Little Dorrit*, who 'had been in his time the experienced surgeon carried by a passenger ship', but was most remarkable for being 'amazingly shabby, in a torn and darned rough-weather sea-jacket, out at elbows and eminently short of buttons, the dirtiest white trousers conceivable by mortal man, carpet slippers, and no visible linen'; it was a recognizable pen portrait of a surgeon on an emigrant ship.[26]

Although the surgeon on an emigrant ship was 'called upon to exhibit more practical knowledge of surgery and midwifery than can be possessed by any unqualified person',[27] a survey by *The Lancet* in 1875 found that 224 men sailing in passenger ships as surgeons were not on the Medical Register, since they only held qualifications from the Society of Apothecaries, which would not entitle them to serve as a surgeon in a hospital or the armed forces, and that fifteen of them were under the age of twenty-one, which meant that they were totally unqualified.[28] It concluded that

> The medical service of the mercantile marine ... has too often been a refuge for the destitute of our cloth; and some ship owners, whose only objective is to screw and pinch as to expenditure in every possible way, get a cheap article in doctors as in other things and do not care to enquire if he be qualified to kill or not.[29]

The only way of finding men willing to take on the post was by lowering the qualifications required, and in 1899 colonial medical qualifications were recognised for the role of ship's doctor, as they already were on the coolie ships.[30]

The government-chartered emigrant ships to Australia, with their emphasis on the importance of the surgeon, offered a model for other private emigrant vessels. This had in turn been based on the medical services provided on the ships of the Royal Navy. The Admiralty had stipulated that convict ships should carry a surgeon since 1815, and from the 1830s government-chartered emigrant ships adopted similar regulations. The health and dietary systems used on convict ships indeed offered a model for maintaining health on the government-assisted emigrant passages to Australia which started in 1831, and were funded by the sale of land in the colony to wealthy settlers. However, it was not until the passage of the 1854 Merchant Shipping Act that all British ships were required to carry medical equipment and stores, and all British passenger ships with more than one hundred people on board were required to carry a qualified surgeon.[31] The 1855 Passenger Act made it mandatory for all passenger ships to have a medically qualified doctor, proper dispensary, and hospital accommodation, all of which were examined by the port authorities at the start of the voyage. Other ships were not required to carry a doctor, but were expected to have the necessary medical supplies.[32] After 1867, ships without doctors were issued with medical guides, giving plain instructions as to treatment and the dispensing of medicines, by the Board of Trade.[33] At the same time, a scale of medical supplies and comforts was laid down for ships according to the number of passengers carried,[34] but many shipping companies prided themselves on exceeding the regulations both in diet and medical supplies,[35] though others complained that 'the new scale is quite out of proportion with the requirements of a voyage of ten or fourteen days duration to Canada or the United States and, if insisted on, will materially add to the already long list of expenses which the steam ship owners are called upon to pay.'[36] The scale was perhaps less adequate for the longer journeys to Australia and New Zealand.

Many members of the medical profession, unlike their employers in the shipping companies, considered that the government medicine chests which all ships now had to carry were 'altogether antiquated', since they contained some drugs no longer required, while better modern drugs were not included.[37] The Board of Trade responded quickly to these criticisms, and in November 1888 issued a revised scale of medicines, medical instruments, and medical comforts to be carried on passenger ships, with the advice of the Royal Colleges of Physicians and Surgeons: 'We have been actuated by a desire to bring the scales to a level with the advanced position of modern medical and surgical practice in order to give to the medical officer of a ship the means of efficiently performing the duties to which he has been appointed.'[38]

Not surprisingly, most surgeon superintendents were 'not treated as a gentleman and had no authority.'[39] Some of them would have preferred to be seen as a gentleman, and accordingly neglected their duties towards their poorer passengers, preferring the company of cabin passengers and attending to their own interests. Samuel Archer, the twenty-one-year-old surgeon on ss *Great Britain* in 1857, was far more interested in natural history, a suitable pursuit for a gentleman scholar, than in any of his passengers, and had to be recalled to the ship from the beach where he was searching for shells during a stop at Mindelo, in order to treat a man who had fractured his skull when struck by a winch handle. He was perhaps more concerned that on the previous day his white trousers had been soaked and caked with sand so that he 'much resembled a bricklayer' more than a surgeon, not smart enough to suit the self-image of a dashing young gentleman.[40]

However diligent, well qualified and competent in professional fields, the surgeon superintendent was nothing if he lacked a strong personality, as he had to exert his authority over passengers and crew if he were to perform his duties efficiently. Yet his powers were limited:

> The Surgeon is to understand that he is not only charged with the medical care of the emigrants, but that on him devolves also the maintenance of discipline among them, and subsequently the enforcement of any regulations for securing cleanliness, regularity and good conduct ... As his means of coercion are limited ... he will have to trust very much for the attainment of these objects to the moral influence which he may acquire over the emigrants ... By scrupulously regulating his own conduct and demeanour, and by a firm and decided but kindly and conciliatory exercise of his functions, by a considerate attention to the feelings of the people, and an impartial and just bearing in any questions which may arise among them, and by showing an interest in their well-being and comfort, there can be little doubt that over persons so circum-stanced an officer in the position of Surgeon Superintendent may acquire a very great influence. But it is equally evident that any want of temper or justice or attention on his part will alienate the emigrants from him.[41]

The surgeon on the emigrant ship *Lady McNaghten* in 1837, although 'a man of very excellent character, and of respectable acquirements with regard to his professional knowledge, was quite inexperienced in respect to the duty he undertook.' Totally unable to enforce the proper sanitary regulations and the rules for keeping order, cleanliness and ventilation, he failed to prevent the 'dirt and filth accumulated in every direction, and disease naturally was the consequence'.[42]

Every hour of the day was tightly regulated as far as possible to maintain discipline and good conduct on the ship. In 1848 emigrants had to rise at 7am and air their bedding on deck. Breakfast was at 8am and by nine o'clock the deck and berths were to have been cleaned and any children got ready for classes with the schoolmaster. Dinner was at 1pm and tea at 4pm. After 8pm all lamps were to be extinguished, except for a general lamp, and all steerage passengers had to be in bed by 10pm.[43] In such circumstances there was 'no doubt that a three-months journey in an emigrant ship, under the most favourable circumstances, will make large demands upon the patience, temper, forbearance and hopefulness of the emigrants', but they were expected to accept that, when faced with all the inconveniences of the voyage, 'the best thing that emigrants can do is to make up their minds to bear them cheerfully.'[44]

Sunday services held at sea were expected to be attended by all emigrants who could go on deck, and many men and women would make efforts to look respectable in honour of the Sabbath. However, inevitably the congregation would include 'scoffers', while the Anglican services did not appeal to Nonconformists or Roman Catholics. Moreover, 'prayers at sea, notwithstanding that the situation is so well calculated to add to their solemnity, are yet mingled with such sounds and scenes – at least in an emigrant ship – that the effect is not what one would expect or wish.' There were inevitably distractions from the boatswain's whistle, the noise made by the crew going about their business, the orders being shouted by officers, the preparation of food, and the chatter of 'groups of unconcerned lookers-on.'[45] John Hillary, a Wesleyan Methodist lay preacher taking his family from Tow Law in northeast England to the 'promised land' of New Zealand on the clipper *Westland* in 1879, considered that on board ship 'we have much wickedness, but no prayers, no Christian fellowship, no Sanctuary', and prayed that 'this journey was ended, and its godless associations.'[46] He himself was reluctant to preach because most emigrants only attended services when the captain or doctor presided, because they thought that was expected of them; and the captain indeed failed to give a moral lead, for 'Captain Wood asks me to preach on the Sabbath, and himself reads the lessons, yet during the week he sings songs, leads off the dance, allows much profane swearing among his crew, and himself sets the example.'[47]

The role of the surgeon in maintaining discipline could become impossible, and 'a troublesome post' without the support of the captain when 'an emigrant ship is a hotbed of iniquity'.[48] When relations between the captain and surgeon broke down, the surgeon super-intendent was most vulnerable. On the *Mandarin* in 1843, 'the language of the captain to the surgeon (all loud out and in the presence of his passengers) was full of "By G[od] and D[am]n" and he designated the latter a "boy", a "child"'.[49] Fearing violence from both captain and passengers, taking their cue from the captain's public display of contempt for the surgeon, 'the surgeon is obliged to carry about a life preserver for his own defence in case of assault.'[50]

On the *Lady Kennaway*, a farmer tried to break into the women's area of steerage. Although he was recognised by many of the emigrants, none of the men in steerage would reveal his name, but the women had no hesitation in pointing him out to the surgeon superintendent, who wanted to clamp him in irons to make an example of him. The captain considered this too severe a punishment and merely stopped his allowance of meat for a short period of time as his punishment.[51] The result of such leniency was that another emigrant later challenged the authority of the surgeon when he insisted that the women go to their berths at the regulation hour, and 'violently attacked him' with abusive and insolent words. The captain only agreed to have the man put in irons and have his rations reduced to bread and water, a harsh punishment for the offence, when the cabin passengers rallied in support of the surgeon, and it was obvious that there would be no opposition from 'the other emigrants, as I first somewhat apprehended from their front and bearing.' The emigrants themselves were split along nationality lines with the Irish emigrants taking sides with the surgeon, and the English with the troublemaker, whose language 'appeared to be directly calculated to stir up the worst passions in the large mass of his brother emigrants, and to create riot and insubordination in the ship.'[52]

With such a mixture of people from a variety of backgrounds conflict was inevitable. On the *Lady Kennaway* in 1841:

> the scene below decks baffles description, – Irish, Scotch, English, Germans, French – mechanics, cottagers, watchmakers, and ladies of all descriptions, young, old, and middle-aged. Some were tolerable in appearance; but the majority, chiefly Irish, were of the coarsest fabric of woman kind.[53]

Some of the migrants spent most of their time lying on their berths and, 'though in perfect health, it is with difficulty the surgeon can expel them from their lairs.'[54] If they went on deck it was merely so that they could smoke, a habit which distressed other passengers. A lady complained in 1862 about passengers smoking on the starboard side of the *Great Britain* because 'the practice is in itself offensive, and leads to expectoration, which, unfortunately, is swept up by our dresses'.[55]

The only way in which emigrants on the *Juliana,* sailing from Gravesend to Sydney in 1838, could be driven off the lower decks so that they could be cleaned was by closing the hatches and smoking them out with the fumes of sulphur and cayenne pepper.[56] Other emigrants wished to prevent steerage from becoming 'an Augean stable' and made attempts to keep up standards of cleanliness and respectability. In this they had to contend both against slovenly passengers and the rodents that infested all ships. The crew could also be abusive towards the passengers. The chief mate on the *Lady McNaghten* in 1837 'was very rough in his language to the emigrants', and he carried a small stick with which 'I have seen him strike the women and boys.'[57]

Before boarding, the luggage of each emigrant in steerage was inspected to ensure that he had with him the bare minimum of clothing required for the voyage: two suits of outer clothing, six shirts, six pairs of socks and two pairs of shoes for the men, and two dresses, two flannel petticoats, six shifts, six pairs of stockings and two pairs of shoes for the women.[58] It was considered especially important that the clothing for the journey should be suitable for the extremes of temperature to be found on 'so long and varied a voyage as that to Australia', since 'at sea, as on land, nothing contributes more to personal health and comfort than a good supply of suitable clothing'.[59] Travellers were advised to take only the shoes they would need on the journey as the leather would be in a poor condition by the time they reached Australia 'from the damp and mildew they are sure to collect on board ship, and which rots them to an extent which renders them unfit for use.'[60] However, checks that the emigrants had adequate clothing for the voyage were not always carried out. Edward Mallins, a painter from Tralee with his wife and three children on the *Lady McNaghten,* had one box containing 'the proper complement for a change, but no medicinal man nor other person examined to see if I had the proper quantity or not.'[61] Once a week, passengers were allowed access to their luggage 'for effecting the necessary changes of clothing.'[62]

Two days were set aside each week when passengers could wash their clothes in rainwater collected from the awnings in butts, or in seawater, but they were not allowed to do this between-decks nor could they hang up their clothes to dry there.[63] Meanwhile, on Saturdays all their bedding was taken on deck and aired, while the berths were disinfected with chloride of lime.[64] It was essential that 'the between decks were kept perfectly dry during the whole period of the voyage', through daily dry scraping and sanding of the decks and occasional fumigation 'by pouring hot vinegar over the chloride of lime, which at all times had the effect of destroying any latent or unpleasant effluvia.'[65]

When a ship was overcrowded, conditions in steerage became impossible. Alexander Aberdeen, an agriculturist sailing with his wife and three children on the *Lady McNaghten* from Cork to Sydney in 1836, was adamant that 'I consider the greater part of our sufferings in the passage arose from the want of air.'[66] He, his brother, and nephew occupied a berth, four and a half feet wide at one end and three and a half feet at the other, in the bows of the ship, while his wife and three daughters had one three and a half feet wide. Although children were not considered to need as much space as adults, more astute observers were aware of the necessity of providing for large numbers of very young children 'who, to permit of proper attention to that cleanliness which is absolutely necessary for the preservation of their health, require nearly as much room as adults.'[67] On the *Lady McNaghten* the problems of overcrowding were made worse by the obstruction of the ventilation by passengers' luggage because the hold had been filled with cargo. As well as commercial cargo, the hold was also full of the potatoes which made up the bulk of the emigrants' diet, 'to the exclusion of the emigrants' luggage, which was consequently stowed between decks, obstructing ventilation and causing an accumulation of filth, to which may be attributed many of the evil consequences that have ensued.'[68] Not all the emigrants were given the accommodation they had booked, nor allowed to board with all their luggage. Daniel Kennedy, a clerk and steward from Tipperary, had booked three berths, one for himself and his son, one for his wife and youngest daughter, and the third for his two eldest daughters. Once on board he was only allotted two of these berths, having been prevented from bringing all his luggage with him. The chief mate had threatened that 'he would throw both the box and myself into the sea' if he attempted to bring a chest containing clothing worth £4 15s 8d on board. Despite losing a valuable part of his luggage, 'I had still a sufficiency of clothing for myself and my family for the voyage', but Kennedy was even more indignant that 'I had not sufficient accommodation on board.'[69] Henry Bingham, one of the cabin passengers, observed that conditions in steerage were intolerable as a result of the overcrowding and bad ventilation, and that 'as we advanced in the voyage, the effluvia arising from the hatchways was so offensive that I avoided going near that part of the deck.' He also noticed that the women in steerage 'were very much disinclined to go below on account of the great heat.'[70] It was not surprising when ten adults and forty-four children died of fevers during the passage of 111 days.[71]

Steerage passengers were issued with cooking and eating utensils. They would form themselves into messes of between four and eight people. It was the duty of one of the members of each mess to go to the purser to receive the provisions and water for that mess. Fresh water was issued daily, but preserved meat, flour and dry biscuit were issued two or three times a week, and tea, coffee, sugar, pepper and mustard only once a week. Sometimes 'the biscuit is now very hard, being damp and mouldy',[72] and the water 'which has been collected from the decks and rigging' could be undrinkable and of a 'very low character' which meant that 'especially in tea it is very nauseous.'[73] Many of the emigrants would have agreed with Margaret Donovan on the *Lady McNaghten* that 'if we had got good water, I should not have felt aggrieved.'[74]

The British government laid down the dietary scales of food and drink that must be carried, based on the Royal Naval allowances for ratings. Half rations were issued to children under fourteen years of age, while infants under a year were issued only with a quart of water daily, it being the responsibility of the mother to feed her child. A gill of lime juice was issued each week to prevent scurvy.[75] It was a diet which was not always familiar to the emigrants. The surgeon on *Amity* in 1825 thought that tea and cocoa should be dropped from the diet scale, and peas replaced by more oatmeal and potatoes, since 'the class of Irish which comes under notice for emigration is known to subsist upon the lowest species of provisions', and did not adapt well to the change to a 'very abundant and very varied supply.'[76]

However, unscrupulous captains and pursers often cheated the emigrants of their full allowances. Sometimes the flour was maggoty. When Margaret Donovan, a passenger on the *Lady McNaghten*, complained about the poor quality of the drinking water, Captain Huswick told the steward to give her water from the hold, and 'called me a troublesome wretch and threatened to send me down below.'[77] On the same voyage, the captain authorised the issue of flour, raisins and suet on Christmas Day 1836 and New Year's Day 1837, where 'that on Christmas Day was said to be a gift to us from the Captain but there were three pounds of meat stopped from each mess for the serving on New Year's Day.'[78] Roger Meehan, a twenty-two-year-old rope-maker from Limerick, volunteered to serve out the provisions when the emigrants began to complain of being cheated of their rations: 'I did it voluntarily as the people had begun to complain of the shortness of the provisions. I did it with a view of seeing that justice was done.'[79] When 'a deficiency in the supply of provisions for the emigrants' was noticed on the *Mandarin* and reported to the captain, excuses were quickly found such as 'that the mistake had originated with an officer in charge of the stores, and who in ignorance of the weight of the meat in the tins had issued a smaller number than the scale justified.'[80] The emigrants were at all times prey to being cheated, and 'the refusal of the captain to give up the scale for the use of the emigrants leaves us still exposed to imposition.'[81]

However generous the dietary scales may have been, when full rations were actually issued on the orders of the captain it was not always possible for a ship to provide for a longer than expected voyage, especially if the ship were to become becalmed in the doldrums around the equator. Although shipping companies often advertised sailing times to Australia of four months, few ships actually achieved this, and a voyage of five or six months was not uncommon. The usual route was for a ship to sail due south to Cape Town, where it would reprovision before sailing across the Indian Ocean to Australia. Sometimes it was necessary for ships to call in at Rio de Janeiro, rather than Cape Town, to take in more water and food, if they had been stuck in the doldrums for a long period. After the mid 1850s a new non-stop route was adopted which reduced the sailing time by picking up the Roaring Forties for a high-speed dash across the Southern

Ocean. By this time many of the sailing ships were also fitted with auxiliary steam engines powered by a single screw, which enabled them to avoid becoming becalmed in the doldrums and made sailing times of between seventy-five and eighty days a realistic target. However, this route brought new hazards for the traveller, of heavy seas, and even icebergs. In high seas the hatchways were battened down, making conditions in steerage airless and stifling, though it would have been even worse had the hatches been left open. This happened on the *Lady Kennaway* during a storm when 'the main hatch, being generally left open for air to the emigrants below, was in the confusion forgotten to be closed and down the torrent rolled into their apartments over their beds', so that where 'fainting, sickness and misery were there before ... now the terror of approaching death was added.'[82]

Accidents on board emigrant ships were common, involving both passengers and crew. One of the boy emigrants on the *Mandarin* in 1843, Baylis, 'who had received a fracture at Parkhurst, and who had been complaining some days previously of his head ... in which he has a plate', knocked his skull against a spar lying on the deck. All that the surgeon could do for him was to shave his head and bleed him, leaving him 'in a precarious state, having little sleep and scarcely taking any nourishment.'[83] On the *Great Britain* in 1866, a carpenter was 'ill some time in consequence' of a large piece of beef tied high on the mast falling on him.[84] On an earlier voyage to Melbourne in 1866, William Wheatley, an eighteen-year-old sailor, 'steady, honest and in every way a credit to those connected to him', was swept overboard, and no trace 'could be found after nor the mop or bucket with which he was working at the time.'[85] The previous year the ship had been so crowded that the stewards had to sleep on the tables and, after one particularly rough night, one of the stewards, Jeff, had fallen off the table and, panicking, had run along the corridor melodramatically shouting, 'Oh I've been killed – all my ribs are broke, I'm killed, I'm killed.'[86]

Minor illnesses were prevalent on the ships, especially diarrhoea, constipation and seasickness, for which the cure on the emigrant ship *Adam Lodge* in 1839 was the issue of a gill of wine daily to each adult.[87] If a more serious infectious illness struck, the surgeon had to act swiftly to control it. When scarlatina was found on board the *Maitland* two days out from England on 26 June 1838, John Smith, the surgeon, immediately examined all the children as soon as he had diagnosed the first case and ordered every sufferer to be sent to the hospital. However, 'there was a great reluctance evinced by some parents to the admitting of their children into the hospital', and the surgeon could do nothing to stop the parents from defying his authority, 'all remonstrance having been unavailing, and all attempts at coercion were interdicted'.[88]

Children, not surprisingly, formed the majority of the fatal casualties on these assisted passages to Australia. Three-quarters of all the assisted migrants dying at sea were under the age of six.[89] In 1838 Sarah Brunskill, sailing from Plymouth, lost her son from diarrhoea and her daughter from measles in the course of one single day when only two weeks into the voyage: 'two little angels they looked, so beautiful in death'.[90] Death also became a commonplace for another mother, Ellen Moger, in 1839. She lost three children, even though at first her husband 'Edward and the children suffered but little from sickness'. As the voyage went on the 'dear children' were 'gradually getting weaker and, for want of proper nourishment, became at last sorrowful spectacles to behold.' The loss of her children 'overpowered me and from the weakness of my frame, reduced me to such a low nervous state that, for many weeks, I was not expected to survive.' Sarah Brunskill was to witness twenty burials at sea and Ellen Moger thirty, mainly of children. Mrs Moger indeed was greatly troubled by 'the sad tolling of a bell informing you some poor victim to sickness and privation was about to be launched to a watery grave; such events are not uncommon, but the mind, I assure you, soon becomes hardened and callous on board a ship.'[91] Such callousness did not affect the bereaved parents. When the son of Mr Benningfield, a passenger on the *Medina*, died of typhus in February 1830, his father 'became like a madman at the loss' and the surgeon's mate 'remained up with him during the night applying restoratives.'[92] Even saloon passengers were not spared from such losses, like the mother on the *Great Britain* who in June 1866 had given birth to a stillborn girl, the mother having 'been ill ever since we sailed, she has one little girl though she is just twenty.' Shortly after, a child was born healthily in steerage, and an old man of eighty died there without any family with him.[93]

Funerals at sea were sombre affairs. The Benningfield child who died on the *Medina* from typhus was consigned to the deep the day after his death, though his father was still so shocked by his loss that he 'was brought on deck insensible and remained so all day':

> The coffin is placed on a hatch with the union jack over it. When the Captain came to read the usual service with a black velvet cap on his head, all the crew were ordered aft to witness the ceremony. At a signal given by the Captain the end of the hatch is tilted up when the coffin slides into the sea.[94]

Inevitably, funerals were a recurrent event on long voyages, despite the best efforts of the captain and doctor to keep their passengers healthy and alive.

On such a long voyage it was essential that the passengers should be kept amused. It would otherwise have been too easy for bored passengers to fight with each other and the crew, become mutinous towards the discipline exerted by the captain and surgeon superintendent, or sink into a depression. Suicide could also follow, such as on the *Conflict* headed for New Zealand in 1875 when a Lincolnshire farmer, Alfred Button, threw himself overboard seven weeks into the voyage.[95]

Dancing was a popular entertainment 'to keep all in good humour':[96]

> No dance on shore can give the slightest idea of the real fun and enjoyment, though rude and boisterous it may in part appear, which are the invariable characteristics of a 'folly night' at sea. The sounds of the fiddle heard on board at the right time at once 'makes the whole ship kin.' From the refinement of the saloon to the boisterous hilarity of the steerage – from the lady of refined manners to the simpering hoyden – all join the merry throng, and mingle in the mazy whirl with an earnestness of devotion unknown in other circumstances.[97]

The surgeon superintendent was encouraged to seek out passengers with violins, flutes or accordions who could form orchestras to play at these dances.

The ceremony of crossing the line was observed in time-honoured fashion by the crew and passengers of many emigrant ships where members of the crew, dressed as King Neptune and his retinue, would shave passengers crossing the equator for the first time with a razor and lather of tar or treacle, then duck them in salt water. Such a rite of passage offered novelty and broke up the monotony of the voyage as much as it pandered to superstitions and tradition. It was also an opportunity for revenge against any unpopular passengers, for 'if the sailors have a grudge against any particular fellow they pass the word and you may be sure he gets an awful dose.'[98] On the *Medina* in February 1830, 'all the passengers were ordered below who did not choose to be shaved and battened down', and 'many were cowardly enough to go down but the cabin passengers were allowed to witness the ceremony from the poop in forfeiture of a bottle of rum each.' John Pocock, the ship's surgeon's mate, and his friend Walter, son of the captain, were 'predestined for extra punishment'. Walter was blind-folded and 'a mixture of tar, fat and other filth was then dashed over his face and afterwards scraped by two blunt razors of enormous size made from an iron hoof by the carpenter', before he was 'soused over head and heels, and was kindly kept under by the officers a long time.' Pocock, 'the d[amned] doctor's mate', was given even worse treatment for 'on opening my mouth the brutal brush was pushed in. I could not get the taste out of my mouth all day.'[99]

On a long voyage where there was little to do, it was inevitable that young men and women would flirt with each other and become closer than they might have done at home. There was frequently 'a good deal of romance about, or rather just starting, the fellows having got as far as the waists.'[100] However, for some men the presence of young women posed too great a temptation, especially to the crew for whom women in steerage were a constant prey. Travelling to New Zealand in 1895, Joanna Harper, a cabin passenger, commented disapprovingly of 'a great row last night in steerage, two women in the engineer's cabin'.[101] On the *Waitara* to New Zealand in 1879, the scandals multiplied as first a young man and woman were caught on deck at midnight, then a married man was discovered to be having an affair with one of the single women, and finally the captain and surgeon were both found to be 'free' with the single women under the effects of concerts and wine. Meanwhile on the *Hermione*, also bound for New Zealand in 1879, the steward was caught in bed with a male passenger from steerage.[102] However, when George

Hunter, a bricklayer travelling to New Zealand in steerage on the *Chile* in 1873, tried to rape his heavily-pregnant wife Bridget, the surgeon superintendent Millen Coughtrey moved her into comparative safety of the hospital, and merely 'remonstrated with him about it as his wife was nearly at her full period of pregnancy.'[103] First- and second-class men also courted young women confined to what the crew often dubbed the 'virgin's cage' in steerage, invariably to the scorn of their own social class, who thought that there was 'rather a little more spooning, and in some parts the passengers had got further than that.'[104]

By the 1870s steamships were regularly carrying emigrants to Australia, although sailing ships continued in use until the end of the nineteenth century, and there still remained a need to break up the monotony of the voyage. The introduction of improved triple and quadruple expansion engines driving twin and triple screws allowed ships to maintain a steady rate of 15 knots, cutting the journey down to six weeks. By the early twentieth century oil-fuelled ships were also being used, thereby making for easier and more comfortable travel. Most ships continued to use the traditional route around the Cape of Good Hope, but the opening of the Suez Canal offered the opportunity of cutting the total journey by a thousand miles, and even gave the opportunity for sightseeing en route. Fresh fruit and vegetables were also available in the Mediterranean coaling ports and in Port Said.

For a devout Wesleyan such as John Hillary, returning home in 1880 by the steamer *John Elder* via Australia after New Zealand had failed to live up to its promise, the opportunity to read the Biblical account of the Israelites' exodus from Egypt thrilled him as he sat on deck 'looking into the sea for some of Pharaoh's chariot wheels as we must be very near the spot where the Lord took them off Pharaoh's 600 chosen chariots of Egypt with which the Israelites were pursued.' Just as interesting for him was the sight of the Arabs and gypsies at Suez climbing up ropes with baskets full of merchandise in order to sell their wares, such as coral, shell necklaces, alcohol, apples, figs, pomegranates, salmon, sardine, tobacco and cigars. He noted that these hawkers 'did a good stroke of business especially in the brandy.' Even more memorable were 'the Arab boys, clad in Eden's luxury of dress, viz a rag to cover their nakedness, who ran by our side on the bank of the Canal for three or four miles crying "Backsheesh" money "Backsheesh".'[105]

As on the transatlantic passenger ships, steerage was now giving way to third-class accommodation, with spartan but clean, and even roomy, cabins. The communal galley gave way to mess or dining halls and third-class passengers could even enjoy their own music and smoking rooms. It was not until after the Second World War, when a new wave of immigrants put pressure on the shipping system, and ships that might otherwise have been scrapped after war service were brought into use, that dormitories again became common on emigrant ships to Australia. Men now were separated from women and children, with the result that families were no longer kept together on the ships as they had been in the days of steerage. On the *Volendam* in 1950 emigrants were sleeping in bunks three high, with 250 passengers in each hold.[106] It was a throwback to the days of steerage and a temporary response to the difficulties of the immediate post-war austerity years, and tourist-class accommodation again became the norm in the 1950s until 1977, when the last assisted-passage ships landed in Australia, most immigrants having arrived by aeroplane since the 1960s. It was a world away from the days of the long passage 'down under' that so many had taken before them.

now giving up, and yet depressed enough in means, to have to put up with the discomforts and humiliations incident to a vessel 'all one class.' The husband broods bitterly over blighted hopes and severance from all that he has been striving for. The young wife's grief is of a less cankerous sort, probably confined to the sorrow of parting with a few friends of early years. The circle of her love moves with her.[2]

Class distinctions were rigorously maintained and snobbery prevailed, not surprisingly when 'we were left to form a little world of our own, a copy in miniature of the big world we had left behind'.[3] Middle-class emigrants expected better conditions and to be given more respect than was enjoyed by steerage passengers. Joseph Sams, a clerk sailing from Gravesend to Melbourne on the *Northumberland* in 1874, was very conscious of the differences in social class aboard ship. The nineteen-year-old son of the landlord of the Blue Posts public house in St Pancras, London, Sams was travelling second class alongside fellow passengers whom he characterised as 'with a few exceptions all in the Middle Class of Life'. They included farmers, bakers, merchants, innkeepers, miners and gentlemen and their wives, the majority of whom he considered 'more or less agreeable'. His views on steerage were less complimentary, dismissing those passengers as being 'on the whole a rough looking lot, a great many being Germans, some of whom have between 1000 and 2000 canaries on board.' He was particularly scathing about these German emigrants, 'an ill-assorted lot, and awfully dirty common wretches'. His attitude towards passengers travelling in saloon class was no less snobbish: 'some from a distance seem very seedy but that matters not; they are there so I suppose can dress how they like'.[4] Sams's own relaxation of middle-class dress codes in warmer weather, when he was 'going about with shirt all undone showing my noble (never mind)', and appeared one morning at breakfast 'in rowing attire ... flannel trousers and gauze vest, no sleeves', was later to offend at least one of the ladies travelling with him in second class, but his less than gallant response was to suggest that she sat somewhere else.[5] Envious of the luxury and good food the first-class passengers enjoyed, Sams considered that 'the first class live like fighting cocks and it is rather galling to see all the pastry etc and the good things being taken under your very nose from the galley to the Chief Saloon.'[6]

If a wealthy emigrant wished to avoid contact with his poorer brethren in the days of sailing ships, travelling as a cabin passenger on the packet ships between Europe and America was the way to sail. With the exception of the Le Havre lines, which served German emigrants to America, the packets carried very few steerage passengers until after 1840. Until then it was only if the 'tween decks did not have enough freight that the ship's carpenter would fill the space with temporary bunks for a human cargo taken on almost as an after-thought and definitely as a stopgap. Generally, most of the cabin passengers were textile merchants, businessmen and army officers who 'endeavoured to amuse ourselves as best we could and, for want of work, turned boys again, and went to play', with target practice on deck, gambling, singing and heavy drinking.[7] Ralph Waldo Emerson, the austere philosopher of Transcendentalism with its emphasis on individualism and living in harmony with the natural world, was unable to escape the masculine jollity of shipboard life, and confessed that 'these are the amusements of wise men in this sad place; I tipple with all my heart here.'[8] Alongside alcohol went copious food. On the Black Ball ship *Europe,* breakfast in 1833 offered ham, bacon, eggs, mutton cutlets, fish, rolls and cognac. Dinner consisted of three courses, dried fruit, and seven different alcoholic drinks.[9] This was in contrast to the sparser fare in steerage where passengers had to bring their own food and cook for themselves.

After the hearty meals and comfort of the lounge, the cramped, poorly ventilated cabins often proved a great disappointment. The novelist Frederick Marryat thought them 'about as big as that allowed to a pointer in a dog kennel ... I thought there was more finery than comfort'.[10] Harriet Martineau, writer and social reformer, made the best of the lack of space, when travelling on *United States* to New York in 1834, by being aware of the need to 'put everything away in tight, orderly fashion.' Similarly, she accepted seasickness as 'an annoyance scarcely to be exaggerated while it lasts',[11] and she was not bothered by the children from steerage looking over her shoulder when she was writing on deck, and watching her from behind chests and casks.[12]

Harriet Martineau's views of steerage were limited to the glimpses she had of the children on deck receiving instruction from a clergyman, and to them gathering like the cabin passengers to see the sunsets at sea. She was also stirred by the parting they gave to the cabin passengers who were disembarked first: 'The crew and steerage passengers assembled on deck, and gave us three parting cheers, which might be heard all over the harbour. Our gentlemen returned them, and our hearts yearned towards our beautiful ship, as she sat dark upon the evening waters, with all her sails majestically spread.'[13] What she failed to do was observe the disparity between their conditions and those in which she was travelling.

By contrast her fellow writer and reformer Charles Dickens was only too aware of such class distinctions. He had exposed some of the horrors of steerage on journeys to North America in *Martin Chuzzlewit* when he sent his eponymous hero to the United States in steerage, but for the return voyage allowed him to travel as a cabin passenger. It was as if he could not permit his hero to suffer the pains of steerage a second time round, even if the passage is to be paid by his manservant Mark Tapley signing on as a ship's cook to allow his master to travel like a gentleman. Martin Chuzzlewit is exhorted by his friend Bevan to 'take your passage like a Christian; at least as like a Christian as a fore-cabin passenger can be', and to go into the ship 'without actually being suffocated'. Bevan also advises the returning emigrant Martin that 'if ever you become a rich man or a powerful one, you shall try to make your Government more careful of its subjects when they roam abroad to live', and to 'tell it what you know of emigration in your case, and impress upon it how much suffering may be prevented with a little pains!'[14]

Although Dickens does not expand on this return journey in his novel, elsewhere he had recorded his own less than comfortable experiences on transatlantic ships, which would have been familiar to the more affluent emigrant. When he set out on the Cunard Line's steamship *Britannia* in 1842 for a lecture tour in the United States, his fellow passengers included a Scottish woman on her way to join her husband in New York, and 'an honest young Yorkshireman, connected with some American house, domiciled in that same city, and carrying thither his beautiful young wife to whom he had been married but a fortnight, and who was the fairest example of a comely English country girl I have ever seen.'[15] Days were long and tedious with passengers lounging around talking, reading and dozing in the intervals between meals of 'another dish of potatoes' and assorted hot meats, 'not forgetting the roast pig, to be taken medicinally.' Evenings were filled with games of whist and glasses of wine or brandy and water. On a 'rough night' when 'the cards will not lie on the cloth, we put our tricks in our pockets as we take them.' The other daily occupation was gossip about 'this passenger is reported to have lost fourteen pounds at Vingt-et-un in the saloon yesterday; and that passenger drinks his bottle of champagne every day, and how he does it (being a clerk) no one knows.'[16] Dickens was not impressed either with 'what may be called the domestic noises of the ship: such as the breaking of glass and crockery, the tumbling down of stewards, the gambols, overhead, of loose caskets and truant dozens of bottle porter, and the very remarkable and far from exhilarating sounds raised in their various staterooms by the seventy passengers who were too ill to get up for breakfast.' That the cabins were too small and uncomfortable to spend much time in, and that the saloon was 'not unlike a gigantic hearse', was not what a bestselling author and journalist might have considered suited to his ambitions and self-esteem.

Dickens may have preferred sailing ships to the new steamers, but a shorter journey was what most emigrants wanted, whether in cabin class or in steerage. The new steamships, such as Isambard Kingdom Brunel's *Great Eastern* and *Great Britain*, seemed to offer speed and greater comfort – or at least discomfort for a shorter time. The steamers only really started to challenge the domination of sail after 1837 once Brunel's paddle steamer *Great Western* had reduced the advertised time of the Atlantic crossing to fifteen days. Despite the much-vaunted advantages of the new steamers, most of the early steamships continued to rely on sails as a fallback since the early steam engines were unreliable and there was an ever-present danger of stocks of fuel running out before the end of the voyage.[17] Although the new steamships promised cleaner journeys, their griminess was constantly bemoaned in the early days. Ladies travelling in 1862 on Brunel's second steamship, *Great Britain*, the first oceangoing, iron-hulled, screw-driven ship, were concerned about the lack of privacy, despite a passage connecting the cabins assigned to them with a 'commodious boudoir' so that 'ladies who are indisposed or in negligé will be able to reach their sleeping berths without the slightest necessity for their appearing in public.'[18] Even so, the cabins of saloon- and second-class passengers were not free of visits from ship rats, a constant problem among all classes. On her honeymoon on the *Great Britain*, travelling from Melbourne to Liverpool in 1866, Mary Crompton was frightened when a large rat 'came into my cabin as I was going to bed, I jumped onto the berth and waited until Joe came down, then he and one of the stewards had a grand rat hunt but the gentleman escaped through a hole.' Another passenger was less fortunate in her encounter with a rat when she was 'wakened by one biting her toes.'[19]

There was no guarantee that fellow passengers would be any more congenial than the rats. The cabin passengers on the *Moravian* in 1874 included 'a great number of mercantile men going out or returning home on business', as well as 'families, including a plentiful supply of children, with servants.' There were also 'several young married couples going out to start new homes for themselves in Canada.' As well as these first-time emigrants, there were a number of young men who 'having established themselves there have returned to their old sweethearts in England, and are now taking them out as their wives.'[20] Some of these young men, having prospered, were able to honeymoon in cabin class. William Morris, a journalist who had got to know these successful migrants on his voyage out to Canada, was less impressed by some of the steerage passengers he encountered on his return voyage on the *Circassian*, who 'appear to have gone out to Canada expecting to be enabled to live without work, and not having succeeded, are going home.'[21] In general, he felt that the outward voyage gave an indication of how successful an emigrant would be in their future lives. Those who complained about the ship, did not make the most of the voyage, and who were miserable during the voyage out, 'are hardly the people to go out to a new country and carve out fortunes for themselves.'[22]

Many of the better-off emigrants, just like their poorer fellow voyagers, were unsuccessfully trying to escape their demons. For those men trying to escape their addiction to drink, an emigrant ship merely exposed them to further temptation. Joseph Sams made friends with a fellow passenger because they both preferred drinking port to attending a church service organised for second-class passengers by a lady from the first-class saloon. They had sat together with their bottle of port at one table, 'while at the next they were praying', and it was 'rather amusing to see some of the fellows making believe to be religious and all the time laughing', so much so that one of them 'whilst singing a hymn felt dry so he went into his cabin, applied a bottle to his lips and then with renewed vigour returned and attacked the hymn.' Sams's new friend Charley Woollens had been 'a great drinker and profligate owing to the fault of having none to guide him', and was going out to Australia 'to try to break himself of drinking'.[23] Sams was not perhaps the best person to take him in hand as he himself was to injure his hand when the neck of a bottle he was uncorking broke, and he was 'obliged to get Charley to help me wash on account of finger' and he was 'also forced to have breakfast cut up', as he was 'as helpless with my left hand as a baby, which goes against the grain.'[24]

Sams, the son of a pub landlord, also organised heavy and boisterous drinking sessions with his fellow passengers, priding himself that whereas his drinking companions retired to their cabins 'to lay down regular slewed', he 'your humble servant was all right.' One of his fellow drinkers 'sat ... with his eyes dilated, mouth wide open and as still as possible for about one and a half minutes, and then be jabbers', the alcohol 'at last escaped through his nose, much to our amusement and his discomfiture.'[25] Sams was to impress his fellow passengers by his practical joke played on a drunken member of the crew who, after his failure 'to get into some of the girls' cabins in third class, but under threats of a hiding gave it up', had entered the cabin of 'a married woman and her husband and wanted to take liberties with the wife.'[26] This drunken storekeeper had got off with 'a hot caution' from the captain on this occasion, but Sams had on the previous day found the man naked and drunk in his berth, and had 'poured best part of a bottle of blue ink over him, much to the amusement of the middies[27] and the passengers.'[28]

Eating was as much of a distraction for better-off travellers as heavy drinking and the boorish behaviour resulting from overindulgence. For cabin passengers, fresh milk, cream, eggs and meat were provided by cows, goats, sheep, pigs, ducks, geese and chickens kept in special pens on deck. Joseph Sams described the forecastle of the *Northumberland* as 'like a young farm yard.'[29] While this might have helped to provide a balanced diet on a long voyage, it could cause other problems. On ships carrying goats, there was a problem that passengers who drank goats' milk could be struck down by Mediterranean fever, characterised by intermittent feverishness, anaemia and rheumatic pains and caused by a bacterium, *Brucella melitensis,* which was spread by drinking goats' milk. An outbreak of the illness on the cargo steamer *Joshua Nicholson* in the summer of 1905 was found to have been caused by passengers and crew drinking the milk of infected Maltese goats, whilst those who either disliked the taste or with whom the milk had disagreed when first they had tried it remained well.[30]

Inevitably, given human curiosity, many of the middle-class passengers were fascinated by their glimpses of their fellow passengers in steerage. On most ships it was impossible to be unaware of their presence. Robert L Stevenson was only too well aware on the *Devonia* in 1879 that through the thin partition of the second cabin 'you can hear the steerage passengers being sick, the rattle of tin dishes as they sit at meals, the varied accents in which they converse, the crying of their children terrified by this new experience, or the clean flat smack of the parental hand in chastisement.'[31] Edgar Howe travelling in 1913 on the *Canada,* carrying almost two thousand in steerage, complained that 'the decks were black with emigrants and they were still going up the gangways as thick as ants.'[32] Mary Poynter, accompanying her husband to the Far East in 1914 on *Graz,* found that 'the picturesque element is to be found, as always, in steerage', people who were much more interesting than 'the bronzed Anglo-Indian officers' and 'earnest looking' missionaries of her own class:

> When tired of book and steamer chair we go to the forward railing and look down upon the really 'simple life' – upon a venerable green-turbaned hajji just returning from Mecca ... brightly if scantily clad little companies of natives sitting cross-legged, their chins resting on their knees, before small charcoal mangals, cooking their evening meals.[33]

The querulous Devon antiquarian Charles Luxmore was not so enchanted when the *Hildebrand,* on which he was sailing to South

America in 1927, took on board at Lisbon 'over 300 steerage ... mostly Portuguese, who with their children, turned out to be a very rowdy lot.' These Portuguese emigrants 'seem to have bought the ship, very noisy, make a beastly noise in the music room, babies squealing', which irritated Luxmore and spoiled his trip.[34]

However, some first-class passengers took a keen interest in the lives of some of the steerage passengers, especially when romance was involved. One of the second-class passengers travelling on the *Northumberland* in 1874 was 'in the habit of going into the third cabin to court a woman there.' On one of his romantic visits, the two lovers had flour thrown at them, completely covering the woman, who complained to the mate, 'but, of course, he can do nothing as they have no jurisdiction in rows between the passengers.'[35] When Captain Bertram Hayes of the *Majestic* was informed in 1906 that 'there were a couple of Norwegians in the third class who, judging from the appearance of the lady, ought to have been married some months previously', a delicate condition which would have meant that the pregnant woman would have been refused admission to the United States, and would have had to be returned to her port of embarkation by the White Star Line, he was able to seek and gain the interest of the first-class passengers. A clergyman among them performed the wedding ceremony and the rest of the first-class passengers 'made a collection for a wedding present.'[36] Cabin passengers could be equally generous to the crew. When a sailor on the *Great Britain* fell and fractured his skull in 1866 while painting the anchor, the passengers collected £50 for him, as he was 'one of the best on the ship', and was supporting his parents from his wages; the passengers thought that 'the poor young man may get well but I am afraid there is not much chance.'[37]

Not all interest in steerage was so well-meaning. For many wealthier passengers there was amusement to be had from watching the less fortunate. Robert Louis Stevenson was understandably resentful, and felt that he and his fellows 'had been made to feel ourselves a sort of comical lower animal', when two young ladies 'with little gracious titters of indulgence and a Lady Bountiful air', accompanied by a superior young gentleman, visited steerage as if it were one of the tourist sights on the ship. He felt that 'there was no shadow of excuse for the swaying elegant superiority with which these damsels passed among us, or for the stiff and waggish glances of their squire.'[38] Such visits contravened the 'etiquette of the sea life' that it was 'a shocking exhibition of bad manners and low inquisitiveness for passengers to visit unasked the quarters of an inferior class.'[39] As it was, many emigrants travelling in steerage on liners did not get a good deal, because 'too much had to be given to the higher classes for their comfort and luxury, preventing the due care that was to be given to the ragged emigrant population.'[40] For the emigrants' confined space then to be invaded by cabin-class sightseers was unacceptable. Edward Steiner, a professor at Iowa College, was a frequent transatlantic traveller and a critic of the upper- and middle-class patronising attitude towards immigrants in steerage. After one storm at sea, he noticed that cabin passengers on the upper deck found their amusement in watching the unkempt steerage passengers emerging from the hold wrapped in the grey blankets issued by the shipping company, and 'getting some sport from throwing sweetmeats and pennies among the hopeless looking mass.' Steiner condemned the social stratification revealed by such condescending behaviour:

> This practice of looking down into the steerage holds all the pleasures of a slumming expedition with none of its hazards of contamination; for the barriers which keep the classes apart on a modern ocean liner are as rigid as in the most stratified society, and nowhere else are they more artificial or more obtrusive. A matter of twenty dollars lifts a man into a cabin passenger or condemns him to the steerage; gives him the chance to be clean, to breathe pure air, to sleep on spotless linen and to be served courteously; or to be pushed into a dark hold where soap and water are luxuries, where bread is heavy and soggy, meat without savour and service without courtesy ... makes one man a menace to be examined every day, driven up and down slippery stairs and exposed to the winds and waves; but makes of the other man a pet, to be coddled, fed on delicacies, guarded against draughts, lifted from deck to deck and nursed with gentle care.[41]

Nowhere was this social contrast starker than on the luxury liner *Titanic*, which officially was an emigrant ship, although now it is more often remembered for the gilded opulence enjoyed by its more aristocratic passengers. One of the most popular and sentimental depictions of its sinking on its ill-fated maiden voyage in April 1912, *Women and Children First* by the artist Fortunino Matania for *The Sphere*, reinforces the image of doomed high society. A dinner-jacketed young man, clutching a lifebelt in one hand, blows a kiss to his wife who reaches out to him as she is lowered in a lifeboat. Another lady is reluctant to enter the lifeboat despite the pleas of a man in pyjamas who has left his overcoat on the rail while he persuades her to leave. Another man holding a small document case, standing next to the man in the dinner jacket, looks down sadly at an abandoned woman's shoe. The whole picture is infused with the gallantry and self-sacrifice of the gentlemen allowing women and children to be saved first. Matania based his picture on the recollections of a survivor, a steward, who corrected him on details before the picture was completed:

> The scene was vividly impressed on the steward's mind and he was able to correct costume and grouping as the reconstruction proceeded, down to the smallest detail ... The shoe lying on the deck is no artist's invention. The passenger in his dinner jacket stood here as shown, not wearing his lifebelt, but holding it as he kissed what was to be a last farewell to his wife.[42]

Matania obviously went to great lengths to ensure the accuracy of his picture of the last hours of the *Titanic*, even checking the position of the stars in the sky. He also produced an equally memorable image of the ship going down with lifeboats in the foreground, again filled with society ladies. What he did not show prominently were the steerage passengers. It may have been women and children first for the wealthier, but fewer children were saved among the third-class passengers than in the first. All but one of the six children in first class and all twenty-four children in second class survived, but only twenty-seven out of seventy-nine children in third class were saved. While only four ladies travelling first class and thirteen in second died, eighty-nine of the women in third class were lost. Meanwhile fifty-seven gentlemen of the 175 in first class survived but only fourteen of the 168 in second class and seventy-five of the 462 men in third class. Social class helped to determine who survived.[43]

Class distinction pervaded the whole ship. First-class passengers, accommodated in luxurious suites, staterooms and cabins on the upper decks, were pampered as soon as they stepped aboard. The cabins for second-class passengers were plainer and smaller but were considered to be the equivalent of first-class accommodation on other ships. Steerage passengers, dignified with the status of third class, were on the lower decks in cramped cabins for two, four or six passengers, and in small dormitories reserved for single men. These cabins had little space for more than bunk beds, unlike the comfortable rooms of their social superiors. The first-class passengers enjoyed lavish meals in an à la carte restaurant or in the formal dining room, where dressing for dinner was as strictly observed as on land, before the gentlemen retired to the mahogany-panelled smoking room with its open fire, and the ladies to one of the public reception lounges. The Café Parisien and the Veranda Café offered refreshment in a more informal setting. A library and a writing room offered quiet spaces, an orchestra played in the public areas, whilst the more energetic passengers could enjoy a well-equipped gymnasium, swimming pool and Turkish bath, or take part in deck games. Second-class passengers had their own dining saloon, lounges, library and smoking room, all less lavishly but still comfortably appointed. Third-class facilities were more basic with a general public room, two dining saloons, offering two sittings for meals, a promenade, and a smoking room. Each class of passenger was strictly segregated from the others, separated by locked gates in compliance with American immigration regulations, which later made evacuation from the sinking ship more difficult. After the sinking of this ship there was a suggestion that 'the provision of Turkish baths, gymnasiums and other so-called luxuries involved a sacrifice of some more essential things, the absence of which was responsible for the loss of so many lives', but there was actually enough space for lifeboats amidst the opulence.[44]

Among the second-class passengers was Franz Pulbaum, a twenty-seven-year-old machinist who had emigrated from Bremen in 1907, and was returning to New York from a visit home and a stay in the French capital to inspect the mechanical rides at the Luna Park amusement park. Pulbaum's body was never recovered, but in 1993 his cabin baggage was found on the ocean floor onto which it had fallen after the sinking of the *Titanic*. Amongst his working tools, including a measuring tape,[45] a collection of postcards intended to remind him of his stay in Paris, and such personal items as newly purchased silk socks still attached to each other at the toe, blue garters and a striped grey tie,[46] were documents evoking his aspirations as an emigrant to the United States. With a stock certificate for shares in the Bowery Witching Waves Company[47] which manufactured fairground rides, and a pocket book with useful advice for the businessman,[48] Pulbaum was keen to have a stake in his new country. A German-English dictionary[49] perhaps indicated that he was still mastering his new language, but he had already taken the first steps towards a new nationality. In his cabin trunk was a completed and signed declaration of his intention to become a United States citizen, an ambition destined never to be realised.[50]

Also recovered from the ocean in 2000 was the humbler suitcase of William Henry Allen, a thirty-five-year-old Birmingham toolmaker travelling in third class. Whereas Pulbaum had spent £15 0s 8d on his ticket, Allen's had cost him only £8 1s. Neatly packed for a new life, his case contained his best black woollen three-piece suit, shirt collars, both smart shoes and worn work shoes, socks and darning wool, as well as a pocket watch and sterling silver matchbox still containing matches.[51] Other luggage recovered from wealthier passengers in underwater exploration of the wreck by RMS *Titanic*, the company formed to explore the wreck and granted salvage rights in 1994, bears witness to their prosperity. However, it is the humble possessions of the emigrants that evoke their values and aspirations, though a more affluent emigrant like Pulbaum was obviously better equipped for a new life than those in third class. Even so it was still less than the fourteen trunks, four suitcases and three crates deemed necessary luggage by Charlotte Drake Cadeza travelling in first class.[52]

Even in death the emigrants in third class were not treated as well as first-class passengers. Ironically, it was some members of the crew who managed to subvert the social order. Unable to reach their own quarters in the bowels of the ship to put on warm clothing with which to face their fate in the icy waters, some of them helped themselves to the abandoned Savile Row tailoring in the staterooms of gentlemen travelling as first-class passengers, and in death being well dressed were mistaken for their social betters, and their corpses were treated with greater dignity than would have normally been given to them. Only when their other possessions or their body tattoos were examined was it realised that they were actually members of the crew.[53] On the ships sent out to recover the bodies of victims, identifiable first-class passengers were given the dignity of their own coffins stacked on the poop deck, whereas second- and third-class corpses were simply sewn up in canvas sacks, while members of the crew were unceremoniously stored in the ice-filled holds of the salvage ships, with the result that 'many of the frozen limbs had to be broken', in order to get the corpses of the crews on to stretchers and into coffins when they were eventually landed in Halifax.[54]

Many of the crew and obviously less affluent passengers, as well as those whose bodies were badly mutilated or decomposed, were routinely buried at sea. The body of Thomson Beattie, the thirty-six-year-old Canadian owner of a land company selling farmland to emigrants and travelling in first class, was found, still in full white tie evening dress and lifejacket, on a collapsible raft over a month after the sinking, together with a fireman and seaman; a passenger on the ship that picked them up observed that 'their legs were under the thwarts, and this no doubt held them in the boat. They all had lifebelts on, and we could see their faces were almost black.' Since Beattie's corpse was in no condition to be taken for burial on land, the crew of the *Oceanic,* which had picked up his body, 'then took tarpaulins and big iron weights, and the doctor also went out and read the burial service over them and they were then buried in the sea ... and there was hardly a dry eye on the ship whilst this was taking place.'[55]

The survivors were also treated according to their social status. When taken aboard the *Carpathia,* their names and details were recorded, and then they were dispatched to the dining saloon corresponding to their class aboard the *Titanic,* where they received first aid to treat hypothermia, shock, exposure to the elements, and minor injuries. Even the doctors treating the first-class survivors among the passengers were of higher rank than those assigned to look over the third-class survivors. The first- and second-class passengers were then found accommodation in the public saloons and officers' cabins. Third-class survivors were sent to steerage. However, when the ship reached New York the usual customs formalities were suspended for all passengers, and even the immigrants in third-class were spared the indignities of the expected medical inspections on Ellis Island. Many of them had lost all the possessions they had taken with them to start a new life and, with the loss of husbands and fathers, were forced to seek the help of relief agencies.[56]

A ship such as the *Titanic* was like a floating hotel for the wealthy in which the discomforts of ocean travel were minimised thanks to improved shipbuilding technology. First-class accommodation had been moved amidships away from the vibration of the engines, and where there was less motion from the action of the waves. In this the White Star liner *Oceanic* had led the way in 1870 with its large portholes, electricity, and running water for the first-class spacious staterooms amidships. Fine clothes could now be worn without fear of being soiled by the squalor of the ship or the seasickness of passengers. The tradition of dressing for dinner had started on board the Cunard liners *Mauretania* and *Lusitania*. The *Titanic*, with its grand staircase, sumptuous dining salon, elegant lounges, writing and smoking rooms, gymnasium, sauna, and well-appointed staterooms, had taken this luxury to even greater heights for those who could afford it.

This increase in standards of comfort for first-class passengers trickled down to second-class passengers and even to steerage. Indeed, by the beginning of the twentieth century some steamship companies actually abolished steerage and replaced it with third-class accommodation, or offered it as an alternative on vessels which still had the old steerage areas on board. Fares were higher than for steerage but third-class passengers now enjoyed the comparative privacy of small four- or six-berth cabins, complete with clothes hooks and chests of drawers. They had access to more washing facilities and lavatories than had formerly been available in steerage, although showers and baths were not all that common. One of the duties of the stewardesses on the *Titanic* was to show third-class passengers how to use the toilets. Dining rooms were more comfortable than they had been and 'the stewards performed their duties carefully and thoughtfully; and so gave splendid service', while 'the food, though it offered practically only actual necessities, was sufficient in quantity and properly prepared and decently served.'[57] Yet third class remained spartan even on the newest of ships. Harry Clarke, sailing from Glasgow to Quebec on the newly built *Cassandra* in 1907, found that in his eight-berth cabin 'a straw mattress with a straw pillow and an army blanket is the sum total of our bedding furnishing but I have added my rug and overcoat.' The steerage cabins were two flights of stairs below the wash houses, which could cause difficulties, 'especially when one has to go for water with a china mug and then descend again'. Clarke did recognise that 'one cannot expect home comforts aboard an emigrant ship.'[58] Nor did third-class passengers enjoy any of the other privileges of higher class passengers, as Paul Knaplund, returning to the United States on the *Bergensfjord* from a trip home to Norway in 1916, found to his cost when, 'hearing that the American citizens were to go ashore ahead of the rest', Paul, 'ignorant of the rule that those on third should wait until the first- and second-class passengers had disembarked, was one of the first off the ship, with the result that his haste aroused the suspicion of the customs inspector.'[59] Nevertheless, such improved facilities made them more palatable to emigrants who had fallen on hard times.

The anti-Jewish policies of the Nazis in 1930s Germany resulted in the emigration of many once well-off professional and business families who, in happier days, had themselves been pleasure passengers on the very ships on which they now sailed as reluctant emigrants. Although emigration would have helped the Nazi state in its aim of a Jew-free Reich, obstacles were put in the way of people seeking this escape route. Leaving Germany not only meant a loss of friends and fatherland, social and professional status, but also incurred financial penalties. Taxes, the cost of export permits, limitations on foreign exchange and export bans meant that after 1938 most emigrants lost at least 95 per cent of their assets. More affluent emigrants were charged an emigration fee, assessed according to wealth, 'to finance the emigration of destitute Jews' to 'avoid proletarianized Jews remaining behind.'[60] There were even limits on the number of personal effects that could be exported. Would-be emigrants had to submit detailed lists of all their possessions with valuations down to such minor items as all kitchen towels, neckties and socks, before permission was given for an emigrant to leave with any personal possessions.[61]

Many Jewish migrants preferred, whenever possible, to travel on foreign ships sailing from ports outside the Reich, where they would be treated like any other passenger, rather than on the vessels of German shipping lines which segregated them into Jewish-only quarters, effectively shipboard ghettoes. Erich Sternberg, owner of a clothing store in Aurich, left Germany on uss *Majestic* in January 1936, leaving behind his wife and children with the intention of sending for them once he had established himself in a new business in the United States. When he was able to send for them to join him in Baton Rouge in August 1936, his family's departure from Germany was delayed for two and a half months by his wife Lea's refusal to travel on a German ship. Instead she had booked tickets on uss *Washington*, scheduled to leave Bremen on 27 December 1936. Even then they only received their exit permits forty-eight hours before they were due to leave. Although only allowed to take with her 10 marks for herself and 5 marks for each of her three young children, there were fewer restrictions on sending furniture and household goods overseas than there were from 1938, and Mrs Sternberg was able to send her furniture and some family heirlooms ahead of her. However, even aboard a foreign ship, the Sternbergs were not free from harassment until they had left German waters. Gestapo agents searched their belongings, throwing everything on the floor and destroying biscuits and sausage made for the children by their grand-mother and uncle, and even body-searching Mrs Sternberg as they made her perch on the toilet in the bathroom of the cabin. In protest, Lea Sternberg ordered them to clear up the mess they had made and, to her surprise, her peremptory, 'You took them out, now you put them back', was obeyed. On the voyage out her eighteen-month-old son Hans had double pneumonia and the entire family was seasick, prompting Lea to vow never to board a ship again.[62]

For the 937 passengers on the ill-fated voyage of the *St Louis* in May 1939, later dubbed 'the voyage of the damned', their journey, once they had left Germany, was more like a pleasure cruise than a voyage on an emigrant ship. They had been sold tourist visas for Cuba by the Hamburg–Amerika line, with which they hoped to enter the country whilst seeking ultimate refuge in the United States. However, before they sailed, the Cuban government had closed this immigration loophole and now required a 500-peso bond and written permission from the Cuban secretaries of state and of labour before any would-be immigrant could disembark. The ship was not allowed to dock at

Havana and only twenty-two of the passengers who had obtained full immigration visas in Hamburg before embarking were allowed to land. Refused refuge in the United States, the *St Louis* was forced to return to Antwerp, where the passengers were offered sanctuary by the United Kingdom, France, Belgium and the Netherlands, only for many of them to end up in concentration camps after the German occupation of their new countries. During the voyage, the captain, Gustav Schroeder, had insisted that they should be treated like any other passengers on any pleasure cruise, despite the swastika on the flag flying over the ship, and the portrait of Adolf Hitler hanging prominently in the social hall. As the refugees settled into shipboard life they were able to enjoy deck games, the swimming pool, leisurely dining, film shows, tea dances, cocktail parties and a costume ball, a distraction from their plight. Children played practical jokes on the stewards by putting soap on the door handles so that they would be unable to open the door when carrying a tray for cabin service. Young men and women passengers flirted with the Aryan crew, some of the women passengers being considered 'the hottest ever to come on the ship' by the crew, and many of the young men 'had not been doing too badly with the German stewardesses'.[63] It was an illusion of normality. Aaron Pozner, a passenger in tourist class recently released from Dachau concentration camp, observed 'a feeling of anticipation, of release from the Nazi horror. People laughed and prayed, and the crew smiled, pretending to understand.'[64]

Less comfortable were the luxury liners adapted to transport supposed enemy aliens deported from wartime Britain in the face of the invasion fears of 1940. In many cases this was the forced emigration of men to a new continent from the country to which they had emigrated in search of a better life many years before. Guido Conti had left his native Bardia in the Italian Apennines and settled in Newport in South Wales as a shopkeeper. Following Italy's declaration of war and Winston Churchill's instruction about enemy aliens to 'collar the lot', this young man, aged thirty-two, with the well-tailored elegance of a debonair 1930s matinee idol, was arrested as a citizen of Italy, and interned in the squalor and humiliation of a local police cell, a barracks block in Cardiff, and a disused woollen mill in Bury, where internees slept on the floor and used a bucket as a toilet. Arbitrarily selected for deportation to Canada, he was among the 1,190 British Italians, Austrians and German refugees, many of them opponents of fascism, embarked at Liverpool upon the *Arandora Star,* which at 6.58am on the morning of 2 July 1940 was sunk by a German submarine in the Atlantic. Just before embarking, Conti had received a telegram informing him that his wife had given birth to a son he was never to know. He had every reason to survive but, clinging on to a paltry piece of wood, he offered his life-grasping plank to a friend who was not as strong a swimmer as he, only to lose his own life in the cold waters of the Atlantic.[65] The Rossi brothers from Swansea clung to each other in the cold waters for about eight hours, but when seventeen-year-old Giuseppe was picked up by a Canadian destroyer *St Laurent,* his thirty-two-year-old brother Luigi was long dead and had to be left behind.[66] Many of the Italians aboard the ship were middle-aged cafe and restaurant owners, caterers and waiters, many of them fully integrated into the British communities amongst which they lived and of which they were a part, rather than the dangerous fascist sympathisers with whom they were confused. One of the bodies of the 446 Anglo-Italian victims was that of forty-three-year-old Giovanni Marenghi, impecc-ably dressed in a dapper suit and overcoat, recovered a month later off the coast of County Mayo in Eire, and identified by a receipt for his membership of the Pontypridd Town Bowls Club found in his pocket.[67]

The majority of the men on board the *Arandora Star* were affluent and were travelling in conditions for which their status in their adopted communities at home had ill-prepared them, and which were a shock to their middle-class sensibilities. They were sailing on a luxury ship designed in 1927 for carrying 'happy people to beautiful places in the sunshine', comprising no more than 354 first-class passengers who enjoyed the pleasures of a swimming pool, fine dining room, cocktail bars and dance floors. Uberto Limentani saw it when it visited Venice in 1932 and thought that 'it would be great to travel on that ship one day.' He was not so enthusiastic when, as a Jewish, anti-fascist refugee working for the BBC, he actually boarded it as an internee in 1940, and shared in the feelings of anger of his fellow passengers, 'anger because they left in Britain their wives and sweethearts, their children and parents without being able to say goodbye to them, without even being allowed to inform them.'[68] Cabins for two passengers were

6

Slaves No More?

The abolition of the slave trade in 1807 was potentially a disaster for the economies of many British colonies. No longer could cheap labour be bought in and shipped across the Atlantic from Africa. Sugar planters in the West Indies saw their wealth threatened and put pressure on the British government for aid. However, just as ship owners had found that the transport of emigrants was a suitable, and just as lucrative, replacement for the old triangular slave trade, the movement of indentured emigrant labour from India, China and Polynesia to the West Indies, Mauritius and South America was the solution to this labour shortage. This new trade in the shipment of indentured labour began in 1834 with 41,056 labourers sailing from Bengal to Mauritius.

European emigrants were not considered suitable for labour on the plantations because of their delicate constitutions. The eighteenth-century naval surgeon James Lind had warned that 'the recent examples of the great mortality in hot climates, ought to draw the attention of all the commercial nations of Europe towards the important object of preserving the health of their countrymen, whose business takes them beyond seas.'[1] Although other doctors such as John Hunter thought that Europeans would adapt to tropical climates in time, even darkening in complexion over a number of generations, it was generally accepted that Europeans were unsuited to labouring in the tropics except as overseers, whereas Africans were much more resilient in the heat and so suitable for heavy plantation work.[2] However, with emancipation came the question of how to ensure a good supply of labour suited to work in such hot and sultry climates.

The abolition of slavery not only led to labour shortages on the plantations, but also raised questions about the future of freed slaves who might wish to return to Africa, rather than remain in the colonies in which they had been slaves. This had already arisen in the late eighteenth century when attempts were made to set up a settlement in West Africa for former slaves, a colony that was to become Sierra Leone. In 1787 the first convoy of six hundred ex-slaves, who had been loyal to the British cause during the American Revolution and were of African descent, left London, to which they had fled after American independence, for Sierra Leone. Among them were several white prostitutes who later claimed that they were plied with liquor and brought on board ship at Wapping just before sailing, then married off to some of the black men as soon as they left land. One of these ill-fated women claimed that she 'really did not remember a syllable of what had happened over night, and when informed, was obliged to enquire who was her husband?' She believed that 'to the disgrace of my mother country, upwards of one hundred unfortunate women, were seduced from England to practice their iniquities more brutishly in this horrid country.'[3] Whatever the truth of these unsubstantiated allegations, there were sixty-three 'white women married to black men' and seven 'white women waiting to be married' on the ship, which suggests that not all the girls from Wapping were unwilling victims of kidnap and forced marriage.[4] This first attempt to establish a colony of former slaves in Granville Town soon failed, and in 1789 the settlement was destroyed by the local Temne tribe who took some of the settlers back into slavery, whilst other survivors themselves entered the employ of local slave traders.

Another attempt was made by the Sierra Leone Company to establish the colony on a sounder basis in 1791. The abolitionist Thomas Clarkson's twenty-eight-year-old brother John was sent to Halifax, Nova Scotia, in 1791 to recruit colonists, including 'an old woman of 104 years of age who had requested me to take her, that she might lay her bones in her native country',[5] and organise their voyage to West Africa, a task for which as a lieutenant in the Royal Navy he was well suited. He was described by Anna Maria Falconbridge, wife of the commercial agent of the Sierra Leone Company, as 'being the only man calculated to govern the people who came with him, for by his winning manners and mild, benign treatment he has so gained their affections and attachment that he can by lifting up his finger (as he expresses it) do what he pleases with them.'[6] He involved himself in the planning of all aspects of the voyage, supervising the refitting of the vessels and planning the scale of the provisions, but became so ill that 'the indisposition I felt at times, previous to my leaving Halifax, and the fatigue and anxiety I have had since, has quite knocked me up' and, shortly after setting sail on 15 January 1792 with 1,190 free black emigrants in fifteen ships, 'by the advice of the Doctor I shall not interfere with the management of the Fleet until I get better.'[7]

Clarkson's health did not recover throughout the voyage, but he was not the only one to suffer. When he 'was this day brought upon deck on a mattress, as I was not able to walk or to be moved in any other way', Clarkson found that fever was raging throughout the ships.[8] Many of the migrants were also sick after camping for up to three months outside Halifax, waiting for the ships on which they were to sail to be made ready for them. Sixty-five of them died on the voyage from fevers. Clarkson himself suffered fits and delusions and was unable to offer the leadership of the emigrant fleet that he had promised, even once he was convalescent and well enough to appear in public, an occasion when 'the Black passengers had collected themselves upon deck with their muskets, and fired three volleys, and afterwards gave three cheers, as they had entirely given up all hopes of my recovery, which was to them of the greatest consequence.'[9] Throughout the voyage, reflecting the importance given to hygiene in the Royal Navy at the time, he did ensure that the ships of his fleet were regularly fumigated and holystoned. He reached Freetown on 6 March 1792 to find that, against his will, he had been appointed superintendent of Sierra Leone, a post equivalent to that of the governor of the fledgling colony, and was faced with the problem of dealing with the 'pride, arrogance, self-sufficiency, meanness, drunkenness, atheism and idleness ... daily practised by those who were sent out to assist me.'[10]

Alexander Falconbridge, the commercial agent for the Sierra Leone Company and a former surgeon on a slave ship before his conversion to the cause of abolitionism, had cautioned against what his wife Anna Maria called the 'premature, hair-brained and ill-digested scheme' of bringing such a large number of settlers into a largely untamed and disease-ridden wilderness, 'before they were certain of possessing an acre of land.'[11] A hasty-tempered and hard-drinking man, Falconbridge would perhaps have been more suited to keeping the former slaves healthy on their voyage than he was to developing the profitability of the colony and, after devoting his efforts to the care of the colonists during an epidemic, was dismissed from his post and proceeded to drink himself into an early grave aged only thirty-two, leaving his relieved and ungrieving widow free to marry a slave trader.[12] Clarkson too was dismissed from his post by the Sierra Leone Company, partly because he appeared to be placing his obligations to the settlers above the commercial needs of the Sierra Leone Company.

Just as the British government had funded the ships carrying the first freed slaves to Sierra Leone from Canada, because repatriation to Africa seemed the best solution to the problem of dealing with newly emancipated slaves in a white colony, pro-emancipation members of the American Colonization Society, founded in 1816, thought that, rather than absorbing former slaves into American society when the abolition of slavery became inevitable, it would be better to encourage African-Americans to return to Africa, and in 1821 founded Liberia. The first eighty-six emigrants set sail from the United States for Africa on the *Elizabeth* in January 1820 and, having first called at Freetown in Sierra Leone, attempted to establish a settlement in Liberia, though many of the migrants succumbed to yellow fever and the survivors sought refuge back in Freetown. Only once a second ship was sent was a successful new settlement established.[13]

As well as Sierra Leone, Africans liberated from foreign slavers by the British Anti-Slave Trade Squadron were also transported to St Helena, Guyana, Jamaica and Trinidad. However, conditions on these ships were often no better than on the slave ships from which they had been liberated. Many of the 436 passengers on the *Growler* suffered from diarrhoea and 'African cachexy', a form of malnutrition associated with not only 'bad and insufficient food', but also seen as 'the consequence of great and continued fear' when they were landed in Guyana in 1847.[14] As these freed slaves were not returned to the lands from which they had been seized, and were often taken to countries with which they had no links, this forced migration perhaps differed very little from being enslaved in their eyes.

Similarly, in many respects the system of indentured labour differed little from the slavery system it replaced. In this it greatly differed from

'Leaving Old England', 1870 (Library of Congress, LC-USZ62-118128)

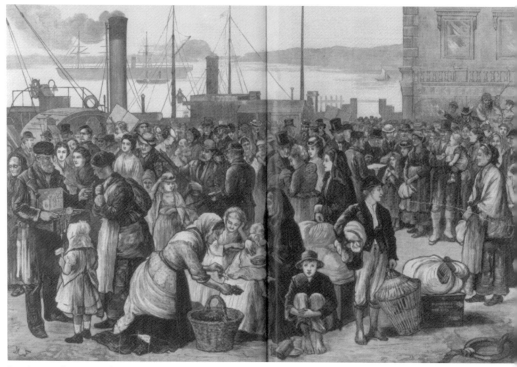

Parting at the port of Queenstown (now Cobh) with Irish emigrants leaving for New York, 1874 (Library of Congress, LC-USZ62-105528)

Poster for the Cunard Line, 1875 (Library of Congress, LC-DIG-pga-01235)

RIGHT: 'The Emigrants' by Jacques Joseph Tissot, 1880 (National Maritime Museum, PAG9432)

BELOW: Equipped for a new life, a Polish emigrant boarding ship with all his possessions, 1907 (Library of Congress, LC-USZ62-23711)

Emigrants boarding a steamer at Göteborg, Sweden, for England on the first leg of their journey to the New World, 1905 (Library of Congress, LC-USZ62-94340)

The White Star Line emigrant ship *Moravian*, built in 1858, bound for Australia
(© National Maritime Museum, Greenwich, BHC3501)

The Hamburg–Amerika Line steamship *Columbia* carrying emigrants to North America, 1889
(© National Maritime Museum, Greenwich, G01447)

Roll call on the quarterdeck of an emigrant ship, 1850 (Library of Congress, LC-USZ62-73506)

'On Board the Screw', Fred Barnard's view of the camaraderie of steerage with Charles Dickens's Martin Chuzzlewit hiding in his berth while his servant Mark Tapley looks after emigrant children, 1871 (Private collection, Tudor Allen)

EMIGRANTS AT DINNER.

Emigrants at dinner in steerage, 1844 (© National Maritime Museum, Greenwich, A2942)

'Horrors of the emigrant ship', the hold of the *James Foster Junior*, 1869 (Library of Congress, LC-USZ62-105130)

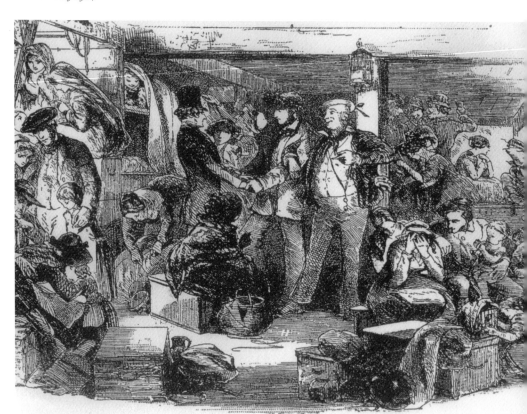

A scene worthy of the painter Ostade when Charles Dickens's David Copperfield visited Mr Micawber in steerage, an etching by Phiz, 1850 (Private collection)

Heedless of any safety hazards, steerage children at play on *Friedrich der Grosse*, 1910 (Library of Congress, LC-USZ62-22340)

Emigrants coming to the 'Land of Promise', 1902 (Library of Congress, LC-USZ62-7307)

Italian emigrants at mess on deck on the *President Grant* (Library of Congress, LC-B2-4929-3)

Steerage passengers 'Taking Life Easy on an Ocean Liner', 1905 (Library of Congress, LC-USZ62-58585)

Emigrants travelling first class enjoying finer dining than those in steerage – except in rough weather, 1904 (Library of Congress, LC-DIG-ppmsca-25848)

The burning of the emigrant ship *Ocean Monarch*, 24 August 1848, painted by the Prince de Joinville who had been involved in the rescue of survivors (© National Maritime Museum, Greenwich, PW7740)

Saving the survivors from the wreck of the *Atlantic*, 1873 (Library of Congress, LC-USZ62-5709)

'Women and Children First', Matania's imaginative reconstruction of a scene on the boat deck of the *Titanic*, technically an emigrant ship, 1912 (© National Maritime Museum, Greenwich, 916_10_UIG-00000102)

The port of Calcutta in 1870 from which many coolies set sail for Mauritius, British Guiana and the West Indies (© National Maritime Museum, Greenwich, C6622)

The coolie ships *Mersey* and *Volga II* in a gale (© National Maritime Museum, Greenwich, BHC2330)

'Preserving the Peace' on a coolie ship, 1864 (Harpers Monthly Magazine)

Chinese immigrants at San Francisco Customs House, 1877 (Library of Congress, LC-USZ62-93673)

Sydney Harbour in the late nineteenth century, the end of a long journey (© National Maritime Museum, Greenwich, C5041)

'Welcome to the land of freedom' – a first sighting of the Statue of Liberty from the steerage deck, 1887 (Library of Congress, LC-USZC2-1255)

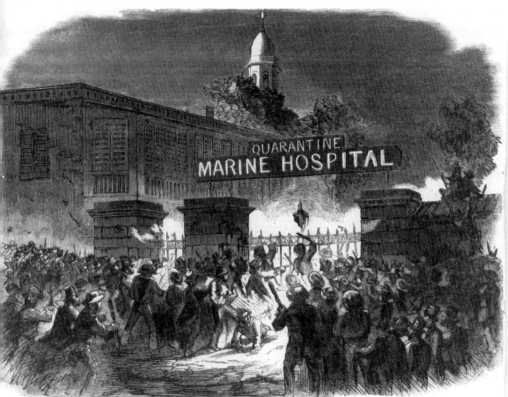

Mob burning Marine Quarantine Hospital, Staten Island, in protest at the health hazard posed by immigrants, 1 September 1858 (Library of Congress, LC-USZ62-57615)

Immigrants on the Battery in front of Castle Garden, New York, the original landing station, 1868 (Library of Congress, LC-USZ61-366)

Dressed in their best for landing at Ellis Island, 1910 (Library of Congress, LC-B2-5202-11)

Newly arrived immigrants in the pens of the Immigrant Building, Ellis Island, 1904 (Library of Congress, LC-USZ62-15539)

The indignity of medical inspection: physicians examining a group of Jewish immigrants at Ellis Island, 1907 (Library of Congress, LC-USZ62-22339)

A friendlier welcome: immigrants being taken by horse-drawn bus to the Immigrant Hostel in Buenos Aires (Library of Congress, LC-USZ62-100773)

Greek immigrants returning from New York on the *Madonna* to fight in the first Balkan War in October 1912 (Library of Congress, LC-B2-2532-9)

previous systems of indentured labour in the British colonies, where many of the men on contract had been white overseers or skilled tradesmen, rather than replacements for slaves. The workers now signed up for a fixed period of five to eight years, during which time they were supposed to receive a monthly wage, housing, food and clothing. Then at the end of the first or second term of service, they were entitled to have their tickets home paid for them by their employers. During the period of their indentures, they may as well have been slaves. Nevertheless, many of the Indian migrants who had returned home after their first or second terms subsequently remigrated, often bringing new recruits with them. Other indentured labourers never returned home but instead settled in Mauritius, British Guiana, Trinidad and Natal, creating substantial and visible Indian communities which reflected the burgeoning internationalisation of the imperial labour market.[15]

The early voyages from Bengal to Mauritius were so horrific for many of the emigrants that suicide was common. On the *Lancier* in 1838, '*malgré toutes les surveillances possibles*' by eight guards, 'five of the Coolies rendered desperate by their situation, destroyed themselves', while on *Indian Oak* there were twelve attempted suicides, though nine of the men who jumped overboard were saved and 'brought back by the boats' sent to retrieve them.[16] In many instances 'the proper allowance of food for the voyage has not been provided, medical inspection has not taken place previous to embarkation, nor medical attendance been furnished during the voyage', all of which contributed to the unhappiness of the coolies, many of them initially from the marshy sloping planes of the Ganges where they were known as *dhangurs*, or 'hill coolies'.[17]

They were expected to assist with the work of the ship and many had been lured on board under false pretences. J P Woodcock, a Bombay civil servant, a passenger on the *Drongan* sailing to Mauritius in 1841 on a voyage lasting two months with 'a cargo of rice and sixty-six Coolies', commented that 'Mauritius was described to them in glowing terms, and advantage taken of their ignorance to provoke the belief that every necessary of life was cheap, labour light, and that the voyage would only occupy them ten days.' On the *Whitby* in 1838, many of 'the men appeared to have no conception as to where they

were going and the length of the voyage; they said they had been told
... that they were to go on board for two or three days, and then land
and march the remainder of their journey'.[18] The actual conditions on
board came as a shock to these men, who came from 'every variety of
caste from the Brahmin to the Choman', and were mixed together
without any sensitivity towards the caste system.[19] In particular, many
of the coolies 'complained of being seduced from their own country by
fine promises; and, they had no idea, when they consented to come
down, that they would of necessity lose caste.'[20] Insultingly, they were
considered less valuable than the other cargo being carried since 'the
lower decks of the *Drongan* were stowed with rice, and the Coolies
were disposed in the waist between the gangways and the forecastle,
where, if the weather had not been remarkably fine, they might have
suffered, being unprotected from every change of weather.'[21]

Such abuses in the system of indentured labour were condemned as
early as 1837 by Thomas Fowell Buxton and Lord Brougham, and in
1838 the East India Company banned any further shipments of coolies.
J P Grant, a member of the committee appointed to investigate the
conditions under which the coolies were being shipped and employed,
urged that legislation be passed to regulate the system, with emigration
being restricted to particular ports and under the supervision of a
protector of emigrants. In 1842 an Order in Council provided for the
appointment of responsible emigration agents in India and a protector
of immigrants in Mauritius. In 1844 emigration to Jamaica, British
Guiana and Trinidad was also sanctioned. All labourers had to be
examined by a magistrate to satisfy him that they had chosen to
emigrate and understood their contracts. Over the next ten years,
107,000 coolies were sent through the agency of East Indies government officers, mainly from Calcutta, to Mauritius.

Before embarkation, the coolies, most of them young and only too
familiar with demanding labour, were herded together in guarded
depots so that they would not attempt to escape after having signed
their contracts, and where they could be examined by the protector of
emigrants, who was concerned that they were well-looked after, fed
and adequately clothed ahead of the long voyage. They were even
weighed and a record kept of whether they had gained or lost weight
during their stay in the depot.[22] Note was taken of 'the slender form,

lank limbs and obvious muscular weakness of most natives of India, as contrasted with Europeans.'[23] A native doctor was also employed to check the emigrants for signs of venereal disease or ruptures before their examination by the medical officer from the ship. It was also the responsibility of the protector of emigrants to make sure that the ship was seaworthy before it sailed.

Conditions in the depots were not always ideal and there were frequent complaints that the coolies were often in an unhealthy state even before they boarded the coolie ship. Emigrants who left the Calcutta depot to board the *India* bound for British Guiana in 1879 were described as having 'in all probability suffered from unhealthy conditions previous to embarkation.' The blame for this was laid upon the 'utter incompetency of the Surgeon Superintendent, Mr Arthur Chundra Doss', a native-born doctor, though great care was taken not to criticise doctors trained in India, since many of the surgeons serving in the coolie trade were the products of Indian medical schools, and 'we do not think that any case has been made out for the exclusion of native doctors.'[24] Had native doctors been excluded, there would have been few doctors at all to undertake the medical inspections.

In many cases, the desire of families to emigrate together meant that sick or ailing emigrants and young children were getting through the medical inspections held prior to embarkation. The able-bodied coolies would not leave their families behind and so the old and infirm were allowed to embark. When typhoid and dysentery killed ten men, eight women and six children on the *Wellesley* on its voyage from Calcutta to Demerara in 1856, 'it is believed that the evil originated in the depot at Calcutta', despite the declarations made by the emigration agent, assistant protector of emigrants and medical officer at the depot that 'with the exception of a few old people, who were objected to, but embarked in consequence of their being members of families, the coolies were fair average lots, and in good health at the time of leaving Calcutta.' Similarly, when cholera struck aboard the *Bucephalus* a few weeks later, soon after it sailed from Calcutta, it was argued that this was unconnected with conditions at the Calcutta Depot:

> The occurrence of cholera in the passage down the river is no proof that the emigrants were in a bad state of health when they embarked,

as similar outbreaks of that inscrutable malady have happened in troop ships, and vessels of all kinds and class, among robust healthy Europeans, strong bodied Lascar crews, pilgrims to Mecca, and even in boats with natives on board, who constantly live on the river, and are proof against all the ordinary exhalations and miasmata incident to its banks.[25]

As the nineteenth century progressed, there was more rigorous selection at the depots, increasing numbers of emigrants were rejected on medical grounds, and in 1894 the protector of emigrants noted in his report that out of 26,707 registered emigrants only 14,865 actually embarked for the colonies. The few not dismissed on health grounds ran away, frightened by the harshness of the depot where the slightest hint of infection could change it into 'a place of sickness and death'.[26] By 1897 the protector of migrants at Port-au-Prince could comment that 'the immigrants that have arrived this year are an exceptionally good lot and indicate a more careful selection at Calcutta'.[27]

Depots were also established in Hong Kong and the Chinese ports for the collection of coolies before embarkation. These were known as barracoons, adopting a term originally used in the African slave trade for the enclosures in which the slaves were confined. Nothing could have shown so clearly the way in which the coolies were regarded. Once in these barracoons, the emigrants were sold on to shipping companies or ship captains at so much a head, and marked with a stamped or painted letter on their breasts to indicate their destination, such as 'C' for California or 'P' for Peru.[28] Since 1855, the Chinese Passengers Act had laid down that all British ships carrying passengers from Chinese ports should be inspected by an emigration officer to ensure that all the passengers were emigrating of their free will and that the ships they were sailing on were well ventilated and free of disease.[29] Yet the barracoons remained full of unwilling emigrants, kidnapped or conned into making unwitting agreements, and, despite successive measures to stop abuses, the exploitation of the coolies remained a scandal. Emigrant brokers had to be licensed and bonded, the barracoons had to be licensed and be operated under rules laid down by the governor of Hong Kong, permits were necessary for passengers and ships, and it was decreed that contract labourers leaving from Hong Kong could only be taken to British colonies.[30] Nevertheless, regulation of contract emigration from Hong Kong remained weak because the West Indian planters still needed labour and Hong Kong merchants were involved in the supply and fitting up of ships, not only sailing from the British colony of Hong Kong but also from Portuguese Macau and mainland China.[31]

Canton had long been imperial China's main point of contact with Europe and until the Opium War of 1839–42 had been the only trading port open to foreign traders. It had also developed as a centre for emigration, at first mainly to Southeast Asia via Macau and after 1848 to California and Peru. Initially, the Cantonese authorities had not interfered with emigration, which was openly advertised, but by the 1860s kidnapping was becoming common. Governor General Lalou in Canton was concerned that the increase in enforced emigration carried out by crimps[32] was the 'offspring of the receiving ship system.' Smaller boats would deliver emigrants to receiving ships anchored off the coast. In 1859 there were three receiving ships flying the flag of the United States moored at Whampoa, the deep water anchorage downstream from Canton, as well as individual vessels registered in Peru, Oldenburg and the Netherlands, all of them acting as feeders for the barracoons of Macau. If an emigrant received by one of these ships insisted that he had been kidnapped, he would be returned to the crimps and tortured so brutally that when presented to another ship he would be too terrified of being returned again to the dreaded crimps not to embark on that one.

Local mobs, outraged by the growing extent of the kidnappings, took the law into their own hands if they found a crimp attempting to coerce someone into emigrating, and lynched or beat to death the crimp.[33] As a result of pressure from the West, Peh-kwei, the governor of the province of Kwangtung, not only made kidnapping an offence punishable by death but also took the radical step of authorising voluntary emigration for anyone compelled by poverty to seek work overseas. This was in complete contradiction to the policy of the imperial Chinese government but meant that an attempt could be made to prevent the horrors of the crimping system, although, as long as shipments of emigrants continued without adequate supervision at Macau and Hong Kong, crimps remained active.

At Macau, the Portuguese authorities attempted to enact ordinances to check the abuses perpetrated by crimps. In 1853 the governor, Isidoro Francisco Guimarães, laid down that sanitary conditions should be provided in the depots ashore and onboard ship, and that any emigrants rejected on the grounds of ill health or old age should be returned to their homes at the expense of the crimps. In 1855 he decreed that all contracts of emigration should be registered and all emigrants should be inspected on shore by the procurator and on ship by the harbourmaster, and in 1856 that all emigration brokers should be licensed. Yet, despite all this legislation, Guimarães admitted to John Bowring, the governor of Hong Kong, that it was almost impossible to eliminate the existing abuses so long as the crimps remained in control of the business of emigration.[34]

In 1860 Guimarães created a post of superintendent of emigration at Macau, paid by the government and independent of vested interests, and insisted that emigrants were not to be confined to the barracoons but must be free to enter and leave as they wished. The British consul Charles Winchester was impressed when he inspected one of the Macau barracoons, which he found to be 'exceedingly well arranged and worthy of imitation' with 480 'stout men and boys well lodged and well clothed and looking clean and comfortable'.[35] Nevertheless, the barracoons continued to be closely guarded by sentries with heavy clubs.

Moreover, the Emigration Convention signed by China, the United Kingdom and France in 1866 limited emigration to the treaty ports, and prohibited emigrants from going to any country not having diplomatic relations with China. This ruled out the Portuguese colony of Macau but, nevertheless, it still continued to be a centre of emigration for the Chinese to South America, though pressure from the Chinese government finally led to a Portuguese ban on emigration from Macau in 1874. Jui-lin, the governor of Kwangtung, had demanded the immediate closing of the Macau barracoons in 1873 after his war junks on patrol in the waters between Canton and Macau had stopped three ships with sixty kidnapped Chinese emigrants and the Portuguese captains had admitted to working for the Macau barracoons.[36] Jui-lin had responded by issuing a proclamation warning against kidnapping and had blamed the Portuguese for this abuse.[37]

For those emigrants still embarking for a new world, whether from India or China, the journey was long. The average length of the voyage from Calcutta and Bombay to the West Indies was twenty weeks, but it only took nineteen weeks from Madras, usually calling at the Cape and St Helena en route. It took only twelve weeks from Calcutta to Natal, and ten weeks to Mauritius. Voyages from Hong Kong to Peru took about 110 days, and to the West Indies about 120 days. Steamers could have cut these journeys by between ten and twenty days.[38] However, the shipowners saw no profit in using newer or faster ships. Often the coolie had no idea of how long he would be at sea, or indeed that he would be a long way from land. Rahman Khan, travelling to Surinam in 1898, 'had the impression that land would be more or less visible throughout our journey', but soon realised that he was wrong and succumbed to seasickness when 'many of us became dizzy and had to vomit'.[39]

The ships on which the Indian coolies sailed were even more crowded and less comfortable than the ships on which European emigrants sailed to their new lands since it was thought that the coolies would not be accustomed to Western ways and comforts and so did not need them:

> The reader who has been to sea must not imagine the 'tween decks of a coolie ship to be arranged like those for European emigration; on the contrary, they are perfectly clear and unencumbered with bunks except just abreast the hatchways, where the forethought of the Bengal Government has caused a kind of broad shelf to be erected, so that those coolies who are berthed opposite the hatchways may not be exposed to any sea or spray while they are lying asleep on the deck.[40]

There was little concern either, about how the emigrants made the most of the limited space available to them, or to ensuring the protection of the modesty of women and children, as on ships carrying European emigrants. The only attention paid to placing the coolies with a nod towards upholding morality was that single men were sometimes sent forward, and families and single women aft. Bamboo-work platforms were raised three feet above the deck on some ships. The women and children would sleep on these raised platforms while the men slept

below them on the deck. This was considered an unhealthy arrange-
ment by Western observers who thought that 'Indian women and
children are more dirty in their personal habits than the men of the
same race, and, their sleeping above the men must have been
productive of nuisances injurious to health and destructive of
cleanliness.'[41] Moreover, the blankets supplied were often of poor
quality and 'of native make, and of a very inferior substance, not wool',
with the result of 'the fluff from them flying about when shaken,
causing much dirt and discomfort.'[42]

Another hygiene problem, 'interfering greatly with the cleanliness of
the between decks', arose from the reluctance of Indian women to go
on deck to relieve themselves. Men could be 'obliged to come on deck
to obey the calls of nature', but it was not so easy to compel the women
to do so. This problem was put down to 'the dirty habits of the Indian
women' and the difficulty of controlling them, rather than to their sense
of personal modesty and their social customs.[43] However, the layout
of the ships themselves also contributed towards the high incidence of
diarrhoea and dysentery, even on ships that otherwise were 'said to
have been well adapted for the service and well ventilated'. On the
Cambodia, carrying emigrants to British Guiana in 1858, 'the privies
were imperfectly placed on board.'[44]

However, other commentators were aware that 'coolies become far
cleaner than any European emigrants can ever be brought to be',
largely because of their lack of possessions, since 'they have no beds,
no other clothes than a koortah (jacket), a dotee, the long flowing piece
of calico which both sexes use though in a different manner, and in
cold weather a pair of trousers.'[45] As a result of this lack of possessions,
there was little that needed cleaning and the decks could be holystoned
and disinfected without any impediment. Apart from cleaning their
own berths between decks, and receiving their food and fresh water at
the hatchways, the emigrants were 'on no occasion to be called upon
to do any work on board the vessel'. When they were cleaning their
berths, 'they shall on no account be placed to draw water from the sea
on the gunwale, in the chains or in any situation which shall endanger
their falling overboard'.[46]

Ships transporting Chinese coolies from Hong Kong to South
America were often cargo vessels modified for the purpose and were

fitted up in a very similar manner to slave ships, rather than like steerage on ships from Europe to North America and Australia: 'they are (to use the phrase known in slave ships) "packed and sold", and merely "paddy" (unclean rice) and oil put on board for their food.'[47] In Joseph Conrad's novella *Typhoon* of 1899, Captain McWhirr, shipping two hundred Chinese coolies home from Southeast Asia, merely reflected the views of many captains when he had 'never heard of coolies spoken of as passengers before', obviously regarding them as little more than the sacks of rice and other commodities also crammed in below deck.[48]

Don Aldus, travelling on a coolie ship from Macau to Havana in the 1860s, noted that 'each shelf simply represented one hundred and fifty in a bed', and that whereas the legal minimum of sleeping space allotted to each man was between 20 and 24 inches, 'they are not over particular in this matter as they seldom exceed twenty one inches.'[49] This merely allowed a passenger to lie on his back in discomfort. The British regulation of 1852 that British ships could only carry one passenger for every two tons registered was generally ignored and the governor of Hong Kong admitted that any attempts to enforce this provision of the Passengers Act would only drive shipping to non-British ports to the detriment of the trade of Hong Kong. Pressure from shipowners led to the Passenger Act being amended in 1853 to allow for 'twelve instead of fifteen superficial feet to be sufficient space for natives of Asia and Africa who may be conveyed from Hong Kong through the Tropics.'[50]

The problem of overcrowding was made worse by the perennial problem of ventilation. In the early days of the coolie trade, the hatches were often the only means of airing the ship. In December 1851 the hatches of the *Futtah Salam*, sailing from Hong Kong to Mauritius, were battened down for three days during a storm and when opened again all 234 emigrants below deck were dead. In 1855, during an attempted mutiny on board the United States ship *Waverley* from Swatow to Peru, 257 of the 450 passengers died of suffocation after they were forced below and the hatches closed on them for up to fifteen hours.[51] On later vessels with more humane masters two or three planks would be lifted at regular intervals along the main deck with watertight coverings raised above them and iron bars running through them to prevent passengers from escaping, Two large pipes at either end of the ship were intended to draw off the foul air from below with the aid of ventilators.[52]

The *Blue Jacket* was praised in 1857 by one inspector of emigrants as 'by far the most perfectly ventilated ship I have yet seen', and in which the cargo was arranged so that 'no leakage of cargo can find its way to the bilge'.[53] Two large ventilators, each about four feet square, were located fore and aft and ran from the hold to the upper deck without communicating with the main deck.

European tastes dictated the food that was served on the ships and at first this rarely appealed to Indians; it was thought that the Bengalese coolies suffered when fed on sea biscuit because they were more used to rice, just 'as is often the case with Irish and Scotch Emigrants who have been accustomed to potatoes.'[54] Moreover, this dry biscuit was considered 'not suitable food for a woman nursing, as bread is considered most injurious for all emigrants, as being the main cause of bringing on dysentery.' Rice and dried fish would have been an acceptable diet to many of the passengers, but sago was generally supplied instead which they tended to dislike. There was also a danger that many of the emigrants would eat too much at mealtimes and 'hide what they cannot eat, and, before they eat it, it turns sour, and brings on diarrhoea; though every means were used to prevent them hiding any.'[55]

Some government tenders stipulated that salt fish, chillies, dhal, ghee and such spices as turmeric and tamarind should be carried, providing food that was palatable to the tastes of the emigrants, and that dry provisions should be stocked for use when cooking was impossible in bad weather.[56] When it was observed that sweetened tinned milk was preferred to unsweetened milk, tinned milk was supplied. The supply of tinned milk was considered especially important for infants since 'from sea sickness, the unaccustomed life at sea and the total change in their habits, women, with children at the breast, rapidly lose, and, in the majority instances, do not again recover their milk.'[57] At the same time, tinned mutton was provided rather than ships carrying sheep on board since 'the pens take up valuable space; the urine and dung get under the pens and are hard to remove and become very offensive.'[58]

On ships carrying Chinese coolies, rice, tea and salted fish and meat were supplied for the emigrants to cook in their own fashion in 'smelting pots' set up as communal galleys on the upper deck, but this food soon became putrid. Diarrhoea and scurvy as a result were common. Some ships took on board fresh vegetables and live pigs and sheep at ports en route. However, the effect of a plentiful diet on many emigrants, more accustomed to the starvation that went with their accustomed hand-to-mouth existence, was also dysentery, which they were unable to fight against in their emaciated and weakened state on boarding.[59]

Water supplies were just as inadequate as the food, a situation made worse by the difficulties of obtaining fresh water in the Indian and Chinese ports. Water would often be taken on board at Anjer, Cape Hope and St Helena. In order to conserve these supplies of water, various stratagems were adopted, including rationing passengers to between a pint and a gallon a day and preventing wastage by storing water in caskets which had reeds inserted in them when an emigrant wanted a drink. On another ship, the water supplies were treated twice a week with six gallons of port wine and one gallon of 'anti-scorbutic medicine', a measure which it was claimed prevented scurvy and which provided water that the emigrants drank with 'great avidity and enjoyment.'[60]

The ships from China were heavily armed to keep the passengers under control. The movement of passengers from the between decks to the main deck was controlled by the fitting of crossed iron bars, arched in the centre with a small opening at the top, over the hatchways. The hatches leading to the provisions of tea, fish and rice in the hold were surrounded by iron bars fitted to both decks both to prevent theft, and also served as cages for armed guards to take up position in, to restore order in the event of a mutiny. The captain's cabin was similarly protected by a barricade firmly bolted to the deck with sixteen-pound cannons poking through the defences. From this defensive structure, resembling a 'floating menagerie for wild beasts', a small number of guards could command the entire deck and subdue the passengers.[61]

In the China Seas there had long been a fear of piracy and it was believed that some pirates would volunteer as emigrants to South America and then hijack the ship.[62] As a result 'in the *Fei Ma*, the Chinese passengers are put down in the hold twelve feet deep and the ladder is taken away', while 'a sailor keeps guard over them with a drawn cutlass.' Meanwhile, 'one of the Yankee ships has an iron cage on deck into which the Chinese passengers are invited to walk and are then locked up.' There was only one way a ship could feel secure from hijacking: 'the Peninsular and Orient boat has a better but more costly precaution; she carries no Chinese passengers.'[63]

There was indeed a real danger of mutiny on these ships. Between 1850 and 1872 there were at least sixty-eight mutinies on ships carrying Chinese contract labourers bound for Cuba, Peru, British Guiana, Australia, India and the United States. Some of the mutineers had been tricked on board and effectively kidnapped, others regretted having agreed to emigrate, some were reacting to the harsh treatment they received onboard ship, and a small number wished merely to plunder the ship.[64] One passenger, E Holden, on the *Norway* shipping 1,038 Chinese labourers to Cuba in 1859, witnessed a mutiny in which the mutineers, having written with the blood of one of their number their demands to be taken to Siam, attempted to set the ship on fire when their initial attack on the crew was repulsed:

> The foiled wretches, maddened at defeat from the outset, rushed with furious yells from one hatch to another, swinging lighted firebrands or striving to wrench away the iron bars that covered them, or hurling bolts and clubs at every face that peered down at them from above. The red glare of the flames lit up the sky, reflecting grimly against the swelling sails, and in spite of a constant stream of water from the pumps seemed scarcely to diminish.[65]

Floggings were as common as in the heyday of slavery, not just as a punishment, but equally, if not more importantly, as a deterrent to anyone considering mutiny on the ships carrying Chinese emigrants. A dozen lashes were given for smoking below deck, theft, or illegal gambling, and up to two dozen for perjury, fighting and 'depositing filth between decks'. The worst punishments were reserved for challenges to authority, and 'any coolie or coolies discovered conspiring to mutiny, shall, when found guilty, be punished with the cats not exceeding four dozens and afterwards be handcuffed and chained to the ringbolts of the deck during the master's pleasure.'[66]

A more effective way of keeping the coolies under control than through violence and stern discipline was to keep the emigrants entertained and 'employed in any way to prevent them from thinking and drooping'. On the *Salsette*, travelling from Calcutta to Trinidad in 1858, Captain Swinton and his wife Jane 'found exercise, such as their native dances, very useful in keeping up a good state of health – an experiment which we tried. Music is also very desirable.' However, they had to be careful about not encouraging immorality among the younger passengers because 'they have no morality whatever: if they fancy each other they become man and wife for the time being, and change again when they please.'[67]

Chinese coolies were notorious for spending their time on deck playing dominoes and cards, but arguments over gambling often ended in fighting. Alternative entertainment was provided by passengers playing on one-stringed violins, clarinets, cymbals, gongs, drums and trumpets. Sometimes these musical instruments were provided as part of the ship's equipment, but many passengers took their own means of making music.[68] Some enterprising captains organised concerts and competitions to keep the passengers amused and occupied, such as the prizes of tobacco and silver dollars for the best piece of basketwork produced on one voyage.[69]

Keeping the passengers entertained depended very much on the cultural characteristics of different groups of coolies. Emigrants from the Madras area were seen as sociable and keen to be involved in what was happening on board ship:

The Madrasee is a lively, singing merry fellow, who delights in remaining on deck, seldom stays below if he can help it, day or night, is always ready to bear a hand in pulling ropes or any other work going on in the ship, and is much less troubled with prejudices of any kind.[70]

Emigrants from Bengal, contrarily, were seen as much less cheerful and active, almost the antithesis of those from Madras:

The Bengali is so much given to remaining below that compulsion is necessary to bring him on deck. He rapidly gives way to sea sickness and depression; when taken ill, always imagines that he must die;

and remains in an apathetic state of torpid indifference, the very reversal of the mercurial propensities of the Malabar.[71]

Such crude racial stereotyping was also applied by Europeans to Chinese migrants. Jane Swinton preferred Indian coolies to the Chinese, whom she considered 'a most determined and self-willed people, who thought a great deal of their joss, and were quite opposed to the others in character.'[72]

Much depended upon the attitude of the captain and his crew to the passengers. Tenders for ships carrying emigrants to the West Indies stipulated that 'the said emigrants shall be treated with kindness by the Master and all the officers and crew of the said ship'.[73] Captain Swinton, 'kind, generous and humane', and his wife Jane both showed great concern for the welfare of their charges on the *Salsette*. Prepared to see that 'the luxuries of his chief cabin, the delicacies provided for his wife's comfort, were dispensed with a liberal hand to men, women and children, when their state of health required them', he did everything possible to look after the welfare of his charges.[74] It was in his interest to do so, apart from any humanitarian considerations, since the death of a coolie represented a loss of £13 from their charter money for the shipowners as the colonial authorities in Trinidad would only pay for coolies landed alive.[75] Jane Swinton believed that it was 'most unjust and illiberal to the owners of any Coolie-ship to be paid only for such as are landed alive, particularly when put on board in such a diseased state by the emigration office in Calcutta.' She further questioned 'why have one law for our Indian emigrants to the West India colonies, and another for our English emigrants to Australia?'[76] Yet the same system of only paying for emigrants arriving in a sound and healthy condition also applied to ships carrying Chinese emigrants.[77] The captain and crew had an incentive to be concerned about the well-being of their passengers.

Not all captains were as solicitous about the coolies in their charge as they might have been. The commander of the *Bucephalus*, which left Calcutta for George Town in 1857, 'seems to have looked upon the condition of the coolies as a matter with which he had little or no concern' and 'left them altogether in the hands of the surgeon, who again had neither aptitude for command nor energy sufficient to contend with the dirty and disorderly habits of the people.'[78] It is not surprising that, though the medical treatment on the *Bucephalus* was satisfactory, sixteen men, fifteen women and fourteen children died on the ninety-five-day voyage.

As on the ships to Australia, each British ship had a qualified surgeon superintendent on board. The captain of a chartered ship was required to 'on all occasions, when practicable, attend to any of the suggestions of the surgeon calculated to promote the health, comfort or well-being of the emigrants'.[79] Jane Swinton, as captain's wife, believed that 'the captain ought to be allowed to nominate a doctor on behalf of the owners, to make the selection of the Coolies in conjunction with the doctor appointed to the ship, and that sufficient time be given to doctors to make the proper inspection.'[80] On board the ship the surgeon superintendent was in charge of the coolies and responsible for keeping them under control as well as keeping them healthy.

Inevitably, many of the surgeon superintendents appointed were not always of the highest quality and many of them were to be blamed for any deficiencies in the treatment of the emigrants. European doctors considered service on a coolie ship to be below them, unless they were desperate for a post anywhere. They were also paid on a less generous scale than their equivalents on government-assisted passages to Australia, because the West Indies colonies could not afford to pay them so generously. In Barbados it was recognised that 'there can be no question as to the advantage of employing competent surgeons on board emigrant vessels … but I fear that the adoption of the Emigrant Commissioners' to increase their remuneration and recruit a superior class of surgeon 'would very materially increase the expenses of emigration, already high.'[81]

As a result many Indian-born and educated doctors took these posts. They were in turn looked down upon by European officers, and even Indian crew. Robert Sinclair, surgeon superintendent on the *India*, shipping coolies from Calcutta to British Guiana in 1879, soon made himself unpopular with the captain and crew of his ship when trying to carry out his duties:

It was mainly in insisting on the rights of the emigrants in my charge and endeavouring to control abuses that I got myself into disfavour with the crew and others aboard. The simple fact is that the commander and officers could not control the crew in their ill-treatment of the emigrants, the crew being an unruly lot, recruited from the back slums of Calcutta, and utterly beyond restraint; and their repugnance to me, in my efforts to defend the emigrants from their ill-treatment, is the surest proof of my determination not to tolerate abuses in spite of the odds against me.[82]

Sinclair was belittled as a 'native surgeon', but highly placed government officials supported him in denying this, and 'the Lieutenant Governor cannot understand how Mr Sinclair is spoken of as a native. He is in appearance a decidedly fair European, though his education was received in the Calcutta Medical College.'[83]

Not all surgeon superintendents were as determined as Robert Sinclair to stand up for their status and the rights of their charges. On the *Bucephalus* 'the surgeon was a mere boy, and unfit to be entrusted with so serious a duty.' A fellow doctor commented on his inexperience that 'I knew him during the whole period of his study in the Medical College of Calcutta and am aware that he was a lad of ability who was well acquainted with his profession; but I should not on that account have considered it right to entrust him with the management of so large a body of emigrants' as the 389 on board the *Bucephalus* in 1856. One of the reasons for sickness among the coolies was 'the excessive and mistaken kindness which induced the surgeon to allow the people to remain below the greater part of the voyage.'[84]

Although native surgeon superintendents were looked down upon as being inferior to European doctors, they did have the advantage of being able to speak to their charges in their own language, depending upon the part of India they came from. On the *Blue Jacket* in 1857 'the surgeon was well accustomed to the management of natives and spoke their language fluently.'[85] The ships did carry interpreters who were essential for communication between the surgeon superintendent and the coolies. These interpreters, known as *sirdars* or *chokedars*, were also supervisors of groups of fifty coolies. An Indian apothecary would also have been helpful as an intermediary between the doctor and his charges. This would have helped overcome prejudices against Western medicines. Otherwise the alternative would have been 'that the ship be supplied with the herbs used by the natives in sickness, as it is next to an impossibility to get them to take our medicine.'[86]

Chinese migrants were also suspicious of Western medicine and preferred treatment for dysentery, scurvy, dropsy, fever and opium withdrawal with traditional Chinese remedies. Although from the 1850s onwards emigrant ships were supposed to have qualified surgeons, a hospital, and adequate medical supplies, these regulations were often ignored and the only doctors that could be obtained were Chinese practitioners, who were unfamiliar with European medicine and often extorted money from the sick in return for their favours or for the supply of opium.[87]

Cholera, in which violent diarrhoea, cramps and vomiting were usually followed by death within hours, was especially prevalent on the overcrowded ships taking coolies from India to the West Indies. The Colonial Office recognised that very little could be done to keep cholera off the emigrant ships, since Calcutta was 'never quite free from cholera and ... to insist on perfect health at the depot would be tantamount to stopping the emigration altogether.'[88] The problem was that, in their eagerness to find employment overseas, many of the emigrants hid any symptoms of disease when they were inspected by medical officers before boarding the ship and then, having brought the disease on board, did not seek medical help until too late. Death rates from cholera were particularly high among children on these coolie emigrant ships, and it was possible that restricting the number of children travelling might have reduced the incidence of cholera. However, if there were restrictions on the size of families allowed to emigrate from India, this would inevitably have resulted in labour shortages in the West Indies. Moreover, the maintenance of good health through well-ventilated accommodation, adequate privies, nutritious food and medical care was 'so important to the future continuance of emigration and to the well-being of the West India Colonies.' Fewer child passengers might have been desirable but few families would have been willing to be split up:

A large number of children, especially if under six or seven years of age, must be undesirable in a sanitary point of view in Indian as in English emigration, and it would therefore be advisable that the

Emigration Officer should as far as possible exclude families having more than a certain proportion of young children. But his doing so will necessarily impede him filling his ships.'[89]

Without coolie emigration from India and China, there would have been severe labour shortages in the colonies and in South America. Such emigration was also accepted by the Indian government as a safety valve for those of its people who could not be provided with work at home, but by the beginning of the twentieth century there was more concern about the exploitation of Indian migrants. Within a year of his appointment as Viceroy of India in 1898, Lord Curzon expressed concern about the situation when he refused a petition from Caribbean planters for the general abolition of the Indian labourers' right to a free return passage at the end of their five-year contract.

Meanwhile, the indentured community itself was protesting against some of the abuses of the system. In Natal, resistance against the system was led by the young Indian lawyer Mohandras Gandhi who convinced Indian public opinion that emigration was detrimental rather than beneficial for India. His fellow campaigner and lawyer Henry Polak described the treatment of Indians in South Africa as 'a record of shame and cruelty that has no counterpart within the confines of the British Empire.'[90]

In the face of such criticism, the response of the British government was to favour reform of the indenture system rather than its abolition. Joseph Chamberlain asserted in 1897 the right of the self-governing colonies to control the influx of Indian and Chinese migrants, who were 'alien in civilization, alien in religion, alien in customs', but insisted that it was necessary 'also to bear in mind the traditions of the Empire, which makes no distinction in favour of, or against, race and colour.'[91]

However, the days of the indenture system were numbered, mainly through a combination of exclusionist policies by the white dominions, rising Indian and Chinese nationalism, and the changing world economy in the aftermath of the First World War, when falls in the profits of sugar plantations made the importation of contract labourers less commercially viable, especially when there was already a pool of more settled labour in those colonies. In 1916 indentured emigration was banned by the government of India, bringing to an end a far from glorious period of imperial migration, but one in which the coolie ships had built up the economy of the British Empire and fostered a multicultural world.[92]

7

In Peril

Overcrowding, poor food, bad water and a foul atmosphere were the least of the fears of the emigrant. Disasters were reported often enough in the days of sailing ships, on which there was a constant risk of fire, so that there was a good chance that an emigrant setting out so hopefully might be fearful of never reaching the promised land. The *Ocean Monarch* had only left Liverpool for Boston a few hours earlier when fire swept through it in August 1848. It was thought that a steerage passenger might have lit a fire in one of the ventilators, that a seaman searching for stowaways had left a burning candle underneath one of the after-cabins, or that the fire had started through careless smoking by steerage passengers, though no one ever knew for certain what had caused the blaze.[1] Soon 'the flames were bursting with immense fury from the stern and centre of the vessel', driving the panicking passengers to crowd into the fore of the ship while some of the women jumped overboard with their children in their arms in their 'maddened despair'. Then, as the fire advanced towards them, 'to the jib-boom they clung in clusters as thick as they could pack – even one lying over another.' As the foremast burned it fell overboard 'snapping the fastenings of the jib-boom, which, with its load of human beings, dropped in the water amidst the most heart-rending screams both of those on board and those who were falling into the water.' Some of them clambered back on board those parts of the ship not yet affected by the fire, others clung to spars, and many of them drowned. While the majority of the 360 on board, including all the cabin passengers, survived, there were still 176 deaths, in a 'most harrowing and appalling' disaster which happened within sight of land, of people 'who, but a few hours before, were buoyed up by bright anticipations of the future'.[2]

Thomas Littledale, Commodore of the Royal Mersey Yacht Club, had been returning to Liverpool from a regatta at Beaumaris when he came across the burning *Ocean Monarch* and he was the first to attempt to rescue the passengers and crew, picking up thirty-two people on his yacht. It was not until an hour and a half later that the rescue attempts were joined in by other ships, the Brazilian frigate *Affonso,* the steamer *Prince of Wales* and the packet ship *New World* sailing for New York. Had these ships not been nearby, there would have been even greater loss of life. The *Affonso* sent four boats, one of them containing the ship's commander, the Marquis de Lisboa, and the other Admiral Grenfell who had been aboard the Brazilian frigate, another of whose passengers, the Prince de Joinville, son of the recently exiled Louis Philippe of France, 'stripped off his coat, and was particularly assiduous in assisting the passengers on board the frigate'. A seaman from Portsmouth on the American ship *New World*, Frederick Jerome, was congratulated and rewarded with a gratuity from the Duke of Aumale, Joinville's brother and fellow passenger on the *Affonso*, for having 'stripped himself naked and swam through the wreckage with a line, climbed aboard the *Ocean Monarch* and succeeded in lowering the last helpless victims into a boat before he, himself, was forced to leave'. Less heroic was the conduct of the captain of another ship, the *Cambria,* a packet running from Liverpool to Bangor, who failed to offer the stricken *Ocean Monarch* any assistance, using the excuse that 'he had 200 passengers on board and his decks were completely crowded with livestock which would have rendered it difficult at any time to render assistance.'[3]

The survivors were in a pitiable state when rescued and 'never did we witness such squalid masses of human beings, most of them are women, some with burns on their necks and shoulders, produced by the blazing masts and spars, and others with black eyes, and contused wounds upon various parts of their persons, caused by frequent surges on the tops of the waves against broken spars and the hull of the burning wreck'.[4] Other survivors were suspicious of some of their rescuers. Henry Powell was picked up by the pilot boat *Pilot Queen* and later claimed that robbery was the driving motive of its crew, who were more interested in salvaging valuables than in saving lives. When the rescued men tried to leave the pilot boat to get on a fishing smack,

Powell had to surrender his silver pocket watch before he was allowed to leave the *Pilot Queen*. Unfortunately, one of the casualties from the *Ocean Monarch*, a young man named Coombes, was left behind, 'naked and too ill to dress himself'. The crew of the fishing smack commented that, 'If they find out he's got money about him, they'll murder him and throw him overboard. They'll never think to be found out.' Coombes 'wasn't heard of again', although Powell did have his own watch returned to him by the police.[5]

Wooden sailing ships were obviously the most vulnerable to the dangers of fire. This was responsible for the loss of 101 emigrants on the *Caleb Grimshaw* in 1849 after it caught fire three hundred miles northwest of the Azores. On Christmas Eve 1852, fifty-one emigrants died when fire got a hold on the *St George* in the mid-Atlantic. Away from land and other ships, the hopes of rescue could be slim and many people were doomed to being burned or drowned. Yet steamships could also burn, and the worst fire disaster in the history of Atlantic crossings was on the steamship *Austria* in August 1858.[6] For the first week of the voyage from Hamburg the weather had been rough and the passengers were kept below. On 13 September 1858 the weather improved and most passengers crowded on deck. It offered an opportunity for the captain and surgeon to order the fumigation of steerage, which was 'foul and foetid' after eight days of closed down hatches and very poor ventilation. The boatswain charged with this task accidentally knocked over the bucket of hot pine tar he was using for fumigation and the wooden deck caught fire. The flames were fanned by the recently opened hatches and ventilators. Although the *Austria*'s hull was made of iron, her gangways, stairways, deckhouses, masts and spars were all made of wood and soon caught alight.[7]

At first the passengers on deck assumed that the cries of 'Fire!' were a false alarm and some men playing shuttlecock ignored the alarm until they themselves noticed thick smoke and flames bursting through the midship. The captain went into action much more quickly, bolting from his cabin to order the ship's fire brigade to their posts. Already the fire had melted the lead pipes of the steam pump, which meant that the fire hoses were useless. Two strings of fire buckets were equally hopeless. Meanwhile, the smoke and fire overcame the engine room crew. When the ship's magazine of ammunition and guns exploded, the captain realised that the ship was doomed, and he was heard to shout, 'My God, we are lost!' The starboard lifeboats by now were on fire, and the crew were only able to get one from the port side afloat. The captain tried to board a lifeboat and perished in the attempt. At the same time, emigrants were jumping into the sea, their clothes ablaze. The screw propellers were still turning and chopped into lifeboats and swimmers. By the time a French bark came to the rescue, the death toll was 471. The surviving crew defended themselves against charges of incompetence by stating that they had done their best in impossible circumstances, and 'we leave it to everyone to judge whether we have done our duty or not.'[8]

The crew were the only survivors after the *Cospatrick* caught fire in November 1874, 250 miles west of Cape Good Hope, on its way to Auckland with emigrants embarking at the emigrant depot at Blackwall near London. The ship was carrying a flammable cargo of turpentine, varnish, methylated spirits, linseed oil and alcohol, and the fire soon got out of control. The captain Alexander Elmslie, his wife, small son, and the surgeon Dr Cadle threw themselves into the sea and drowned. One lifeboat, full of eighty women passengers, capsized and only two of the five lifeboats, holding a mere sixty-two of the 470 passengers and crew, were able to get away from the burning ship. One of these lifeboats drifted away and was never seen again. When the other boat was picked up after ten days, only five men were alive of the thirty originally on board. Two of them, a passenger and a sailor, were out of their minds and died on the ship, the *British Sceptre*, that rescued them. There was no food or fresh water on the lifeboat, and the men had rigged up a sail using a dead girl's petticoat.[9] Charles MacDonald, the second mate, later confessed that 'we were that hungry and thirsty that we drank the blood and ate the livers of two of them' who had already died, and that as the days went on 'we kept sucking the blood of those who had died'.[10] He was at pains to stress that they 'ate no flesh, only the liver', and that in the case of 'Mr Bickersteth, who paid for his voyage ... his body was not touched before it was thrown overboard'.[11] Even in this extremity there were taboos not to be breached and standards of social status to be upheld. Edward Cotter, an eighteen-year-old seaman with a 'fair and good humoured face', observed that 'the biggest, fattest, healthiest looking men went off first', but that 'it was not from them that the blood was obtained'. It was only later that cannibalism was considered as a means of survival. Cotter himself 'only ate twice', but 'I drank whenever a vein was opened'.[12] The horror of cannibalism was enough to discourage emigrants from undertaking the long and potentially hazardous journey to New Zealand for a while after these gruesome events were reported in the popular press.

Fire was not the only hazard at sea resulting in horrendous loss of life. Shipwrecks were also responsible for appalling levels of mortality. The wooden sailing ships had the worst record, just as they had with fire. In 1834, seventeen sailing ships were lost in the Gulf of St Lawrence alone and 731 emigrants drowned. When in April 1847 the *Exmouth,* sailing from Londonderry to Quebec, ran aground on rocks off Islay, only three of the crew survived and about 240 emigrants perished, most of them still below deck:

> There was no cry from the multitude cooped up within the hull of the ill-fated brig; or at least it was unheard, for the commotion of the elements was so furious that the men on the top could scarcely hear each other at the top of their voices. The emigrants, therefore, must have perished in their berths, as the rocks rapidly thumped the bottom out of the vessel.[13]

The *Floridian,* carrying two hundred 'young, respectable German agricultural labourers, with their wives and families, and many mechanics', was wrecked on the Long Sands off Harwich in March 1849, and 'a scene of horror instantly presented itself on deck', to which many of the passengers had rushed in 'frantic dismay'. However, within a few moments of the vessel striking the rocks, the sea broke into her hull, blowing up the hatchways, and 'sweeping many of the poor creatures overboard, while others were drowned in their berths, being unable to rise from the effects of sea sickness.'[14]

Another bad winter was that of 1853–4 when gales and snowstorms wreaked havoc in the Atlantic. As a result, passages were longer than usual and several emigrant ships were severely damaged. The *Jacob A Westervelt,* bound for Canada with seven hundred passengers, reached the Banks of Newfoundland in December 1853, stripped of sails and partly dismantled after weeks of battling against high seas and head gales. Her exhausted crew mutinied and, supported by the passengers, forced the captain to return to Liverpool. The two hundred German passengers who drowned on the *Powhatan* were not so lucky when that ship was driven by a northeast wind onto the shore of New Jersey.[15] The fate of some ships was never known. Perhaps the greatest disaster of the winter of 1853–4 was when the *City of Glasgow* disappeared with 480 on board, 293 of them in steerage, after clearing the Mersey in March 1854 en route for Philadelphia.[16]

When the *Strathmore* ran aground on its way to Otago from London in early July 1875, its forty-nine survivors, many of them scantily clad for winter in the southern hemisphere, some only in their nightclothes, clung to a lonely rock off the Crozet Islands, more than a thousand miles southeast of Cape Good Hope. With no supplies other than two barrels of gunpowder, one cask of port wine, two cases of rum, one case of brandy, two cases of gin, one case of preserves, one case of women's boots, and eight tins of sweets, together with a few blankets, knives and spoons from a passenger's box, they were lucky that there was a freshwater spring on the rock. Only one woman and two children survived the sinking. The other passengers and sailors were polite and helpful towards Frances Wordsworth and her son Charles, but the rougher element among the sailors preyed upon the male passengers, who were mainly from the first-class saloon, and so 'the strong men took from the weak'. They organised themselves into six messes and lived off seaweed, mosses and seabirds, including albatrosses, until finally rescued from their desert island almost seven months later on 21 January 1876. As a result of their unwholesome diet, they all 'got pot-bellied' and suffered from dysentery. Shelters were rigged up from rocks and turf, and a signal fire was kept going with the carcases of dead seabirds. In the view of *The Times* it was 'a gloomy prospect, this, of a lifelong bondage, away from the flesh pots that have before now made bondage tolerable', and 'those seven months of suffering and suspense must indeed have been a sore trial of endurance, physical and mental, of those who were compelled to go through them.' Five of the castaways died on the rocky islet, including on Christmas Day Walter Walker, a three-year-old boy, whose mother had drowned but whose father Alfred had survived to care for him. The survivors were rescued by the *Young Phoenix* bound for

Mauritius and eventually returned to London via Mauritius or Ceylon.[17] Their experiences had had none of the romance of a real-life *Robinson Crusoe*.

Shipwreck survivors had often lost everything when their ship went down and it was beyond the resources of local charity in the areas where they were grounded to give them aid. When over 120 German emigrants bound for New York in a ship chartered by Belgian agents were shipwrecked near Brixham in 1846, it was 'obviously impossible that private charity alone will suffice for the maintenance of the individuals in question and their conveyance to the place of their destination'.[18] The British government accordingly sought the support of the Belgian government in putting pressure on the Antwerp shipping company that had sent out an unseaworthy vessel to provide another ship so that the emigrants could continue their journey. The company concerned had 'acknowledged their responsibility by having sent out to the value of about £50 in provisions.' Meanwhile, attempts to get aid from the German states that the emigrants originally came from proved futile.[19] Similarly, when the Dutch ship *Helen Marie* had landed at Falmouth in February 1828, bound for Brazil but 'in a destitute and diseased condition', attempts to persuade the Dutch government to get the shipowners to fulfil their obligations had elicited the response that 'the Netherlands Government had just forwarded to the Brazils at their own expense another lot of German emigrants who had arrived at Amsterdam without the means of transport and support', and suggested that the British did the same. Prussia had declined to help its former citizens and the British government was forced to provide the funds to send the distressed emigrants on their way, aided by the charity of the mayor and people of Falmouth.[20]

Travellers were advised by handbooks on emigration that the passages to Australia and New Zealand were safer than the shorter journey to North America:

> The number of shipwrecks is much greater of American emigrant ships than of Australian vessels, not perhaps, however, in proportion to the greater number which undertake the voyage. We are bound also to add that these shipwrecks seldom occur from the mere bad weather, but are generally the result of ignorance of the Channel, or

of mistakes in soundings, as it is not at sea that the accidents occur, but generally near the coast either in setting out or on the approach to British America. New Zealand is often reached without any weather worse than a breeze. Perfect candour and impartiality call upon us to observe that opinion.[21]

Many mistakes made by an incompetent captain and poor crew could lead to disaster. An economist, John Ramsay McCulloch, considered in 1839 that 'a third part of the wrecks that have taken place of late years have been occasioned by the dangers of the sea', but that 'the other two thirds or more have originated in artificial causes of which the principal have been ... the incompetency of the masters.'[22] On 28 September 1853 the *Annie Jane,* sailing from Liverpool to Quebec, foundered off the coast of the island of Vatersay in the Hebrides, split into three pieces, and 350 passengers and crew were drowned. The ship had already returned once to Liverpool for repairs after being damaged in a gale. When it again hit stormy weather, some of the passengers petitioned the captain to turn back once more or to put into a port, but 'instead of reading or paying any attention to it, he pitched it overboard, observing that they had got him to put about upon a former occasion, but that he would have the satisfaction out of them the second time.'[23]

The self-regard of the captain and his dislike of being criticised also contributed to Australia's worst maritime disaster, the wreck of the emigrant ship, *Cataraqui*, bound for Melbourne, on the western coast of King's Island, on 4 August 1845 when there were only nine survivors out of the 423 on board. There had been differences of opinion between the captain and surgeon superintendent for most of the voyage. On 3 August Captain Christopher Finlay expected to reach Melbourne the following day and had given permission for the emigrants to have their boxes brought up out of the hold, 'in order that they might look out and select their holiday attire for shore inspection, on their landing'. However, signs of an impending storm had made the captain act cautiously in shortening sail and putting the vessel 'under very easy canvass'. Then he had overheard Carpenter, the surgeon superintendent, criticising such caution and declaring that it was the result of cowardice rather than prudence. Annoyed at such remarks, the captain had counter-ordered the crew to 'shake out the reefs and stand on!' The ship had struck a jagged rock less than a hundred yards from shore. There was no time to launch the lifeboats, the emigrant families did not know what to do, and 'the poor unhappy girls were tossed into the ocean as they were, unclad, unprepared; the wild screaming death shriek mingling with the wilder storm.'[24] The surgeon superintendent whose criticism of the captain had led to the disaster was one of the first to die, but only one of many.

The behaviour of the crew was nothing if not callous when the *William Brown* sank after striking an iceberg on 19 May 1841, five weeks out from Liverpool en route to Philadelphia. Thirty of the sixty-five steerage passengers went down with the ship, while the captain, seven of the crew, and a woman passenger boarded the jolly boat to steer towards Newfoundland never to be seen again. The mate, Alexander Holmes, eight crew, and thirty-three passengers crammed into the longboat and steered south. Under their weight the longboat began to sink so Holmes consulted the crew, who agreed that 'it was necessary to throw overboard those who were nearly dead, until we had room enough to work the boat and take to our oars', and ordered them to throw some of the emigrants overboard to lighten it.[25] Six were tossed overboard without any resistance, but when the crew attempted to do the same with another passenger, Frank Askins, he offered them five sovereigns if they would spare him until the morning. Askins' sister Mary cried out, 'Oh! Don't put out my brother – if you put him out, put me out too!' She and another sister Ellen were thrown out after their brother, despite Ellen's futile plea for a mantle to cover her nakedness. The survivors on the longboat were picked up by the ship *Crescent*, eastbound from New York, and taken to Le Havre. Holmes was later found guilty of manslaughter and sentenced to six months in prison.[26] His offence was not only that 'for an individual to sacrifice the life of his companion in order to make his own secure would be an atrocious outrage on humanity', but that 'the heinousness of the deed was peculiarly aggravated by the circumstance of the parties being sacrificed being persons who had impliedly committed themselves to the protection and safe conduct of the officers and crew of the vessel', whose duty was 'to risk their own lives in their defence instead of being induced by an unmanly selfishness to become their executioners.'[27]

clear one. The coast of Nova Scotia was well charted with no hidden perils. What had led to the disaster was a series of circumstances which may have seemed unimportant enough by themselves, but cumulatively led to catastrophe. The captain, James Williams, was not familiar with the Nova Scotia coast, but had sailed close to it when four days of bad weather had slowed the ship down and its supplies of coal were depleted. It would have been more sensible to have put in at Halifax for refuelling but, fearful of having to pay a hefty penalty if the mail it was carrying on contract with the United States government was late, the captain decided to try for New York. Rather than slow down to take soundings to measure the depth of the water, Williams had preferred to rely on the visibility of navigational hazards.[29] Apart from the human errors involved, there was the corporate culture of pursuit of profit by shipping companies at the expense of compromising safety, not to lose money by delivering the mail late. The solution to this would be to hold the shipowners financially responsible for any negligence. *The Times* had considered at the time of the sinking of the *John* in 1843 that 'if there be no regard for human life among the owners of emigrant ships, perhaps consideration for their own pockets may render them more careful in the selection of competent officers', and ones who would not take risks with lives for financial reasons.[30]

Even when the captain of one ship was careful, little could be done if others were less cautious. The *Northfleet*, with over four hundred emigrants on board, went down off Dungeness in January 1873, after being cut in half by a steamer which 'made off without any attempt to render assistance', and 'disappeared so completely that her name and nationality are unknown', though a Spanish steamer was suspected.[31] In January 1895 the steamer *Elbe* collided in dense fog with the Scottish coaster *Crathie* in the North Sea. The *Crathie* should have given way to a ship coming up to starboard, but she continued on the same course; the *Elbe* did not give way, but sent up warning rockets. The *Crathie* then went into the port side of the *Elbe*, abaft of the engine room bulkhead, and when the coaster pulled free, water poured into the steamer. There was confusion in the darkness, and fights over the inadequate supply of life preservers, with one cabin passenger having to struggle against other men wanting to take his life jacket from him. There were only twenty survivors from the 352 on board when the

Elbe sank, and the master of the *Crathie* deservedly lost his certificate.[32] Losses were on a similar scale in July 1898 when 549 were drowned after *La Bourgogne* was rammed amidships off Cape Sable by a British sailing ship.

The sinking of the *Utopia* on 17 March 1891 was also the result of a collision, this time with HMS *Anson* in Gibraltar Bay. The *Utopia* was sailing from Trieste to New York and had stopped at Naples and Genoa to take on board more emigrants. She carried 880 people, comprising fifty-nine crew, three first-class cabin passengers and 815 in steerage, most of them from Calabria and the Abruzzi, with three stowaways, yet there were only 160 life belts.[33] After rounding Europa Point, the steamer approached the anchorage at Gibraltar, which was full of warships. Captain John McKeague reduced speed and attempted to clear the *Anson* by spinning the helm sharply to starboard and then to port. However, the warship's ram caught the *Utopia* at midship and ripped a hole in her. Five minutes after the ramming, the *Utopia* began to sink. Many of the passengers were on deck at the time but rushed to the hatchways to retrieve their belongings and warn people below. Meanwhile, passengers in steerage tried to get on deck. The result was that nobody could move in or out. The confusion was such that 'the rush from behind carried those who first reached the hatchway, from the deck, onto the top of the crowds who were seeking to escape the inrushing water, till the whole hatchway was choked right up to the top; then, and only then did those behind discover what had happened at the hatchway, and each one rushed to save his life abandoning all hope of rescuing those below.'[34] Some of the people trapped below tried to escape through the portholes but got stuck. Those on the deck were able to jump into the sea, cling to the anchor chains, or climb into the rigging.[35]

The sea was so rough that the vessels in port could not send boats alongside the sinking ship but had to stay at the leeward to pick up survivors and shine their searchlights.[36] A Swedish frigate, the *Freja*, commanded by Prince Oscar Bernadotte, also took part in the attempts 'to save life.'[37] One of the survivors, William Colburn, a New York stockbroker travelling in first class, owed his life to his being a strong swimmer, as 'no person would have a chance unless they could swim well in such a sea', and remembered that 'the stern of the ship actually sank under my feet.'[38] The final death toll was 564. The coroner recorded a verdict of 'accidental death' and ruled that 'the Master had committed a grave error in judgment in attempting to enter the anchorage behind the new Mole before ascertaining that it was occupied by the Fleet and ascertaining what were there, and then in attempting to turn the ship out across the bows of Her Majesty's Ship *Anson*.'[39]

The survivors were taken ashore and many of them accommodated in the Sailors' Home where 'it was a piteous sight to see them landed, utterly exhausted, unable to walk and unable, some of them, to give an account of themselves.' Prince Oscar Bernadotte even gave up his own cabin and bed on *Freja* for some of the women and children.[40] Those in need of medical care were treated at the Old Naval Hospital. Tents for the shipwrecked emigrants were also erected on the glacis of the Landport outside the town.

Meanwhile, attempts were made to recover the bodies, though 'the divers appear to have experienced great difficulty in removing the bodies owing to the number of orange boxes and amount of luggage floating about below, which might cut or entangle their air pipes.'[41] Some of the luggage had been stowed next to a cargo of beans which had swollen when soaked after the sinking, thus adding to the difficulties of recovery of bodies.[42] Noxious gases from the decomposing cargo and corpses impeded recovery attempts. Local fishermen also suffered from the protracted recovery, as 'owing to recent disastrous circumstances, those who earn their living by supplying fish to our markets are, from almost complete failure in its demand, in great want.'[43] Bodies were still being recovered when the ship was raised in July 1891, including a woman found 'clutching an infant to her breast.' Through all of this, 'the Medical Corps are conducting their sickening work with all the tenderness and humanity that circumstances will permit.'[44]

About three hundred of the emigrants on board the *Utopia* survived either to return home or continue their journey. On 22 March 132 returned to Naples, and on 26 March 153 left for New York on another Anchor Line steamer *Anglia*. They had lost all their money and possessions apart from the clothes they were wearing. Any of the personal effects found on the dead and any baggage recovered was to be forwarded to Naples by the Italian consul where the captain of the port and the judicial authorities would see that they were returned to their owners or the families of the deceased. However, a relief fund had been set up in Gibraltar and payments to the survivors ranged from £2 to £10 according to individual circumstances. For those continuing on to New York, the requirement that emigrants without luggage would be barred from entry into the United States was waived. By 28 March 1891, 'with the exception of three emigrants, who are in hospital and not well enough to be moved, and a man and his wife, who decline to again trust themselves to a sea voyage, all those who were saved from the *Utopia* have left Gibraltar.'[45]

The panic among the immigrants as the *Utopia* went down had been great and was unfairly ascribed to the Italian temperament. Alexander Sellar, the surgeon on the *Utopia*, recalled that 'the passengers were very excited, yelling and rushing around.'[46] John Adam, the third engineer, also thought that 'there was the greatest confusion among the passengers – they lost their heads.'[47] The newspapers went further and betrayed a prejudice against immigrants from southern Europe, the *New York Times* averring that:

> The Italians were thrown into a state of complete and cowardly panic. They yelled frantically and fought madly to reach the forecastle. A few of the married men dragged their wives with them, but the bulk of the single men were heedless of the piteous appeals of the women and children ... The only instances of manliness occurred among the people in the rigging. Many men and nearly every woman clasped children to their breasts, but they were gradually overcome by sheer exhaustion and cold ... The majority of the Italians, however behaved more like beasts than like reasoning men.[48]

Similar charges of panicking were made against the Italian emigrants aboard the *Sirio* when it went aground off the Spanish coast near Cartagena, en route for Argentina in August 1906. The passengers were 'in a state of horror and panic', and crowds of them rushed forward with knives, 'fighting for places at the bow of the boat', in the lifeboats and for life buoys, with the result that 'many fell and were trampled to death, and dozens of men and women threw themselves into the sea'.[49] It was claimed that 'the lower class of emigrants from Southern Europe cannot be trusted with knives and pistols at any time', and that 'the officers and crew were powerless to cope with the horde of Italians who fought for the boats.'[50] Such aspersions were resented by Italian-Americans such as Vincent Lattarulo, who responded that 'when it is asserted that the Italian emigrants acted as savages and bloodthirsty men, killing everybody, having no respect for age or sex, abandoning even their dear ones, and simply aiming at their own salvation', this was a slur on 'a people that rightly claims to have been, and to still be, the most civilized and humane of all peoples', and that what should be remembered is 'how deep is the sentiment of brotherhood in the Italian, to what extent the idea of altruism is inculcated in his character, and, above all, how great is the ascendancy the woman ... has over the heart and life of the average Italian man, in whatever stage of society he may be.'[51]

At first the captain and crew of the *Sirio* had been praised for their attempts to maintain discipline, but it was soon revealed that they had been the first to flee the ship and had commandeered lifeboats for their own use.[52] The captain was also accused of having sailed so close to the coast because the ship was 'engaged in the clandestine embarkation of Spanish emigrants along the coast', behaviour which 'left much to be desired.'[53] Captain Piccone was said to have committed suicide a year later out of 'grief' for the loss of his ship and the death of between 150 and 300 people on board.[54] The number of deaths was so imprecise because of poor record-keeping. Piccone's conduct contrasted with that of the Bishop of São Paulo who 'went down with the ship while blessing the drowning passengers'.[55]

The alleged cowardliness of the Italian crew of the *Sirio* was no different from that of the crew of the *William Brown* in 1841, or of the British and American crew of the *Arctic* in 1854, sailing from Liverpool to New York with only cabin passengers, after a collision with the French steamer *Vesta*. The engineers, oilers, firemen and trimmers on the *Arctic* had rushed on deck, brandishing knives, from which point 'all order and discipline ceased on board.' A lifeboat full of women and children slipped its rope and tackle, drowning all its occupants. Meanwhile, the chief engineer seized a small boat, filled it with food, water and cigars and launched it with nine other crew members, who forcibly prevented any passengers from boarding. Another lifeboat was occupied entirely by sailors, and some of the firemen and trimmers pushed passengers aside to take their place in the lifeboats. Of the 281 passengers, only twenty-three men survived, but sixty-one of the 153 crew were rescued in what was referred to ironically as 'a manly spectacle'. Such ungentlemanly behaviour was considered to be 'enough to make us all ashamed of humanity, and envy the better nature of the beasts of the field.'[56]

There were bound to be fights over life jackets and lifeboats when most ships carried too few for the number of those on board. The enquiry into the shipwreck of the *John* in 1855 was critical that 'the boats on board the *John* were not stowed in their proper places, nor were they prepared for service if wanted', but even more so that 'even had they been properly stowed, and had they been prepared for service, there was not in them sufficient accommodation to secure the safety of the passengers.'[57] The 1849 Passengers' Act had specified that there should be two boats for passenger ships of 100 tons and upwards, three for 200 tons and upwards, and four for 500 tons upwards. The Passengers' Acts of 1855 and 1863 similarly based the number of lifeboats on the ship's tonnage, not on the number of people on board, except that if there were more than two hundred passengers one of the boats should be a longboat in addition to regularly fitted lifeboats.[58]

In 1870 after the sinking of the paddle steamer *Normandy*, plying between Southampton and the Channel Islands, when there were too few lifeboats for passengers and crew, it was the opinion of the Board of Trade that 'it will not be possible to compel passenger steamers running between England and France to have boats sufficient for every numerous passenger they often carry', on the grounds that 'they would encumber the decks, and rather add to the danger than detract from it.'[59] It remained an anomaly that 'a passenger ship of 1,000 tons burthen, carrying 300 passengers, is not compelled to carry so many boats as a cargo ship of 2,000 tons, with a crew of 30.' However, any attempt to redress the problem was considered to be too onerous for shipowners. In 1887 a Select Committee of the House of Commons on Saving Life at Sea reported 'that many passenger ships could not, without great inconvenience, carry so many of the ordinary wooden boats as would suffice to carry the whole of the passengers and crew with safety in bad weather.'[60] The Merchant Shipping Acts of 1888, 1894 and 1897 merely provided for increasing the number of lifeboats as the vessel tonnage increased, but it stopped short at the point where the gross tonnage of the vessels reached 10,000 tons and upwards.[61]

The *Titanic* actually had more lifeboats than was legally required of it when it struck an iceberg in April 1912. Instead of the sixteen lifeboats the ship's tonnage required her to carry, there were fourteen lifeboats, four Engelhardt boats with collapsible canvas sides, and two cutters. This gave it a lifeboat capacity of 1,178, yet it was certified to carry 3,547 passengers and crew. In this it was no different from most other ships of the time, even the best equipped of which, *La Provence,* only had lifeboats for 82 per cent of those on board. Lifeboats were seen as cluttering the decks and as being almost redundant at a time when 'the ships are built nowadays to be practically unsinkable, and each ship is supposed to be a lifeboat in itself', according to Arthur Rostron, captain of the *Carpathia,* who was instrumental in the rescue of survivors from the doomed liner.[62] Indeed, Alfred Chalmers of the Board of Trade considered that too many lifeboats might have led to an even greater loss of life than the 1,498 lost, 'for the simple reason that, knowing they had so many boats to trust to, they probably sent the first lot away not fully loaded', and that 'I do not want to criticise the Officers or the Master of the ship at all, but I assume it is probable that that may have been the case; whereas if they had had fewer boats they would have taken good care that they utilised them to the fullest extent.'[63]

William Sowden Sim, a captain in the United States Navy, was more realistic when he commented after the sinking of the *Titanic* that:

The truth of the matter is that in case any large passenger steamship sinks, by reason of collision or other fatal damage to her flotability, more than half of her passengers are doomed to death, even in fair weather, and in case there is a bit of a sea running none of the loaded boats can long remain afloat, even if they succeed in getting safely away from the side, and one more will be added to the long list of 'the ships that never return.' Most people accept this condition as one of the inevitable perils of the sea, but I believe it can be shown that the terrible loss of life occasioned by such disasters as overtook the *Bourgogne* and the *Titanic* and many other ships can be avoided or at least greatly minimized. Moreover, it can be shown that the steamship owners are fully aware of the danger to their passengers; that the laws on the subject of life-saving appliances are wholly inadequate; that the steamship companies comply with the law, though they oppose any changes therein, and that they decline to adopt improved appliances; because there is no public demand for them, the demand being for high schedule speed and luxurious conditions of travel.[64]

Even had there been sufficient lifeboats on the *Titanic,* the crew were not altogether familiar with the procedures since lifeboat drills were rarely held. They were not a Board of Trade requirement and, although the White Star Line scheduled them for each Sunday morning, they were not a regular feature for the crew. George Cavell, a trimmer on the *Adriatic, Oceanic, Olympic* and *Titanic*, testified to the inquiry into the sinking of the *Titanic* that in his eighteen months at sea, 'the only boat drill as I ever had was when we went to New York, on Sunday morning'.[65] Unaccustomed to operating the lifeboats, the officers were also afraid that if they filled the boats to capacity, the davits and tackle for them might buckle. Second Officer Charles Lightoller, in particular, was said by an able seaman, John Poingdestre, to be 'frightened of the falls', and only forty-two women were placed into a boat designed for sixty-five.[66] Others left half-empty.

Many of the passengers were also reluctant to commit themselves to the dangers of the lifeboats, and at first 'there was practically no excitement on the part of anyone during this time, the majority seeming to think that the big boat could not sink altogether, and that it was better to stay on the steamer than trust to the lifeboats', according to Imanita Shelley. Mrs Shelley was not impressed by the lack of equipment on the lifeboats when eventually she did board one, for 'there was none in her boat except four oars and a mast, which latter was useless; there was no water nor any food; that there was neither compass nor binnacle light nor any kind of lantern; that on questioning occupants of other lifeboats they told her the same story – lack of food, water, compass, and lights, and that several boats had no oars or only two or three.'[67]

Captain Edward Smith issued orders to fill the lifeboats and 'put the women and children in and lower away.'[68] First Officer William Murdoch, in charge of loading starboard lifeboats, allowed men in once women and children were in the lifeboats, but Lightoller on the port side interpreted this as meaning 'women and children only', and resolutely excluded men, youths and even some boys, even when 'I could have put more in that boat and could have put some men in, but I did not feel justified in giving an order for men to get into the boat, as it was the last boat as far as I knew leaving the ship, and I thought it better to get her into the water safely with the number she had in; or, in other words, I did not want the boat to be rushed.'[69] Despite fearing that the boats would be overwhelmed by a rush of men, Lightoller admitted that discipline was splendid, and that only had 'the men commenced to climb in when they heard there were no more women.'[70] Indeed, earlier 'the men could not have stood quieter if they had been in church.'[71]

At first the men in third class were not allowed near the boat deck, and were forbidden from accompanying the women and children.[72] It was the responsibility of the third-class stewards to rouse them and give them guidance. Some of these passengers refused to put on their life jackets because 'they did not believe the ship was hurt in any way.'[73] Some of the women when guided through the third- and second-class parts of the ship preferred to return to their cabins when they found the boat deck cold and saw the lifeboats being lowered away, since 'they preferred to remain on the ship rather than be tossed about on the water like a cockleshell.'[74] Many women refused to leave their husbands and were also reluctant to abandon their luggage.[75] They perished alongside them.

On most emigrant and other ships, the crew were most likely to survive a wreck, together with the other men; being stronger and sturdier, they generally had a better chance of staying alive than the women and children.[76] However, the Edwardian consensus about the *Titanic* was that chivalry had prevailed, and that even though 'there is no rule of the sea ... it is customary in cases of this kind for the women to be saved first.' Indeed, 'even the women in the steerage would have been taken off before the men passengers of the first and second cabin.'[77] This was in contrast to the observation made by a survivor from the German emigrant ship *Wilhelmsburg*, which sank in 1863, that 'in such a moment one has enough to do to think of himself, and has also enough to do to save himself.' His experience of 'thus cowering together in the boat, exposed to every sea which swept the vessel, sometimes lying on the dead, at other times packed between corpses, I awaited the dawn of day', was one that left little room for chivalry or altruism.[78] The many tales of gallantry among the first- and second-class passengers on the *Titanic,* however, perpetuated the belief in what constituted a gentleman, epitomised by Benjamin Guggenheim and his valet Victor Giglio donning evening dress to meet their maker, 'dressed in our best and prepared to go down like gentlemen', so that 'no woman shall be left aboard this ship because Ben Guggenheim was a coward.'[79]

What has been less stressed is the equally honourable conduct of third-class passengers such as Olaus Abelseth who, after ensuring the safety of the two girls travelling under his protection, gave up the chance of using his experience as a sailor to take up a place in another lifeboat to stay with his brother-in-law, cousin and friend who had said to him, 'Let us stay here together.' He was the only one of the three who could swim and was saved when he reached a collapsible boat, where the other 'men did not try to push me off and they did not do anything for me to get on', other than to say 'don't capsize the boat.'[80]

Following the sinking of the *Titanic*, there was a general demand that there should be sufficient numbers of lifeboats for everyone on board a passenger ship. The first international conference on safety at sea was held in London in January 1914 and attended by representatives of thirteen countries. It adopted the International Convention for the Safety of Life at Sea, which stated that 'at no moment of its voyage may a ship have on board a total number of persons more than that for whom accommodation is provided in lifeboats (and the pontoon lifeboats) on board.' The convention was to enter into force in July 1915, but with the outbreak of the First World War in Europe in August 1914 it was never formally ratified.[81]

Although maritime disasters were much reported in the press, and still today exert an almost morbid fascination, they were never an everyday occurrence. Even in a year of headline disasters such as 1852–3, the number of ships lost remained small in comparison to the total voyages being undertaken. In the years 1847–52, only forty-three emigrant ships were lost out of the 6,877 which left British ports, and out of 1,421,704 passengers on them, only 1,043 died as a result of shipwreck or fire.[82] Many more fell victim to the epidemics rife on the emigrant ships, which were the true killers.

8

Coffin Ships

Shipwreck, fire and sickness at sea struck all aboard a vessel indiscriminately, though in the case of a ship going down not all classes fared equally. However, sickness knew no social boundaries, especially in the confined world of a ship. Everyone was at risk and social status made no difference, unlike access to lifeboats. All could 'fall victims to the destroying contagion, and the ocean wave becomes their silent tomb.'[1]

When typhus struck on the *India,* crossing from Liverpool to New York in 1847, William Smith, a Manchester weaver, saw 'the tear of sympathy run down the cheek of many a hardened sailor' at hearing the 'heart-rending cries of wives at the losses of their husbands, the agonies of husbands at the sight of the corpses of their wives, and the lamentations of fatherless and motherless children; brothers and sisters dying, leaving their aged parents without means of support in their declining years'.[2] It was commonplace 'to have a friend well this hour, sick the next and in a few hours more, dead, and thrown overboard before his remains are cold'. Smith was struck by 'the baneful influence' that 'such sweeping calamities' had on some of the passengers, where 'every tender feeling of the heart was dried up, while every selfish feeling in human nature seemed called into full play'. Typhus had first struck the ship within a week of leaving Liverpool, carrying off the captain and twenty-six passengers, with a further 122 passengers, including William Smith himself, being stricken during the eight-week-long journey. Cabin passengers were as much at risk as those in steerage, or indeed the crew. In the face of this, 'despair was depicted in every countenance and desolation spread throughout the ship'.[3]

William Smith had thought that seasickness was unpleasant enough, when 'it reduced me so much that I could not walk without assistance, for I felt as weak as an infant.'[4] Typhus, though, was much worse. It started with him feeling listless, which he simply put down to 'suffering from extreme want' on the ship, but then 'I was so dizzy that I could not walk without danger of falling', and 'I was suffering from a violent pain in my head, my brains felt as if they were on fire, my tongue clove to the roof of my mouth and my lips were parched with excessive thirst'. Water was in such short supply that the captain refused to let him have any, despite his raging thirst. Soon Smith was 'compelled to keep to my berth, which was a double one.' One of his bedfellows had died a week earlier, another was also sick with diarrhoea, while the third was 'afraid to come near us, he therefore stayed on deck most of the time ... for, beside the fever, the stench in the steerage was horrid'.[5] Smith continued to weaken, and 'I now gave myself up as lost'. He was unable to sit up in bed, and 'my eyes were dismal and sunken, and my bones seemed ready to burst through the skin.'[6] Soon afterwards the fever went down, and when the ship reached New York he was admitted to the further horrors of the quarantine hospital on Staten Island.

Typhus, also known as ship fever, was believed by doctors of the time to be caused by miasma, or foul air. With so many people crowded together in a small, confined area, perspiration, 'the carbonic acid and moisture from the breath', and 'other offensive excretions' built up, and heated by the warmth of human bodies and any source of heating in steerage, 'become decomposed and produce an effluvium which will react poisonously on the persons living in it.' With little or no fresh air, especially when the hatches were battened down, 'the weakness and enfeebled condition of the emigrants generally at the time of embarkation' made them more susceptible to the effects of the miasma. These seeds of infection then attached themselves to everything they touched, including the clothing, bedding, furniture and walls of the compartment. Having been absorbed in what were called 'fomites', the infection was thought to become 'more virulent in its action in proportion to the length of time during which it is permitted to remain.'[7] The standard medical authorities of the time believed that 'fomites more readily communicate the disease, and convey it in a worse form, than the sick themselves'.[8]

Surgeons on emigrant ships continued to believe that miasma caused typhus and took pains to destroy the fomites. The surgeon on the *James*

Pattison, carrying emigrants to New South Wales in 1839–40, ascribed the good health of his charges to his having kept the between decks clean by daily dry scraping, rubbing them with hot sand, and free-flowing ventilation. The sleeping berths, water closets and hospital were similarly 'cleaned and sweetened daily', and were also occasionally fumigated by 'pouring hot vinegar over the chloride of lime, which at all times had the effect of destroying any latent or unpleasant effluvia'. Perhaps the true reason that the ship had avoided an outbreak of typhus was that the 185 emigrants had embarked 'all apparently in good health and they had more than the usual accommodation from the ship having been fitted for the reception of two hundred and forty'.[9]

In reality, it was not surprising that in the overcrowded conditions of steerage, typhus was prevalent. It was not, however, caused by miasma nor was it spread in fomites. The bacterium now known to cause it, *Rickettsia prowazekii*, is spread by the human body louse and is linked with poor hygiene. Sometimes called gaol fever, it was easily spread in unhygienic conditions where people were crowded closely together and the same clothes were worn day and night for long periods of time. If there was no one to enforce a strict regime of hygiene, the louse found its ideal habitat. The first signs of the disease were sudden, starting with headaches, loss of appetite, general malaise and a rising fever. Chills, nausea and prostration followed, accompanied by a widespread rash covering the limbs and trunk. When the fever began to subside, it was a sign that the invalid would recover. However, in fatal cases the prostration worsened, deafness, stupor and delirium developed before the patient slipped into a coma. Death invariably followed without respite.[10] In 1847, no less than seven thousand died on the crossing to North America from England and a further ten thousand died in hospitals and quarantine stations at the end of their voyage. In 1848, 17.08 per cent of the 89,738 passengers who left the United Kingdom for Quebec died of typhus, 5,293 during their passage, and a further 10,037 in Canadian hospitals.[11] Many of the victims were fleeing the great Irish potato famine of the 1840s or the Scottish Highland clearances. The wretched hulks used to carry them have come to be known as 'coffin ships', a term originally applied to ships with a greater insurance value than they were actually worth, and on which passages were cheap. Lives too were worth little for those in steerage.

Robert Whyte was interested in observing the nature of the fever when it struck on board the ship on which he was sailing to Canada as a passenger in 1848:

> I found it difficult to acquire precise information respecting the progressive symptoms of the disease, the different parties of whom I enquired disagreeing in some particulars; but I inferred that the first symptom was generally a reeling in the head, followed by a swelling pain, as if the head were going to burst. Next came excruciating pains in the bones, and then a swelling of the limbs, commencing with the feet, in some cases ascending the body, and again descending before it reached the head, stopping at the throat. The period of each stage varied in different patients; some of whom were covered with yellow, watery pimples, and others with red and purple spots, that turned into putrid sores. Some of those, who appeared to bid defiance to the fever, were seized in its relentless grasp; and a few who were on the recovery relapsed. It seemed miraculous to me that such subjects could struggle with so violent a disease without any effective aid.[12]

It was often very difficult to identify particular fevers from their symptoms, especially in the days before it was understood how bacterial infections could be spread and, indeed, without any diagnostic tests. It was also inevitable that different infections would be carried on board by different people at the start of the voyage, which was why there might be more than one epidemic affecting a ship at any one time, and why it was quite common for less deadly infections to precede the dreaded typhus.[13]

On the *Lady McNaghten* in 1836, outbreaks of scarlet fever, measles and whooping cough among 412 Irish emigrants sailing from Cork to Sydney were followed by typhus, from which there were fifty-three deaths. It was fairly common for there to be outbreaks of other diseases alongside typhus, perhaps because natural resistance was lowered, but also because overcrowding allowed disease to spread. Diseases did not originate in shipboard conditions, but were brought on board by passengers and crew. The first death on the *Lady McNaghten* was of a boy suffering from scarlet fever, which had been raging in Cork before he 'was brought into the ship on the back of his mother'. Significantly, 'there had been no medical inspection of the emigrants prior to embarkation', although a cabin passenger, Henry Bingham, 'did not observe that any of the emigrants came on board in an ill state of health'.[14] A month after sailing, J A Hawkins, the surgeon, noted that 'the itch is prevalent'. Two weeks later the typhus epidemic began, and quickly after that 'the fever became general throughout the ship', then within two weeks there was the first adult death from it.[15] The surgeon Hawkins was inexperienced, never having been to sea before, although 'a man of very excellent character, and of respectable acquirements regarding his professional knowledge', and was to die himself on the voyage, leaving the mixing of medications and bleeding of patients to 'a young man named David Kirby who had been an apothecary's assistant and was one of the crew'. Hawkins failed to enforce simple precautions against typhus, such as making sure that clothing was clean, which meant that 'many of the women were very dirty from want of change of clothes', and 'that there was no general order to enforce their washing their persons'. As a result, 'dirt and filth accumulated in every direction.'[16]

Equally scandalous was the case of the *Ticonderoga*, sailing from Liverpool to Melbourne with 795 emigrants, mainly from the Scottish Highlands, in 1852. Typhus had taken the lives of a hundred of the passengers, and an equal number of cases of the fever were still suffering, when ninety days out of Liverpool the ship went into quarantine at Port Phillip Heads. A quarantine ship *Lysander* was sent alongside her with stores for three months. The *Melbourne Argus* deemed that such a level of sickness 'clearly exhibits the cruelty and ill-judged policy of crowding such a number of people on board a single ship, no matter her size, for a lengthened voyage'.[17] Even when some of the emigrants were released from quarantine two months later, 'one poor little child died of fever, whilst, on the boat arriving in Melbourne, its mother was engaged in laying out the body of her child on the deck, having left, we hear, her husband on board the ship, still suffering from fever.' Spectators at the wharf expressed their 'disgust and astonishment, mingled with the greatest sympathy, that these poor unfortunate passengers should have been sent on shore while still in so weak and sickly a state.'[18] The appallingly dirty state of the ship was blamed on the failure of the captain and medical superintendent to enforce hygiene regulations, and a lack of concern for the passengers, since 'the captain and crew seemed to look upon them as perfect nuisances, to be got rid of on any terms.' Little thought was given to helping the weakened passengers off the ship, so that 'invalid women were carried over the side on men's backs, and one poor creature was separated from her child of seven weeks old, another child of five years of age died on board the steamer before we reached the wharf', while 'no arrangements were made at the wharf for the reception of the sick, and two women in a dying state, were taken away in common wharf drays'. The citizens of Melbourne asked, 'Why is this ship allowed to come and vomit her diseased and dying freight in the midst of an overcrowded city?'[19]

The official report on the case of the *Ticonderoga* blamed the emigrants themselves for their plight, since 'looking to its structure and capacity, no vessel could have been better suited to the purpose, and there can be no doubt but that under circumstances securing the unbroken maintenance of order, cleanliness, and general discipline, a yet larger number of persons might have been conveyed in safety to the colony', whereas 'with an unorganised body of emigrants of the classes selected for the *Ticonderoga*, little surprise can be felt that no ordinary exertion of abilities could suffice to introduce at once system and order, and overcome that repugnance to cleanliness and fresh air which distinguished certain classes of the labouring population of Europe', and that 'it would appear as if from the commencement of the sickness the prostration of the whole body of emigrants was such as to overcome all feelings of decency and propriety and even of self-preservation.'[20]

When typhus broke out on the barque *Oxford* in 1883, on its way to New Zealand from Plymouth, killing three young people, some of the passengers suspected that it might be linked to 'the dirty state' of the Emigrant Depot at Plymouth, though 'it would appear that good health prevailed among its inmates previous to the voyage.' However, there had already been an outbreak on the previous voyage of the *Oxford*, and it was feared that the ship had not been adequately cleaned. The passengers complained of 'the wet and dirty condition of the main or passenger's deck' on boarding. The assistant cook had also gone down with symptoms 'not incompatible with a mild attack of typhoid.' The ship had been fumigated more than once at Cardiff, but 'that the hold was not affected or purified is shown by the survival of numerous rats which made their appearance shortly after.' Otherwise, the ship itself was 'roomy and airy between decks and certainly gives the impression that she is well suited for the conveyance of immigrants.'[21]

Yet despite all the problems facing the emigrant to Australia and New Zealand, the regulatory framework of assisted passages meant a higher chance of survival than on the shorter, unregulated crossing to North America.[22] The death rate was particularly heavy on the *Virginius*, sailing from Liverpool to Canada in 1847, which lost 158 of its 476 passengers during the voyage. Of the surviving passengers, 106 were unloaded at the quarantine station at Grosse Island suffering from typhus, 'ghastly, yellow-looking spectres, unshaven and hollow-cheeked, and without exception the worst looking passengers I have ever seen, not more than six or eight were really healthy and able to exert themselves'.[23] 'Feeble and tottering' as they landed, the survivors were a reminder that 'the worst horrors of the slave trade which it is the boast or the ambition of this Empire to suppress, at any cost, have been re-enacted in the flight of British subjects from their native shores.'[24]

If a typhus-stricken ship had not progressed far into its voyage, it would put into a convenient port, not always to a warm welcome from the local people fearful of disease. However, the people of Belfast were more humane in showing great concern for typhus patients on the *Swatara* when she put into that port in March 1847 with a sick passenger, who was admitted to the local hospital through the efforts of Lieutenant Starke, the local emigration agent. By early April there were twenty more fever cases on the ship and the Roman Catholic bishop assisted Lieutenant Starke in persuading all the passengers to disembark, so that the ship could be properly cleaned and fumigated, while the public authorities of Belfast opened up empty buildings for the sick passengers. By this time the passengers were exhausting their own stores of provisions bought for the voyage and had no money to restock them. Lieutenant Starke raised a public subscription to help them and the people of Belfast responded generously. On 17 April the *Swatara* sailed for Australia, leaving behind all passengers showing any signs of typhus, although 'the misfortune of the sick was that they lost their passage and had no right to demand a return of their passage money.' The only assistance that they received was from the captain of the ship who had filled the vacant berths with new emigrants from Belfast, and had used the proceeds for the benefit of the sick passengers left behind.[25]

On a fever-ridden ship, the other emigrants did not always show the same kindness to their fellow ailing voyagers as the citizens of Belfast had shown to the sick on the *Swatara*. William Smith on the *India* observed 'Big Roger', a well-built Irishman, remove the can in which a ten-year-old girl was cooking gruel for her dying mother, with the callous remark that 'everyone must take care of themselves and that he would have his meal in spite of any one'. Another more fair-minded and sympathetic passenger had defended the girl's right to cook her meal before the man's, as she had been first in the queue, her father was confined to his bed, and her mother, for whom she was cooking the gruel, was only expected to last a few hours. The captain, witnessing the argument, threw the bully's can off the fire and punished Big Roger by ordering the steward not to give him his ration of a pint of water the following day. Some men abandoned their sick wives and slept with a friend, getting their children to take them food 'in their fear of the epidemic.'[26] Women, though, tended to be more ready to help not only their families but others who needed their help.

Robert Whyte also noted that 'some entire families, being prostrated, were dependent on the charity of their neighbours, many of whom were very kind; but others seemed to be possessed of no feeling'. The clothing of one victim of typhus was sold by auction by his friend who had promised to take care of his two orphaned children. Whyte was scandalised by the joking, swearing, fooling around and laughter at the auction. Meanwhile, the dead man's seven-year-old son had been given his father's coat, and 'seemed quite unconscious of his loss, and proud of the accession to his scanty covering.'[27] This child was fortunate in having a family friend willing to look after him. On the *Leibnitz*, carrying German migrants from Hamburg to New York in 1868, 'during the voyage some families had died out entirely; of others, the fathers and mothers are gone; here a husband had left a poor widow with small children; and there a husband had lost his wife.'[28] Back in 1848 it was 'no unusual occurrence for the survivor of a family of ten or twelve to land alone, bewildered and broken-hearted, on the wharf at New York; the rest – the family – parents and children, had been swallowed in the sea; their bodies marking the course of the ship to the New World'.[29]

Cholera was even more malignant and inspired greater fear than typhus. Originating in the area around Calcutta in the 1820s, cholera spread rapidly from India through Asia, Russia and Eastern Europe before reaching Western Europe in the 1830s. It first appeared in England in October 1831, brought to Sunderland by ship from Hamburg or Riga. By February 1832 there were epidemics in Newcastle, Edinburgh and London. It soon spread throughout Ireland, possibly prompting some people to try to escape the cholera by fleeing to America. It was a vain precaution. They simply took it with them. The disease probably first crossed the Atlantic with emigrants on the brig *Carrick* sailing from Dublin in April 1832. Of the 173 passengers, forty-two died of cholera before arriving at Quebec on 3 June. By 23 June cholera had entered the United States through the ports of New York and Philadelphia. In a later epidemic in 1848, cholera again crossed the Atlantic by ship to New York and New Orleans before spreading through North America. It reached San Francisco in 1850 by ship from Panama. As with so many other infectious diseases before it, cholera spread rapidly on the ships plying the oceans and, not surprisingly, it took a heavy toll on the crowded emigrant ships.[30]

The *Brutus* set sail from Liverpool on 18 May 1832 with 330 apparently healthy emigrants. At first 'everything promised a favourable and pleasant voyage', but soon passengers started to die when cholera broke out on 27 May.[31] The first victim was a thirty-year-old man who recovered. However, the next passenger to succumb, a sixty-year-old woman, died within ten hours of first showing symptoms. In one day ten people died, and by 3 June there had been so many deaths that it was decided that the ship should return to its port of origin. By the time it reached Liverpool again on 13 June, there had been 117 cases of cholera and 81 deaths.[32]

The disease struck quickly, with violent diarrhoea, cramps and vomiting leading to dehydration and complete exhaustion. It usually resulted in death after a couple of days, and occasionally within hours. Now known to be caused by the comma-shaped bacterium *Vibrio cholera,* isolated by the pioneer of modern bacteriology Robert Koch in Cairo and Calcutta in 1883, it is spread in food and drinking water contaminated by human faeces. John Snow had demonstrated the waterborne nature of cholera in 1854, but many physicians continued to attribute it to miasma, just as they did with typhus, although they recognised differences in the nature of the two diseases.[33]

Nineteenth-century doctors considered cholera to be 'an epidemic which typhus never is.' Whereas ship fever always seemed to abate in the open air, cholera went on unchecked, 'but wings its deadly flight over the prairie and prison-house alike.' Doctors and public health officials did associate it with poor quality food, but did not make the connection with contaminated food at first. In New York Dr Griscom, an agent of the Board of Commissioners of Emigration, thought that 'the miasm of typhus is the direct product of the vitiated excretions of the human body, pent up in a small space', which caused a fever by being inhaled, but that 'cholera, by disabling the system, renders it liable to be overcome by the choleric at an earlier period than that at which typhus fever makes its appearance.' There were two alternate views as to how it caused infection on a ship. One was that it arose 'from the virus of the disease having been imbibed by the persons or clothing of passengers, previously to embarkation.' The other was that it was the result of the shipping passing through miasma in certain zones of the sea. Critics of this theory pointed out that 'it frequently happens that vessels leaving the same port on or about the same day, and arriving at their point of destination about the same time, are differently affected by sickness', yet 'if there be anything in the atmosphere of particular zones or belts, it must be encountered alike by ships probably sailing within a few miles of each other, propelled by the same winds and standing on the same courses.'[34] By seeing cholera as something that struck arbitrarily, doctors could not see the obvious way of preventing or treating it.

Modern treatments for cholera are based on the idea of replacing the lost waters and salts, a notion that was first proposed in 1830. After the German chemist R Hermann had observed that the change in the balance of fluids in the blood was reflected in the contents of cholera excreta, one of his colleagues had injected six ounces of water into a patient dying of cholera; although the patient still died two hours later, this rehydration had induced a temporary quickening of the pulse. In Britain in 1832 W B O'Shaughnessy suggested the intravenous replacement of salt and water, inspiring Thomas Latta to try the procedure out on patients with mixed results. Only after Leonard Rogers perfected the therapy in Calcutta in the early 1900s did this become the standard effective treatment for cholera.[35]

None of this knowledge was available to the ships' surgeons working in the heyday of the emigrant trade. Instead, many of them produced their own cures and mixtures. John Adamson administered to his patients a draught of castor oil, oil of cinnamon, and tincture of laudanum, in a wineglassful of brandy made into a warm punch.[36] Half a glass of such a mixture was to be taken night and morning in case of any debility of the bowels, which was seen as a 'general premonitory symptom.' Small wine glasses of the mixture were given every hour, together with purging and vomiting, until there was some relief. Spasms and cramps, meanwhile, were to be relieved by rubbing the affected limbs with warm spirits or turpentine.[37]

John Adamson administered his remedy to Captain Maxwell of the barque *Industry* when the seaman contracted cholera in 1834, and was seized with violent vomiting and faintness. Maxwell had 'endeavoured to warm himself by walking smartly up and down the wharf' in the port of Halifax. When Adamson administered his draught, Maxwell began to perspire, and 'he looked as red as a lobster'. Although he would have lost more body fluids by all this perspiration, Maxwell recovered after twelve cholera draughts, as did all the sailors on his ship when given similar draughts. Maxwell also observed that many of the men with early symptoms of cholera got well after a brisk run, and 'consequently afterwards I directed all the single men who came to go up to the race course and run two or three times around until they perspired freely, then to return again to the dispensary and record progress, when each was served with a brimming tumbler of hot brandy punch, well spiced with ground cinnamon and ginger, or hot port wine negus.'[38] Very much the old idea of sweating out disease was being followed, which would have led to further dehydration, and most cholera cases were far too weak to even think of running. If such a treatment was actually as successful as Maxwell claimed, his diagnostic skills were less sure than his remedy.

The ship's surgeon, reliant on his copy of the standard text on medicine for merchant vessels at sea by the surgeon Thomas Spencer Wells, often not only lacked therapies, but also had to work in unsatisfactory conditions.[39] Hospital accommodation on an emigrant ship was often inadequate, and was dismissed by one MP in 1889 as 'in many cases scarcely any larger than that covered by the table in the House [of Commons].'[40] Yet every British passenger ship after 1855 was expected to have a compartment on an upper deck fitted out as a hospital, which was not allowed to be used for any other purpose.[41] Not withstanding the legal requirements, all too many emigrant ships ignored the rules and used them for other purposes, including the accommodation of first-class passengers, ship's officers, and other members of the crew. At the same time, the surgeon himself was often put up in inferior quarters, sometimes being given a small, dark, badly situated cabin, and at times even having 'to stow himself away in the dispensary, surrounded by medicines and drugs, having no other place to sleep in.'[42] On better lines, the hospitals were not used for other purposes. On ships of the Union Line, the hospital was usually fitted within the surgeon's quarters, though on one steamer it was adjacent to the surgeon's room, and in another completely separate from it. Infectious cases were housed in hospitals on the upper deck, where 'they are consequently more or less exposed', and accordingly well-ventilated.[43] It sounded good, but faced with fevers on an epidemic scale, even such provision would have been too little.

Cholera was endemic on the ships taking coolies from India, where the disease had its origins, to the West Indies, but it was thought that very little could be done about this, since 'the origin of the evil is in the state of the emigrants before they embark', and 'after a ship is fairly at sea cholera is not likely to be generated in itself if the people are properly fed and the ship is well ventilated and kept clean.'[44] Many of the coolies concealed the fact that they were suffering from the disease when they boarded, for fear of being prevented from making their journey. They, and their fellow passengers, were to pay the price dearly, as indeed were emigrants on ships from Europe who did the same.

In 1853, of the seventy-seven ships that set sail from Liverpool for New York, forty-six were stricken with cholera and 1,328 emigrants died of it. On the *Washington*, 100 of the 898 passengers died. On the *Winchester* the mortality rate was even higher, as seventy-nine out of 490 died.[45] During the next major epidemic in 1866, the newly-built steamship *England*, carrying a thousand passengers from Liverpool to New York, lost fifty passengers at sea and 150 at Halifax, where it put into port. There were thirty-two deaths on the *Virginia* during the crossing to New York, and fifty-seven deaths from the 171 patients transferred to hospital in New York. Similarly, there were thirty-five deaths on the *Peruvian*, and a further sixty-five in hospital in New York, with thirty-five deaths on the *Union*, and twenty-eight in hospital. When *Helvetia* put back to port after four days out of Liverpool, there were forty-four deaths before she reached port. On the *England*, 'in consequence of the appearance of cholera on board, all the bedding was burnt in Halifax, and the personal effects of most of the passengers were destroyed, and in consequence they were exposed on the deck and subjected to great privations the remainder of the voyage.'[46]

Significantly, many of the passengers on these ships, and indeed many of the other vessels with outbreaks of cholera from 1853 onwards, came from Germany or central European regions where cholera was already raging when they left home. The *Atlanta*, beginning its voyage to New York from London in 1865, picked up about four hundred German passengers at Le Havre, and on the second day one of the children taken on board there died of exhaustion from diarrhoea. Several other passengers also showed symptoms, of whom fifteen died. As the disease was 'entirely confined to steerage, none of those in the cabin suffering in the least', the surgeon decided to avoid panic by not telling the steerage passengers what the disease causing the deaths actually was. The cabin passengers soon discovered that there was cholera aboard, but 'adopted the plan not only of making themselves as comfortable as possible, but of diverting their minds from the subject by amusements of various kinds' and, apart from being careful about what they ate, 'lived without any apparent regard to consequences'. The steerage passengers faced with so many deaths were at first more subdued, but many of them followed the example of the cabin passengers, and 'occupied their time in the manner most likely to banish melancholy thoughts'.[47] Generally, it was unusual for cabin passengers to venture anywhere near steerage when disease was rife there, with the result that 'they knew as little of what was going on in the steerage as the inhabitants of the West End did about what was going on in the slums of the metropolis.'[48]

The steamer *Dorunda* carried cholera to Australia in 1885. The ship had left London on 20 October with 290 passengers bound for Brisbane, calling at Malta, Port Said, Suez, Aden and Batavia. Despite all precautions to prevent contact between the passengers and crew and the people of Tandjong Priok, Batavia, where cholera was endemic, some of the passengers had managed to buy fruit from the shore boats, and two of the crew had gone ashore. The day after the ship left Batavia, an old man showed the symptoms of cholera but recovered. Then a man definitely suffering from cholera first became ill at ten o'clock in the morning and died that same day at half past seven in the evening. Two of his children died the following day. Six more people went down with cholera, six with 'choleraic diarrhoea', and fourteen with diarrhoea. The ship sought refuge in the anchorage at Townsville but, as the quarantine station there was not equipped to deal with such a serious epidemic, the ship was sent to Moreton Bay and the quarantine station on Peel Island. There were seventeen deaths and at least fifty cases of cholera, all confined to steerage passengers.[49]

Quarantine was the inevitable knee-jerk reaction of most governments to the threat of infectious disease, to prevent infection spreading through the country. The immigrant was indeed seen as a source of contagion, and it was recognised that:

the maintenance of an efficient maritime quarantine, which is the most important wholesale protection of a country against the scourge, has at its base, it must be confessed, a principle which at first seems to savour not a little of the direct and bold application of the barbaric instinct of self-preservation at whatever cost, since the detention of infected ships with their passengers involves the principle that the few must, if necessary, suffer for the universal good.

For those being protected by the segregation of those exposed to contagion 'it would be well if we who are safe ashore realized a little more fully that those detained in quarantined ships are suffering at least annoyance and apprehension, and perhaps peril, not for their own sakes, but largely for ours'.[50]

Quarantine also should have promised a chance for the infected person to recover, though in reality in times of epidemics it brought new horrors after those of the voyage. William Smith, suffering from typhus on the *India*, was relieved when the ship approached New York and quarantine on Staten Island. As he was taken to the Marine Hospital he was filled with 'buoyant feelings of joy ... that I should have plenty to eat and drink, and medicine to ease my bodily sufferings, a little nourishment to revive my exhausted frame.'[51] He was soon to be disillusioned by the rough, if not callous, treatment given to him by the nurses as he found himself 'in the hands of the most hard-hearted and cruel set of men it ever was, and I hope ever will be, my lot to mingle with'.[52] The bed was uncomfortable, the food meagre and unappetising, the wards were cold and 'from the doctor down to the lowest menial, the poor immigrant is treated with contempt and cruelty, which seemed to be the order of the day.' Smith was especially indignant that 'this treatment is the more uncalled for, when the fact is borne in mind that this hospital is supported by immigrants, each one having to pay one dollar, which is charged to them in their fare.'[53] His experience was perhaps happier than other emigrants had of quarantine. At the quarantine station at Point-St Charles in Montreal in 1848, fever victims lay in the fever sheds 'as if they were in their coffins'.[54]

The quarantine station on Grosse Île in the Gulf of St Lawrence had been established in 1832 as a hurried response to the cholera epidemic of that year, to try to prevent cholera from devastating Canada. Its inadequacies were highlighted by the number of ships landing there in 1847, all with typhus cases on board. All ships arriving at the St Lawrence had to reassure the quarantine officers at Grosse Île that they were free from disease before they were permitted to sail on to Quebec. By midsummer 1847, there were so many ships arriving and so many sick that it was 'physically impossible' to enforce the quarantine regulations. George Douglas, the chief medical officer at the quarantine station, thought that simply washing and airing the ships to rid them of miasma would be enough to stop the contagion spreading between passengers. He also believed that many of the ships' doctors he saw were totally unqualified.[55] The hospital and the sheds for the healthy were soon full, and tents were set up, but there was still not enough, and to reach them 'the miserable patients were drenched by the spray; after which they had to clamber over the slimy rocks.'[56] Around the sheds lay 'groups of half-naked men, women and children, in the same condition – sick or dying. Hundreds were literally flung on the beach, left amid the mud or stones, to crawl on the dry land how they could'. Some, unable to reach dry land and 'drag themselves out of the slime in which they lay', ended up 'dying like fish out of water'.[57]

Robert Whyte and his fellow passengers expected their journey to be nearly at an end when they arrived at Grosse Île. They dressed in their best clothes and cheerfully helped the crew to clean the ship. Their medical inspection was perfunctory and then they were to be 'left enveloped in reeking pestilence, the sick without medicine, medical skill, nourishment, or so much as a drop of pure water', even though ostensibly they were 'within reach of help'.[58] Families were separated, as the sick were taken off to the hospitals. Whyte, disturbed that 'the screams pierced my brain', hoped that 'may I never again witness such a scene' as he saw, including 'the husband – the only support of an emaciated wife and helpless family – torn away forcibly from them in a strange land; the mother dragged from her orphan children, that clung to her until she was lifted over the bulwarks, rending the air with their shrieks; children snatched from their bereaved parents, who were perhaps ever to remain ignorant of their recovery, or death.'[59] As deaths on board ship mounted there was 'a continuous line of boats, each carrying its freight of dead to the burial ground' of which 'some had several corpses so tied up in canvas that the stiff, sharp outline of death was easily traceable'.[60] The condition of the Irish on Whyte's ship contrasted forcibly with that of some German emigrants, 'comfortably and neatly clad, clean and happy', who were 'singing a charming hymn in whose beautiful harmony all took part, spreading the music of their five hundred voices upon the calm still air that wafted it around'.[61] By contrast the Irish survivors from Whyte's ship 'wandered over the country, carrying with them nothing but disease.'[62]

So serious was the situation in Canada in the summer of 1847, with Grosse Île overwhelmed by 'more than 2,000 patients, of whom scarcely more than half could find shelter on the island', that the Archbishop of Quebec appealed to his fellow Roman Catholic bishops in Ireland to 'endeavour to dissuade your diocesans from emigrating in such numbers to Canada, where they will but too often meet with either a premature death, or a fate as deplorable as the heartrending condition under which they groan in their unhappy country', and to try to 'prevent the honest, religious, and confiding Irish peasantry from being the victims of speculation and falling into irretrievable errors and irreparable calamities.' Archbishop Signay considered that if the emigrants wished to realise the 'ardent hopes they so fondly cherished of meeting with unspeakable comfort and prosperity on the banks of the St Lawrence', mass emigration from Ireland could not continue unchecked, as the emigrants 'should possess means which the greater number have not, and which cannot be rendered available and efficacious, unless emigration be conducted on a more diminished scale.'[63]

Thomas Mooney, a writer on the history of Ireland and himself an immigrant in Canada, considered that one of the causes of mortality at the quarantine stations was the very fact that ships were quarantined, and that healthy emigrants might be infected by the sick people that they came into contact with on Grosse Île. He cited the case of a ship that:

> was allowed by the Government agent in Liverpool, to pack into the hold seven hundred passengers; yet they arrived all healthy save a few children; and for this trivial cause the whole passengers were obliged to remain in quarantine nineteen days, in the course of which time, half of them became sick, and many died, though had they been permitted to land, they would all have gone to their destination in spirits and health.[64]

Archbishop Joseph Signay had also felt that the quarantining of the healthy with the sick could cause serious problems, especially when there was not enough space for all the emigrants on the quarantine island, and 'the others were left in the holds of their respective vessels, in some cases abandoned by their own friends, spreading contagion among the other healthy passengers who were confined in the vessels, and exhibiting the heartrending spectacle of a morality three times greater than what prevailed ashore.'[65]

Grosse Île was forever to be damned by association with its grim record in 1847, but it continued in use as a quarantine station until 1937. Frederick Montizambert served as medical superintendent from 1869 until 1899 and modernised the facilities and buildings, to turn what had been a disgrace into an efficient and modern quarantine station. As a bacteriologist, Montizambert was familiar with the revolution in the diagnosis, prevention and treatment of infectious diseases of the late nineteenth century, and was able to introduce more effective and stringent controls. All arriving vessels and luggage were inspected and disinfected, passengers were examined and, where necessary, vaccinated, the sick and the healthy were kept separately, and it was possible to use the latest in laboratory techniques to diagnose any suspected infections. First-, second- and third-class hotels were also built to make the whole process more humane and comfortable.[66]

Most of the quarantine stations began as ad hoc solutions to a particular crisis and then were made more permanent. Just as in the early days at Grosse Île, tents were also used at first to accommodate emigrants arriving at Manly Quarantine Station at Spring Cove in Sydney Harbour, which opened in 1828 in response to the increase in the number of emigrant ships to New South Wales, and after the son of Governor Darling had died of whooping cough brought to the colony on the *Morley*.[67] Queensland did not quarantine any vessels until 1862 when, following the death from typhus of several passengers on the *Erin-go-bragh*, the ship was placed under surveillance at the anchorage in Moreton Bay, and the passengers were prohibited from landing until it was certain that this would be 'without risk to the general health of the colony.' A quarantine station was established on the island of St Helena in Moreton Bay, 'in order to facilitate measures to be adopted for the fumigation of the vessel and the washing of linen and other clothing used during the voyage as well as to afford the passengers the means of necessary exercise and change.'[68] Although ships carrying infection had been quarantined since the early days of settlement, New Zealand, compared with Australia, was relatively late in establishing quarantine stations, not designating Somes Island, or

Matiu, as a quarantine station until 1869. Even then it was not used as such until 1872, when passengers suffering from smallpox on the *England* were put up in makeshift buildings. Then more permanent buildings were erected.[69]

At Queenstown in Ireland, there was discussion in 1853 at the height of a cholera epidemic over the desirability of stationing a hulk there that might act as a quarantine station, and also offer aid to any ship that might be compelled to 'seek refuge' in the harbour. Over the years emigrant ships from England, Scotland and Germany, some of them carrying up to eight hundred passengers, sailing for both America and Australia, had been forced into Queenstown by damage to the ship, disease or contrary winds, 'but from whatever port they may have sailed, or to whatever country they belong, it rarely happens that an emigrant ship is compelled to take refuge in Queenstown, that her passengers are not afflicted with contagious disease, and that generally of a malignant character'. When the disabled emigrant ship *Ella,* carrying 250 Germans suffering from ship's fever, smallpox and scarlatina, landed at Queenstown in 1851, 'all that humanity and skill could do for their relief was done under the circumstances, but the result was that not only did a large proportion of the emigrants perish but numbers of the inhabitants fell victims to the diseases'.[70]

Similar 'fatal consequences' to the people of Queenstown were also feared with the arrival in November 1853 of the *Kossuth,* on which cholera had broken out among the 606 emigrants on board, with twenty-one deaths in the eleven days since leaving Liverpool. The chairman of the Queenstown Committee of Health was concerned that 'this district is at present free from cholera but one must fear, considering what has happened in other places, if the passengers are landed, that the disease will be spread through the town and neighbourhood'.[71] The lack of suitable quarantine facilities at such a port, where not only did emigrant ships set out, but vessels in distress called, also affected the stricken passengers. When the *Hercules* was 'driven in distress' into the harbour in January 1853, with eight hundred Scottish emigrants suffering from typhus and smallpox, many of the emigrants died because of the lack of 'that accommodation which a large commodious and well appointed hospital ship (one of those useless or dismantled men of war lying in the naval ports of this country) would so well afford'. The sick could have been transferred to the hospital ship easily without coming near land, and the vessel could be 'cleansed, purified or refurnished as circumstances might require', thus 'many lives could be saved which otherwise would be sacrificed, and the properties and lives of our industrious population preserved from danger'.[72] However, there would have been a cost to the public purse in setting up and maintaining such a quarantine facility, and instead 'cases of such a nature might be removed to the public hospital at the respective port at which the emigrant vessel might arrive'.[73]

Quarantine as a response to infection at sea anyway was not entirely successful in keeping out disease, nor was it the favoured option of everyone, least of all in Britain with its liberal and laissez-faire traditions. In 1849, the General Board of Health of the United Kingdom suggested that the quarantining of ships and passengers infected with cholera, yellow fever and typhus should be suspended, on the grounds that such diseases were caused by 'epidemic atmospheres' which might potentially cover thousands of miles, though only affect unwholesome spots within that great area. Sir John Simon, Medical Officer of the Privy Council, in 1865 criticised the quarantine regulations as 'a mere irrational derangement of commerce', which interfered with foreign trade but could do nothing effective to prevent the importation of infectious diseases from abroad.[74] By the end of the nineteenth century the British quarantine system, originally laid down in Acts of Parliament passed between 1710 and 1825 and administered by Customs officials, was in decline and was finally abolished by the 1896 Public Health (Ports) Act. Port Sanitary Authorities were now made responsible for the medical inspection of ships and were given the power to detain vessels carrying infectious diseases, until the vessels could be disinfected and provision made for the isolation of the sick.[75] Many continental European states, especially the German and Austro-Hungarian empires, preferred to uphold their hallowed policies of a cordon sanitaire against the importation of infection from abroad. The regime at overseas quarantine stations became less draconian too, partly because infectious diseases were no longer such killers at sea.

Although the confined environment of a ship meant that any contagious disease taken on board would soon spread among the passengers, the shorter length of voyages and the improvement in conditions on the ships themselves, as steamships replaced sailing ships, and as standards of hygiene aboard improved, meant that outbreaks could be contained and were no longer so devastating. Some of that improvement was down to technological advances such as water purification and waste removal. However, the deadly typhus and cholera epidemics of the mid nineteenth century too had done much to focus attention on the need to reform conditions in steerage, and arouse public demand for legislation to end the scandal of the emigrant ships, and to ensure that disease was no longer such a hazard on the vessels. Governments responded with greater regulation of the emigrant traffic, despite a reluctance to insist on anything that might raise fares, and thus discourage emigration or burden shipowners and impede business. By the mid nineteenth century every European maritime state and every country receiving migrants had built up an elaborate code of regulations. The various Passenger Acts limited the numbers of emigrants that could be carried, laid down the space each one should occupy, specified the amount of food and water that should be carried and issued, and stipulated minimum standards of ventilation and sanitation. This did much to improve the health, safety and comfort of all those travelling on emigrant ships, whose only dream was of a safe and speedy arrival in their new land, like the German migrants in 1750 for whom 'the sight of land makes the people on board the ship, especially the sick and half dead, alive again, so that their hearts leap within them'.[76]

9

Strangers at the Gate

There was a great sense of exhilaration as the migrant ship approached the New World. Dickens captured it when he depicted the imminent arrival of his eponymous hero in New York in *Martin Chuzzlewit*:

> And now a general excitement began to prevail on board ... There was infinitely more crowding on deck and looking over the ship's side than there had been before; and an epidemic broke out for packing up things every morning, which required unpacking them every night. Those who had any letters to deliver, or any friends to meet, or any settled plans of going anywhere or doing anything, discussed their prospects a hundred times a day; and as this class of passengers was very small, and the number of those who had no prospects whatever was very large, there were plenty of listeners and few talkers ... An American gentleman ... walked the deck with his nostrils dilated, as already inhaling the air of Freedom which carries death to all tyrants and can never (under any circumstances worth mentioning) be breathed by slaves. An Englishman who was strongly suspected of having run away from a bank, with something in his possession belonging to its strongbox besides the key, grew eloquent upon the subject of the rights of man and hummed the Marseillaise Hymn constantly. In a word, one great sensation pervaded the whole ship and the soil of America lay close before them.[1]

Fictional immigrants were not the only ones to be stirred at the first sight of the new country. A British steerage passenger on seeing the New Jersey shore on 3 June 1848, his thirty-eighth day out of Bristol, was rapturous about what he saw, writing in his diary 'glorious morning! ... What a fine country', and deeming that 'the sight before us compensates for all our toil and trouble'.[2] Similar feelings were expressed by Italian immigrants to Brazil on first sight of land. In 1878 'when after a long crossing, after thirty days, at last on the morning of 11 January, we spotted the mountains of Brazil, we all burst out shouting hooray, long live America.'[3]

Just as disappointment and disillusionment faced the fictional Martin Chuzzlewit, many immigrants, as they now were rather than emigrants, did not at first find what they expected when they arrived at the end of their long journey. Progress to the landing place was not always as quick as it might have been. Ships arriving at New York in the 1840s had to wait for a pilot at the entrance to the harbour to guide them around the shoals. Then the ship would be moored at the quarantine station at Seguine's Point on Staten Island, where federal customs officers would board, inspect the ship's list of passengers and make perfunctory enquiries into the property being brought by the immigrants. More to be feared was the inspection by the quarantine station's health officer, who had the power to detain ships and their passengers if there had been too many deaths at sea on the voyage, epidemics in the port of origin, or if passengers were found to be suffering from an infectious disease on arrival. Everyone in steerage went on deck where 'each passenger's name was called over, and everyone had to pass in review before him.' The doctor then went below to inspect the cabin passengers and 'the ship being pronounced healthy, was permitted to pass.'[4]

This customs and medical inspection procedure was standard at most ports. On the east coast of the United States, New York was the busiest and most popular port of arrival for immigrants, but New Orleans, Philadelphia, Baltimore and Boston also took in a large number of immigrants, all of whom had to be processed. In Canada, Quebec and St John, New Brunswick, were the main points of entry. At St John the Partridge Island Immigration Station, established in 1785, was in the centre of the harbour. However, Grosse Île, thirty miles below Quebec, was the principle Canadian quarantine station, established in 1832 at the time of a cholera epidemic. All vessels sailing up the St Lawrence were obliged to stop at Grosse Île, where there was a battery of three guns under the control of the 32nd Regiment. The quarantine station had a staff house, bakery, two large sheds for immigrants and a hospital, but for many years lacked a wharf.[5] For those immigrants who did not spend much time there it was a beautiful place. William Fulford, emigrating from Devon to Canada in 1848, considered that 'through the mercy of God it was fortunate for us: we were the most decent and healthy passengers the doctor has ever seen or examined. So we were detained only two hours.'[6] William Gliddon, a young man from Barnstaple, had a similar experience with the doctor in 1855, when 'we were all summoned on deck and ranged before him like a lot of soldiers about to be drilled', after which 'he gave us a clean bill and we are allowed to proceed'. Further clearance by medical and customs officials took place in Quebec itself before anyone was allowed to land. Gliddon was interested to observe through binoculars borrowed from the captain of his own ship, the *Appledore*, two ships at Grosse Île whose passengers had been taken ashore 'to undergo a cleansing process'. He was able to see 'a big fellow with a rake and a pair of tongs turning over the clothes and making the people clean them. They are scattering about the island, washing and scrubbing like fun'.[7]

Emigrants to Australia also had similar health and customs checks before being allowed in. If there were no major health problems on board a ship, its passengers had few problems in landing. On the *Northumberland* on 16 November 1874, Joseph Sams and his fellow passengers rose early on the day that they were due to land in Melbourne, so that they could get their first sighting of their new home, and 'the sun rising this morning was most magnificent and nothing has presented a more beautiful sight than it has done this morning.' While the passengers packed, the ship approached the quarantine ground in 'a fine open bay', where 'the medical officer came on board but only stayed about ten minutes and we were allowed to go on with a free pass.' The *Northumberland* then continued on to the Sandridge Pier where Sams 'then wished the ship a goodbye as far as inhabiting her went, and entered the great and prosperous city of Melbourne.'[8]

If there was illness on a ship, she and her passengers could be quarantined for forty days. Those found to be suffering from disease on arrival were confined to the hospital on the quarantine station, a facility funded by a poll tax levy on all entering immigrants. In New York in 1845, this hospital money levy for the Maritime Hospital on Staten

Island, founded in 1797, was set at 50 cents. Quarantine was a disappointment for the immigrants who, after the ardours of a long journey, had looked forward to reaching their destinations. John Hillary was relieved in February 1880, the eighty-sixth day of the voyage of the clipper *Westland* from Plymouth to Lyttelton on the South Island of New Zealand, to reach the end of his journey where 'all my hopes of the beauty of the place and the fineness of the climate are fully realized, and the discomforts of the voyage seem already to be disappearing'. He had welcomed the arrival of fresh provisions, including meat, vegetables, bread, eggs and milk which, after being deprived of them for so long, he regarded as 'dainties'. However, an outbreak of measles on the voyage, to which his own children succumbed, meant a disappointment and with Wesleyan stoicism he wrote in his diary, 'that we are ordered into quarantine is another trial, however, we hope it won't last long before we have our liberty again.'[9] The Hillarys were taken from the *Westland* and landed on the Quarantine Station on Ripa Island, opposite Lyttleton, on 22 February 1880, and remained there until 12 March when they were at last able to complete their journey to Canterbury. Their stay on the Quarantine Station, with its clean, neat wooden buildings with corrugated iron roofs, was preferable to their stay at the Government Depot at Plymouth at the start of their journey, which Hillary denounced as a 'den of disease' where 'the bad arrangements and crowded state of that wretched place arose from the fact that the officials admit some of the filthiest specimens of the human race, whose dirty persons must engender disease'.[10] By contrast on Ripa Island 'we can fish, bathe and enjoy ourselves.'[11]

The health and customs checks on immigrants in the early days of mass migration were concerned with keeping disease out, but otherwise speeding newcomers on their way, so long as they were unlikely to become a burden on public poor relief. In the United States the regulation of immigration was the responsibility of individual states rather than of the federal government, which often meant that procedures were stricter in one state than another. In 1824 the State of New York required captains to report the names of all their passengers to the mayor of New York and give bonds of $300 for each to guarantee that they would not become public charges in the next two years. Regulations were less stringent in the nearby state of New Jersey so, to dodge the bond requirements of New York, ships were offloading passengers in the small New Jersey port of Perth Amboy. However this bond-dodging came to an end in 1837 after the Liverpool vessel *Phoebe* had landed sick passengers at Perth Amboy, leaving them to lie outdoors in a rainstorm, before wagons took them on to New York where they became a charge on the almshouse commissioners who were successfully able to sue the passenger agents.[12]

The State of New York established an Emigration Commission in 1847 to check abuses of immigrants at a time when thousands of fevered Irish immigrants were arriving each day at the height of a typhus epidemic, and only state action could be at all effective. The management of the Marine Hospital at Staten Island was taken over by the Emigration Commission, and an Emigrant Hospital and Refuge was established on Ward's Island in the East River, but New Yorkers were hostile to the landing of any passengers suffering from any disease. When an attempt was made to lease a pier for a landing depot, local residents took out an injunction because the landing of immigrants 'would bring into a quiet part of the city a noisy population without cleanliness and sobriety ... endangering the health and good morals of the ward, and seriously affect the value of real estate'.[13] Indeed, such attitudes were so strong that in 1858 the Marine Hospital on Staten Island was burned down by its neighbours, who feared 'that the Quarantine as it was, and had for a long time, been conducted was a public nuisance dangerous to the health, and in many cases fatal to the lives of the community where it stood, and that therefore the acts complained of were done in obedience to a great public necessity'.[14]

In the United States immigrants were blamed unthinkingly for having brought in disease. This was part of a nativist Anglo-Saxon Protestant response to an influx of Roman Catholic and Jewish incomers from southern and eastern Europe. Not only were these groups of people blamed for having imported cholera, typhus and even plague, but they were seen as reservoirs of infection which made them as much a threat to public health as they were to the moral character of the United States. The Irish were blamed for the cholera epidemics of 1832 and 1849 and their Catholicism was actually linked with poverty, corruption and disease. The direct connection between the importation of epidemic disease and immigration was also given added force by the acceptance of the germ theory of disease at the end of the nineteenth century.[15] The Marine Hospital Service, originally founded to provide medical care for merchant seamen,[16] took on the role of being 'watchdogs at the gate', charged with screening out such undesirables as 'all idiots, insane persons, paupers or persons likely to become public charges, persons suffering from a loathsome or dangerous contagious disease'.[17]

On 1 August 1855 an Emigrant Landing Depot was opened at Castle Garden in Manhattan, where medical inspections could take place and the arrival of the immigrants could be handled in an orderly fashion. Originally a fort built to defend New York from the British in the war of 1812, Castle Garden had been used as pleasure gardens and a fashionable concert hall until its conversion to the world's first emigrant landing depot. Here it was possible for a proper record to be kept of newly arrived emigrants, and for the speedy identification of the blind, cripples, lunatics and paupers likely to become public charges. Only licensed runners and agents were allowed to enter, which made the whole process of arrival more orderly than hitherto. Inside the giant rotunda of the main immigration hall, capable of holding two to four thousand people, immigrants could find refreshments, booking agents for accommodation, and railroad or riverboat tickets, money exchanges, and an office where they could collect letters. A labour exchange was opened in an adjoining building in 1867. By 1871, the *New York Times* could claim that 'Castle Garden is now so well-known in Europe that few emigrants can be induced to sail for any other destination' and that 'their friends in this country write to those intending to emigrate to come to Castle Garden where they will be safe, and, if out of money, they can remain until it is sent to them.'[18]

However, there were problems with the management of Castle Garden. Officials were accused of bullying the immigrants, and the railroad agents and money changers were charged with defrauding then. It was also increasingly felt that it could not cope with the scale of immigration passing through New York at a time when, in 1888, 418,423 of the 546,889 new arrivals in the United States arrived at Castle Garden. Officials, faced with such a volume of immigrants, found it 'impossible to inspect properly the large number of persons who arrived daily during the immigrant season', with the result that 'large numbers of persons not lawfully allowed to land in the United States are annually received at this port', where the local administration was 'a perfect farce'.[19]

It was imperative that the federal government, which since 1882 had taken over from the states responsibility for immigration, take control and establish a new emigration depot in New York. On 1 December 1892 the Federal Bureau of Immigration, set up in 1890, opened a new immigrant depot on Ellis Island, whose isolation made it easier to screen and keep out undesirables. Ellis Island had been occupied by a naval powder magazine since the Civil War and was now doubled in size by landfill. Imposing buildings were erected at a cost of half a million dollars. Whereas the now closed Castle Garden had been intended to protect emigrants, Ellis Island, soon described as 'a cross between Devil's Island and Alcatraz', was meant to exclude undesirables and regulate the admission of future Americans.[20]

For most emigrants their experience of Ellis Island was 'the nearest earthly likeness to the final Day of Judgement, when we have to prove our fitness to enter Heaven', according to Stephen Graham who had travelled to New York with Russian immigrants in 1913.[21] First- and second class passengers were excused the ordeal, merely being asked a few cursory questions by immigration officials before being taken on to the docks, while those in steerage were despatched to Ellis Island. There was outrage when an attempt was made in January 1892 to treat them the same as everyone else. The first- and second-class passengers on the *Carmania* were interrupted in the middle of dinner when the ship was boarded by immigration officials who ordered them to queue up and answer immigration questions. The inspection lasted forty-five minutes, and six of these passengers were sent to Ellis Island for further investigation as suspected prostitutes or embezzlers. As well as objecting to having had their meal spoiled, the cabin passengers were upset that they should be treated like their social inferiors and by the implication that '"first class" passengers are not one whit better in the social scale than those horrid people who cross the Atlantic in the nauseating and ill-smelling steerage.'[22]

Steerage passengers were disembarked onto barges which ferried them to Ellis Island. The Statue of Liberty was visible before them, a tangible symbol of the land of liberty to which they were coming, which 'some emigrants were disposed to cheer, some shed a silent tear', while some had no idea of what it was, one Russian thinking it to be 'the tombstone of Columbus.'[23] As soon as they stepped over the bridge from the barge to Ellis Island, the immigrants, many of them dressed in their smartest clothes to mark the start of a new life, had an identification tag pinned on to them corresponding to their numbers on the ship's manifest. They then proceeded to the baggage room to reclaim their luggage, which had to be carried up a long flight of stairs with doctors waiting at the top to see whether their breathing was too heavy and laboured for them to be perfectly healthy.

On arrival in the imposing red-brick main inspection hall, built in 1898 after fire had destroyed the original wooden building, the immigrants patiently queued up before two United States Public Health Service doctors, the first of whom inspected them for physical or mental abnormalities. He then chalked a mark on the right shoulder of anyone suspected of a defect: 'b' for back problems, 'c' for conjunctivitis, 'g' for goitre, 'k' for hernia, 'l' for lameness and 'x' for mental illness were among the most common marks made. This inspection was necessarily a rapid one based on a visual examination. According to Victor Safford, one of these doctors, 'we used to like to have passengers while under inspection make two right angle turns, the scheme served to bring the light on both sides of a passenger's face. The turns also helped bring out imperfections in muscular co-ordination.'[24] The second doctor was specifically looking for the symptoms of any contagious disease. He would examine the scalp for evidence of lice or scabs that might indicate the presence of the contagious skin condition fauvus. Buttonhooks were used to inspect the linings of the eyelids for signs of trachoma, a blinding disease that was so prevalent that it was responsible for more than half of the detentions, although many cases went undetected because there was little time for symptoms to develop on a relatively short steamer journey between inspection on departure from Europe and on arrival at Ellis Island. Trachoma was especially prevalent in Russia and Poland, and was viewed as a Jewish disease by many prejudiced immigration officials.[25]

Any emigrant failing the initial examination, including anyone suspected of mental deficiency or feeblemindedness, had to undergo a more thorough examination. Stethoscopes and, after 1910, X-ray machines were used to diagnose pulmonary tuberculosis. The tools of bacteriology, such as microscopes, slides, stains and culture methods, were used to diagnose gonorrhoea, syphilis and hookworm. All immigrants suffering from an infectious disease were admitted to the infirmary on Ellis Island and would later be examined by a three-person board of special enquiry with the power to issue certificates of ill health, which amounted to deportation orders. Yet between 1890 and 1924, less than 1 per cent of immigrants were returned to their ports of origin on medical grounds, with never more than 3 per cent in any one year in that period.[26] This was a sign of how successful the initial medical screenings in Europe had been, or perhaps merely that there had not been enough time for an illness to develop on the voyage.

Those immigrants sent to the infirmary were unnerved by the experience and 'they cannot understand by what stroke of scurvy fortune they have been selected from among all the others and forbidden to enter the Promised Land'. Milton Foster, one of the medical officers, also observed that 'the more excitable burst into tears, wring their hands and protest loudly against this great and unexpected injustice', and that 'it is useless to try to calm or reassure them.'[27] Anyone suffering from an infectious disease, such as measles, mumps, diphtheria, and whooping cough, was immediately sent to the infirmary. The Peterson family from Denmark was detained in 1920, because their six-year-old son Carl Heinrich had been diagnosed as suffering from acute osteomyelitis in his left leg as a result of a fall shortly before the family sailed on the *Sweden*. The boy had been operated on, but the surgeon in charge of the case would not allow the family to enter the United States until it was clear whether or not Carl Heinrich would be left with a permanent disability, which might mean that he could become a public charge if unable ever to work. When it was obvious that his leg was healing, Carl Heinrich caught measles, which further delayed any decision about whether or not the family would be admitted or deported. He was then diagnosed as a diphtheria carrier, and finally he caught scarlet fever. His mother, seeing a window wide open next to his bed, was convinced that he would next catch pneumonia.[28]

Katie Schultz was returned to Hungary in 1913 after being identified as 'feeble-minded to such a degree that she would be unable to protect herself; and as she is a pretty girl, it seems extremely dangerous for her to be at large.'[29] Margaret Heckert was refused admission in 1914 because she was unmarried and pregnant, but the man she was travelling with, the father of her child, was allowed in, a decision which seemed unjust as 'it excludes a helpless and friendless girl, and admits a man who is responsible for her condition and for bringing her to this country.' The man, Leopold Koenig, had been 'almost wild' when he learned that his girlfriend had been detained, as he had planned to marry her when they reached America from Germany, where they had been unable to marry because he had not yet completed his military service. For once, common sense won through and the young lovers were both allowed to stay once they were married, since Koenig had a good trade as a bookbinder and could easily support his family.[30]

For those emigrants who had successfully got through the dreaded medical inspections, the ordeal of examination was not yet over. It was all too much like a production line. Stephen Graham objected that 'it is not good to be like a hurrying, bumping, wandering piece of coal being mechanically guided to the sacks of its type and size, but such is the lot of the immigrant at Ellis Island.'[31] Ahead lay the Great Hall, divided into pens of iron railings through which families and individuals slowly filed towards the registration desks where clerks questioned them on their names, age, marital status, nationality, place of origin, who they were travelling with, how much money they had with them, where they intended to settle, and whether they had a job waiting for them. The registry clerks also asked whether the immigrant had a criminal record or was a polygamist, prostitute or anarchist, all grounds for exclusion. After 1917 there was also a literacy test. Pierina Gasperetti, who was from Pavia and had sailed from Genoa in 1912, could not understand why 'they wanted to know a bunch of things ... Probably they were afraid that I wasn't even able to buy myself a piece of bread', and was insulted that 'they stuck a label on us, here, with my name on it, like for livestock.'[32]

For most people this interrogation was brief and they could get on their way, possibly having used the facilities at Ellis Island to exchange money, purchase tickets to their final destination, or send telegraphs to family in the United States. Having collected their luggage again, they could board the tenders to the Battery, a mile away. For others, questioning was much more intensive. It was often difficult to tell whether immigrants were dissembling or whether in particular cases actually complied with the Immigration Laws. Paupers were refused admission, but so were contract labourers who had lined up jobs before their arrival, with the result that 'the immigrant must summon all his ingenuity and subterfuge to dodge the two extremes ... If he cannot support himself he is sent back as liable to become a public charge. If he has provided beforehand for self-support he is sent back as liable to displace an American workman.'[33] Fiorello La Guardia, an interpreter at Ellis Island, saw the paradox, since 'common sense suggested that any immigrant who came into the United States in those days to settle here permanently surely came here to work', yet 'under the law he could not have more than the vague hope of a job'.[34]

There were about two thousand detainees at any one time held on Ellis Island in the heyday of its operation between 1912 and 1914. They were put up in long halls lined with tiers of narrow iron bunks. If there were not enough beds they had to sleep on benches, chairs or even the floor. Clothes had to be washed by hand in the wash basins of the latrines, while the lavatories were filthy and often flooded. There was only six hours' exercise in the open air allowed a week, less than a prisoner would have been permitted. William McUllagh, a British doctor detained for four weeks after being denounced by the father of the girl he wished to marry against parental wishes, was indignant that 'a government by the people for the people has devised this means of humiliating and torturing its immigrants and visitors.' Detainees would 'lie with fever rather than report sick and be sent to Hospital which they dread, and because they will postpone their freedom of this awful place.' The detainees were often afraid of the staff as 'men are assaulted and threatened by the orderlies.'[35]

Progress through Ellis Island was stressful and immigrants were often bullied by officials. Monsignor Giovanni Battista Scalabrini, Bishop of Piacenza, witnessed in 1901 an official aim a stick at the legs of an Italian immigrant, laden with two heavy suitcases, because he was not quick enough in moving when ordered to do so; the bishop feared that the force of the blow could have broken the man's legs. The unfortunate immigrant had then put down his cases and hit the official in retaliation, swearing that 'if I had a gun I would have killed him.'

Scalabrini reflected that it would be better if the officials in their treatment of new immigrants could 'instil in them a sense of confidence in their new country on arrival, instead of treating them like animals or worse', though he admitted that his fellow countrymen, in particular, were generally regarded as rough-mannered 'without any protection from the contempt of others'.[36] One of the crew of a barge taking the immigrants to Ellis Island explained that he was 'driving these animals back', and 'that you've got to be rough with this bunch.' He was 'so sick of handling these dirty bums coming here to this country.'[37] Even the cleaners looked down on the immigrants. Paul Knaplund felt that he had been treated more like a commodity than a human being, and remembered the scornful expression on the face of a black cleaner looking down at him from the gallery running around the Great Hall so much that even years later when he 'was treated condescendingly' on account of his Norwegian origins, he 'saw behind the face of the disdainful person the contemptuous expression of the unknown Negress at Ellis Island.'[38]

Even more restrictive than Ellis Island was its equivalent on the west coast, Angel Island in San Francisco Bay. Opened in 1910 as a receiving depot for all immigrants, it was used as an interrogation and detention centre to enforce the restrictions on Chinese immigration. The first large-scale Chinese immigration had been to San Francisco during the Gold Rush of 1849, followed by a second wave during the construction of the transcontinental railroad by Union Pacific and Central Pacific in the 1870s. Unlike many of the Chinese emigrants involved in the forced labour coolie trade to the Caribbean and South America, those that went to California did so voluntarily. If they could not fund their own travel, brokers advanced credit-tickets for the voyage, to be repaid at an exorbitant rate where a $40 passage could rapidly turn into a $3,000 repayment. Many of the workers were employed as contract labourers and paid as members of gangs. The Chinese were ineligible for naturalisation and contract labour was barred in 1875. Then in 1882 the Chinese Exclusion Act banned Chinese immigration entirely for ten years. This Act was renewed in 1892 and made permanent in 1902.[39] After the passage of the exclusion law, only merchants, professional people and tourists of Chinese nationality could enter the country.

After a three-week journey across the Pacific, Chinese immigrants might be detained at Angel Island in prison-like conditions for three months and more, up to two years in some cases, while their eligibility was determined. There they could be separated from their friends who might coach them on how to pass the entrance questioning, and detained in an escape-proof facility from which it was 'impossible for anyone to escape by swimming to the mainland', in the opinion of Hart Hyatt North, the San Francisco Commissioner of Immigration.[40] Different ethnic groups were strictly segregated from each other in separate waiting rooms, hospital wards and detention blocks. Men and women were also separated from each other. When Jung Look Moy and her three children arrived at Angel Island from Australia in 1916 on their way to join her husband Louie Gar Fun, a Chinese merchant in Idaho, they were detained for three months. He had to verify his status as a merchant exempt from the Chinese Exclusion Laws and prove that he could support his family. His wife then had to prove that they were legally married, and that their children were really their offspring. She was even asked about what kind of floor there had been in her husband's house in China. White travellers on the ship *Tenyo Maru* that Jung Look Moy sailed on were quickly cleared for entry, though one of them complained about being kept overnight and herded with 'the lowest type of Oriental races', because the ship had arrived after the immigration officers had finished work for the day.[41]

The checks on newly arrived immigrants in Latin America were less rigorous than those in the United States. Very soon after landing, the emigrants were taken to immigrant hostels, *Hospedarias de Imigrantes*, very similar to the ones they may have stayed in before their voyage. The hostel at Santos, Brazil, consisted of large dormitories separated by courtyards in which the accommodation was free of charge. However, everything was very basic with mats on the floor serving as beds. Food was little more than soup and bread, whilst in 1908 'the sanitary conditions are so far from flattering that they are even mentioned in the country's official papers.'[42]

British emigrants to South America were also often disillusioned by what they found compared with what they had been promised by the agents. One group of agricultural labourers soon returned home from Brazil in 1873 after suffering from the debilitating heat, diarrhoea, and a diet of rice, black beans and dried or jerked beef. Frederick Crawford, a retired naval officer, the agent who had sent them out from Rio de Janeiro to a remote settlement, accused them of ingratitude towards his employer, the Brazilian government, in return for 'the kind treatment they had received, the excellent and wholesome food and lodgings supplied to them, and the medical care given to them', all at the expense of the government. He even said that the only reason one of the returning emigrants had lost a child was that, despite all advice, the man and his family had gone to Rio, where yellow fever was raging. Crawford professed to 'grieve at the ungratefulness of my countrymen and women, who spent their time in vicious idleness, abusing in no uncertain terms their benefactors', and whom he doubted would have been satisfied with 'champagne and mushrooms and feather beds'.[43] Another group of British emigrants to Paraguay were 'almost in a state of mutiny' after having arrived in Asunción in November 1872 to find that 'no preparations had been made to receive them'. They were kept waiting in the railway station for two days and then sent on their way with no refreshments. The only shelter provided for the women and children at the end of their train journey was in the railway station. An advance group of men had been sent to prepare houses and tents in the place 'where it is proposed to locate the emigrants', but after a fortnight the group was still waiting to move on and expressed themselves 'dissatisfied with their treatment.'[44]

It was easier for people arriving in Australia. The 1852 Passenger Act allowed emigrants to stay on board the ship free of charge for forty-eight hours after arrival in Australia, which allowed many of them to save on expensive lodgings, and gave them more time to find somewhere decent to live and even the chance to be offered a job. Even if they had not found somewhere to live and a job immediately on landing, there were immigrant depots at Melbourne, Sydney and Port Philip where they could stay free of charge.[45] Unlike the United States, which was in many ways a passive and sometimes reluctant recipient of immigrants, the British colonies and the Latin-American countries were keen to encourage settlers to develop their countries, and so made it easier for them on arrival, albeit in not too luxurious surroundings.

Prospective employers swarmed on board the ships to hire the emigrants with the most sought-after skills, and in several cases 'nearly all the emigrants had been engaged within forty eight hours after the government muster or inspection of the people was over'. There was usually a 'scramble' for housemaids because of the scarcity of female servants, which was a result of most eligible young women finding husbands within a short time of arriving in Australia, but 'however agreeable it may be to the girls to get permanently settled, it is doubtless very inconvenient to families to be thus frequently deprived of good servants', and 'there is no remedy for it except patiently waiting the arrival of the next emigrant ship and hence the necessity of employing men as general house servants both in Sydney and throughout the colony.'[46] When passengers arrived at Adelaide, they were handed over to the care of the emigration agent who gave them advice on finding employment. Emigrant guides warned that 'all persons are strongly advised to adopt the course pointed out by that officer, disregarding the opinions (too often given unasked) of designing persons and proceed at once to carry into operation their intended objects'.[47]

Young women were warned against marrying the first settler they met in Australia, since 'when a ship arrives with emigrants the town's people flock on board some to employ labourers and some to obtain wives', and 'many unhappy marriages are made in that Colony through haste and ignorance of each other.' One young woman from Newcastle was approached soon after her arrival in Port Philip by a young squatter, who 'with a courteous and gallant air made her an offer of marriage.' Her immediate response was considered more sensible than that of her friends who very quickly 'had already chosen their partners for life' from the first men to ask them: '"Nay nay hinney," said she, very cavalierly, "nay, my hinney I'se mean to wait a wee and see what turns up."'[48]

For many immigrants, arrival in the port meant reunions with family members who had gone before them and encouraged them to join them in the land of plenty, in many cases sending them the money for their tickets. The nature of these joyful reunions varied from family to family. The novelist Henry Roth resorted to national stereotypes to describe such scenes on the quay in New York:

The most volatile races, such as the Italians, often danced for joy, whirled each other around, pirouetted in an ecstasy; Swedes sometimes just looked at each other, breathing through open mouths like a panting dog; Jews wept, jabbered, almost put each other's eyes out with the recklessness of their darting gestures; Poles roared and gripped each other at arm's length as though they meant to tear a handful of flesh; and after one pecking kiss, the English might be seen gravitating towards, but never achieving, an embrace.[49]

Not all family reunions were lasting. One of Mary Antin's neighbours in Lithuania asked her mother to try to trace his son who had emigrated 'fresh and well and strong with 25 roubles in his pocket, besides his steamer ticket, with new phylacteries and a silk skull cap'. The young man had written from New York to tell his family 'how well he was received by my uncle's son-in-law, how he was conducted to the baths, how they bought him an American suit, everything good.' However, that was the last his family had heard of him in eighteen months and it was 'just as if he had vanished, as if the earth had swallowed him.'[50]

The newly arrived immigrant was as much the prey of the petty criminals at the port of arrival as in the port of embarkation. Italian immigrants in Brazil complained that 'incredible thefts of the emigrants' luggage are committed scot-free in the ports of Santos and Rio de Janeiro; I'd need five sheets of paper to describe them all in detail.' One man was robbed of all his cases only to be told that 'he could do without them, that clothes are available here as well'.[51] Runners were just as active in New York as in Liverpool or Hamburg, snatching up the luggage of new arrivals to force them to follow them to an insalubrious, predatory lodging house. Phony transportation agents tried to sell them tickets for non-existent steamboats or railroads, or else tickets that would only cover part of the journey. A common route to the interior of the country was by steamboat up the Hudson River to Albany, where canal boats could be taken along the Erie Canal to Buffalo, where a steamer could be picked up for cities and towns around the Great Lakes. Many an immigrant bought a ticket for the whole trip, sometimes in New York, and sometimes from agents in the country he had left, only to find it valid as far as Albany alone. Such frauds beset the new arrival:

Many of the steamboats that land immigrants from Quarantine land at the docks in the Third Ward. There they are immediately visited by the runners from the emigrant boarding-houses, backed by bullies to assist in soliciting the passengers to go to the different houses. As the emigrant attempts to take his luggage from on board the boat, the runner will endeavour to get it from him, and by force, unless there is a sufficient police to protect him, representing that they will keep them at sixpence sterling for each meal, and sixpence sterling for lodging, and no charge made for cartage or storage for luggage. When the emigrant comes to pay his bill, he is never able to get off at the contract price, but is compelled to pay from three shillings to fifty cents for each meal and lodging, one dollar and fifty cents for cartage, when, if it was paid at the time, it could not, under the law, be but thirty-one cents and fifty cents per day for storage for an ordinary sized chest, and other things in proportion.[52]

In the absence of adequate protection from the state, the immigrants were often dependent upon the support of immigrant aid societies, especially when 'large numbers of these unfortunate emigrants, as soon as they quit the decks of the vessels, having no home to which to direct their movements, wander through the streets in a state of utter desolation until some benevolent hand, appalled by the misery and wretchedness before him, guides their prostrated frames and tottering frames' to the alms house or an aid society.[53] In New York, representatives of these societies would often be waiting at the docks to forestall the runners. Many of them aimed their work at groups of particular nationalities, such as the Irish Emigrant Association, founded in 1817, the Irish Emigrant Society of 1841, and the venerable German Society of New York, which had been established in 1784. The Irish Emigrant Society and the German Society had jointly lobbied New York State for the creation of a Board of Commissioners of Emigrants in 1847, on which both societies were represented, together with the mayors of New York and Brooklyn, and appointees of the state governor. The Netherlands Emigrant Society and the British Protective Emigrant Society were also active in New York. Baltimore too had long-established immigrant aid societies. The German Society of Maryland had originally been founded to protect indentured servants, but had adjusted to the increased patterns of immigration in the nineteenth century to provide employment services for German newcomers. The Ancient Order of Hibernians, founded in Baltimore in 1803, likewise arranged housing and employment for the Irish arrivals.[54]

The German Societies of New York and New Orleans were supported by German-American merchants with trading links to the Hanseatic ports and often with direct involvement in the emigration trade in the homeland. These and similar societies in other ports had the protection of the immigrant as their mission. Transatlantic travellers were advised to seek them out for guidance on employment, transport and other practical help. The aid societies also forged contact between immigrants originating from similar backgrounds in the same country, helping to ease the assimilation of the recently arrived.[55]

The Hebrew Immigrant Aid Society, founded in New York in the 1880s, was of great importance to Jewish immigrants from Eastern Europe as it searched out jobs and housing for the newly-arrived Jews. In 1909 it merged with the Hebrew Sheltering House Association, founded in 1889, offering destitute immigrants shelter, food and clothing. After 1892 representatives of the Hebrew Immigrant Aid Society regularly went to Ellis Island to collect Jewish immigrants, help them deal with the formalities of immigration, act as interpreters, and even prevent 'unwelcome' Jewish immigrants from being sent back to Europe.[56]

The case of the Aronoff sisters was particularly protracted. In 1914 Joseph Aronoff's wife and four younger children set out to join him and his eldest son and daughter in Chicago. However, ten-year-old Rachel and eight-year-old Kazia had ringworm of the scalp, and Esther Aronoff and all her children were detained in Baltimore. The Hebrew Immigrant Aid Society arranged for the girls to be admitted to the Hebrew Hospital if the family could meet the hospital expenses. As it would be cheaper for the girls to receive treatment for the ringworm in Bremen or Antwerp, the eldest brother, twenty-year-old customer peddler-tailor Nathan, offered to accompany his sisters, so that his mother and the youngest children could go to Chicago to join his father and sister. All that the family could collect together to fund the expenses of the journey was 10 dollars, so the social case worker advanced Nathan 25 dollars which ought to have been enough for the trip and to last him until he could contact an aid society in Bremen. Unfortunately, the *Friedrich der Grosse,* on which they were sailing, had no choice given it but to turn back to New York on the outbreak of the First World War. The Aronoffs were not even allowed to disembark on Ellis Island; however, the Hebrew Immigrant Aid Society intervened on their behalf to arrange for Rachel and Kazia to be treated in the infirmary on Ellis Island. Nathan welcomed this, since at first he had thought that Ellis Island was 'like the Russian jails; but now I am on board of ship not far from New York and nevertheless so far from human beings – to be so near and yet unable to reach them is too sad and too horrible.' The Hebrew Immigrant Aid Society urged trying X-ray treatment when there seemed to be no improvement in the girls' condition, and then in July 1915 arranged for them to be released for treatment at the New Hospital, New York, in the hope that there might be quicker progress than at the infirmary on Ellis Island. Finally, the girls were cured and able to join their family in Chicago in July 1916.[57] Without the intervention of the Hebrew Immigrant Aid Society, the girls, their mother and younger siblings might all have been deported to Russia, and the family separated without any hope of appeal.

The Roman Catholic Church took on the task of protecting the interests of Italian immigrants. Giovanni Battista Scalabrini had first become aware of the problem of emigration when he was appointed as Bishop of Piacenza in 1876, and discovered that 11 per cent of his diocese had emigrated. His first response was to urge his flock to remain in Italy, but in 1880, after seeing a group of emigrants at Milan railway station, where 'not without tears they bid farewell to their native village, to which many sweet memories bound them', he had realised that 'they were disposed to leave their country without regret, since they did not know it save under the hateful guise of conscription and the tax collector, and since for one who is disinherited the fatherland is the land that gives him bread, and yonder, far far away they hoped to find it.'[58] It became his mission to find a solution to the plight of the Italian emigrant. In 1887 he founded the Congregation of the Missionaries of Saint Charles to protect emigrants from disreputable emigration agents, help them to find work and homes in the United States, Brazil and Argentina, oppose the white slavery and prostitution traffic, and provide spiritual guidance to the migrants ensuring that they did not lapse from the Roman Catholic Church. In this work for the 'religious, civil and moral care of our expatriate brothers and sisters', the missionaries were assisted by lay members of the Saint Raphael Society and, after 1895, by an order of nuns, the Congregation of the Missionary Sisters of Saint Charles Borromeo. In 1900 he sent the Apostles of the Sacred Heart to work with the Italian emigrants to Brazil. The Scalabrinian priests opened houses in Genoa, New York, and the other ports through which Italian migrants passed. Some priests even travelled on the emigrant ships to offer spiritual guidance to the migrants. Italian churches were founded as social, welfare and spiritual centres to keep the immigrants in the fold, many of whom were met at the port, 'for in everything concerning migration, it is impossible to separate religious, civil and national interests, public and private interests, without damage'.[59]

Just as the Scalabrinians hoped to keep Italians loyal to their roots and their religion, other immigrant aid societies also wished to maintain ties between immigrants and their homelands for the benefit of the old country. The Pan Hellenic Union, founded in 1908 in Boston, had the twin aims of helping Greek emigrants in distress, and promoting the interests of the Greek state in the United States. With its branches all over the country, it aimed at cementing links between the emigrants and their homeland. When the Balkan War between Greece and the Ottoman Empire broke out in 1912, the Pan Hellenic Union took a leading role in mobilising Greek reservists living in North America and in organising their return to Greece to fight.[60] It was not only Greek citizens in the Greek reserve forces who answered the call of patriotism. Many Greek-born United States citizens also volunteered and returned to defend their homeland, boarding such ships as the *Madonna* and leaving behind businesses, jobs and families until they could return at the end of the war. This provoked questions from opponents of immigration about their divided national loyalties since a naturalised American was expected to stand by his 'decision to become a citizen by remaining strictly neutral when his government is neutral'.[61]

By the early twentieth century the United States was no longer as welcoming to immigrants as it had once been. Since the Chinese Exclusion Act of 1882, there had been successive restrictions laid down on who could enter the country. In 1891 sufferers from congenital or chronic medical conditions, idiots, paupers and anyone 'likely to become a public charge' were barred. In 1903, epileptics, prostitutes, polygamists, anarchists, and anyone seeking the violent overthrow of governments were all excluded. A literacy qualification was introduced in 1917, with the implicit aim of reducing immigration from southern and eastern Europe. In the same year the Asiatic Barred Zone was created to exclude indigenous emigrants from India, Burma, Siam, the Malay states, Polynesia, Afghanistan and eastern Russia. Then amid fears that the end of the Great War would unleash a new wave of immigration, the Quota Act of 1921 capped immigration at 358,000 a year and introduced individual country quotas based on nationalities, set at 3 per cent of the foreign-born individuals of that nationality recorded in the 1910 census. The 1924 Immigration Act was even more stringent. New immigrants from northern and western Europe were favoured above those from southern and eastern Europe.

It all fitted in with the nativist views and eugenic assumptions of the Immigration Restriction League, founded in 1894, that 'we should exercise as much care in admitting human beings as we exercise in relation to animals or insect pests or disease germs. Yet ... we are today taking more care in the selection ... of a Hereford bull or a Southdown ewe ... than we are taking in the selection of the alien men and women who are coming here to be the fathers and mothers of future American children.' The League also urged that 'we should see to it that we are protected, not merely from supporting alien dependents, delinquents and defectives, but from ... that "watering of the nation's life blood" which results from their breeding after admission.' Restriction on immigration was necessary because 'a considerable proportion of immigrants now coming are from races and countries which have not progressed, but which have been backward, downtrodden and relatively useless for centuries', and because 'there is no reason to suppose that a change of location will result in a change of inborn tendencies.' The charge was also made that 'the efforts of steamship agents result, moreover, in the immigration of many of the least desirable specimens of these backward races.'[62] It was a pessimistic view of migration rooted in racism. Yet the great age of immigration to North America was effectively over, and the gates at Ellis Island, Angel Island and elsewhere had been narrowed.

Canada, Australia and Argentina continued to operate liberal immigration policies and to encourage immigration with assisted passages well into the 1930s. There the needs of the labour market continued to make government and employers do everything that they could to make immigration appealing and accessible with financial lures. Nevertheless, even these countries were restricting immigration to favoured groups. One of the early acts of the new Federation of Australia in 1901 had been an Immigration Restriction Act which laid down a dictation test for new immigrants designed to keep Australia a 'white' country. This was repealed in 1958 to allow skilled or wealthy immigrants from Asia to enter, and in 1973 all the remaining barriers against non-white immigrants were removed, which has led to a more diverse and Pacific Rim orientated Australia, yet as late as 1982 migrants from the British Isles continued to be favoured and encouraged through assisted passages that were open to them alone.[63] Canada too continued to offer assisted passages to British emigrants until 1936, when economic depression led to the end of the programme. In a world equally beset by economic crisis, unrestricted migration perhaps no longer had the answers.

For the immigrants who had arrived to build a better life, the hope of great opportunities remained strong. Having survived the journey from port to port, they now needed the strength to establish themselves. The difficulties of the journey had been a rite of passage from one stage in life in the old world to another in the new, one which was to profoundly influence the destinies of those who had undertaken it, but it was only the start of a new life and a longer journey to build a new world. It was not the end of their story but only the interlude before the beginning of a new life, which might take many years to establish. Paul Knaplund, a migrant from Norway in 1906, considered that 'he had weighed anchor and left the home port. A new harbour with a good anchorage had been found, but the change had been very gradual.

Notes

CHAPTER 1

1. C Dickens, *David Copperfield* (1907), pp773–4.
2. Ibid, p775.
3. Ibid, x.
4. C Dickens, 'Home for Homeless Women', *Household Words*, 1/33 (23 April 1853), 169.
5. W Collins, *The New Magdalen* (2004), p285.
6. O Handlin, *The Uprooted* (2002), p47.
7. An Act for the More Effectual Relief of the Destitute Poor in Ireland, 1 & 2 Victoria, c. 56, 31 July 1838; An Act to Amend the Acts for the More Effectual Relief of the Destitute Poor in Ireland, 12 & 13 Victoria, c. 104, 1 August 1849.
8. E Richards, *Britannia's Children* (2004), p138.
9. An Act for the Amendment and better Administration of the Laws relating to the Poor in England and Wales, 4 & 5 William IV, c. 76, 14 August 1834.
10. See H J M Johnston, *British Emigration Policy 1815–1830* (1972).
11. *Illustrated London News*, 21 December 1844.
12. E Gaskell, *Mary Barton* (1850), p283.
13. E Richards, *Britannia's Children* (2004), pp137–8.
14. Papers relating to the Work of the Emigrants' Information Office, C5078, PP 1887, VI.
15. J Harris, *Unemployment and Politics: A Study in English Social Policy 1886–1914* (1972), pp184–7.
16. M Harper and S Constantine, *Migration and Empire* (2010), pp292–3.
17. *The Huggetts Abroad* (Gainsborough Pictures, 1949), dir Ken Annakin (DVD, ITV Studios Home Entertainment, B000MV836K, 2007).
18. W R Johnson, 'Acquiring Emigrants: The Information Chain in Wales 1860–70s', *Proceedings of the University of Queensland History Research Group* (1992), 6–7.
19. J M Bumstead, *People's Clearance,* pp117–18.
20. M Harper and S Constantine, *Migration and Empire* (2010), p288.
21. F Broeze, 'Private Enterprise and the Peopling of Australasia, 1831–50', *Economic History Review,* 25 (1982), 235–53.
22. J Hillary, *Westland* (1979), p56.
23. Ibid, pp60–1.
24. *The Times*, 13 April 1847.
25. Ibid, 20 September 1889.
26. Ibid, 1 June 1848.
27. Ibid.
28. E Dubrovi, *Merika, Iseijavanje iz srednje Europe u Ameriku 1880–1914, Emigration from Central Europe to America 1880–1914* (2008), pp24–6.
29. A Löffler, *Der Entwurf eines Gesetzes betrefend die Auswanderung* (1913), p19.
30. International Labour Office, *Emigration and Immigration*

Legislation and Treaties (1922), pp13–24.

31. S Vere Foster, *Work and Wages, or the Penny Emigrant's Guide to the United States and Canada, for Female Servants, Labourers, Mechanics, Farmers &c* (1855).

32. M McNeill, *Vere Foster 1819–1900: An Irish Benefactor* (1971), p100.

33. *The Northern Whig*, 12 January 1880.

34. *The Economist*, 10/457 (29 May 1852), 589.

35. M Baker, 'A Migration of Wiltshire Agricultural Labourers to Australia in 1851', *Journal of the Historical Society of South Australia*, 14 (1986), 67–82.

36. R Arnold, *The Farthest Promised Land* (1981), pp48–62.

37. W Booth, *In Darkest England and the Way Out* (1890), p151.

38. Report of the Departmental Committee appointed to consider Mr Rider Haggard's Report on Agricultural Settlements in the British Colonies, Cd 2978, PP 1906.

39. Salvation Army, *Empire Migration and Settlement* (1937), pp13, 17.

40. Boy Scouts Association, *The Call of Empire* (1939), pp1–2.

41. *United Empire*, 9 (1923), 43.

42. Cited in J Hitchman *They Carried the Sword* (1966), p64.

43. S L E Barnardo and J Marchant, *Memoirs of the Late Dr Barnardo* (1907), p167.

44. J H Batt, *Dr Barnardo* (1907), clxxii.

45. J Hitchman *They Carried the Sword* (1966), p65.

46. R Kershaw and J Sacks, *New Lives for Old* (2008), pp115–6.

47. G Sherrington, 'A Better Class of Boy: The Big Brother Movement, Youth Migration and Citizenship of Empire', *Australian Historical Studies*, 120 (2002), 267–85.

48. E G Wakefield, *A View of the Art of Colonisation* (1849), p156.

49. General Report of the Emigration Commissioners, C.768, PP1873, XVIII.

50. A J Hammerton, *Emigrant Gentlewomen* (1979), pp99–111.

51. W M Thackeray, *The Book of Snobs* (1869), p344.

52. Ibid, pp345–6.

53. *The Times*, 15 March 1901.

54. Dominions Royal Commission on the Natural Resources, Trade and Legislation of Certain Parts of His Majesty's Dominions, Cd. 8458, PP1917-18, VIII, p173.

55. Ibid, p195.

56. Report from Select Committee on Emigration from the United Kingdom, PP 1826, IV, p296.

57. E Abbott, *Immigration: Select Documents and Case Records* (1924), pp13–14.

58. E E Hale, *Letters on Irish Emigration* (1852), p16.

59. C Erickson, *Invisible Emigrants* (1972), pp152–3.

60. W D Kamphoefner, W Helbich and U Sommer (ed), *News from the Land of Freedom* (1991), p69.

61. Cited in P J Duffy (ed), *To and From Ireland* (2004), pp69–70.

62. J G Alexander, *Daily Life in Immigrant America 1870-1920* (2007), p28.

63. T Blegen, *Land of Their Choice* (1955), p196.

64. O Rynning, *True Account of America* (1917).

65. G Duden, *Bericht über eine Reise nach den westlichen Staten Nordamerika's* (1829).

66. R K Philip, *The Dictionary of Medical and Surgical Knowledge* (1864), p271.

67. J Zucchi, 'Immigrant Friulani in North America', in *Italian Immigrants in Rural and Small Town America, Essays from the Fourteenth Annual Conference of the American Italian Historical Association*, ed R J Vecoli (1987), 62–71.

68. L Carpi, *Delle Colonie e dell' Emigrazione d' Italiani all'Estero sotto l'Aspetto dell'Industria, Commercio, Agricoltura e con Trattazione d'Importanti Questioni Sociali* (1874), p295.

69. J Wilson, *Memories of a Labour Leader* (1910), p195.

70. J Lawson, *Peter Lee* (1936), p57.

71. *Illustrated London News*, 10 May 1851.

72. Ibid, 21 December 1844.
73. R H Billigmeier and F A Picard, *The Old Land and the New* (1965), p191.
74. T Rosati, *Assistenza Sanitaria degli Emigranti e dei Marinai* (1908), p69.
75. United States Immigration Committee, *Reports of the Immigration Committee* (1911), p30.
76. M Antin, *The Promised Land* (1912), p172.
77. M Antin, *From Plotzk to Boston* (1899), pp41–2.
78. Cited in H Rössler, 'The Time Has Come, We are Going to America', in D Knauf and B Moreno (ed), *Leaving Home* (2010), p97.
79. Ibid, p92.

CHAPTER 2

1. *Illustrated London News*, 29 July 1848.
2. *The Times*, 8 January 1852.
3. *Ballou's Pictorial*, 5/8 (1855), 152.
4. *Illustrated London News*, 6 July 1850.
5. A C Buchanan, *Emigration Practically Considered* (1828), p87.
6. R K Philip, *The Dictionary of Medical and Surgical Knowledge* (1864), p273.
7. Ibid, p273.
8. W I Thomas and F Znaniecki, *Il Contadino Polacco in Europa e in America* (1968), p616.
9. H Rössler, 'The Time Has Come, We are Going to America', in D Knauf and B Moreno (ed), *Leaving Home* (2010), p94.
10. Ibid, p93.
11. J M Bergquist, *Daily Life in Immigrant America* (2008), p62.
12. T Feys, *Maritime Transport and Migration* (2007), pp53, 61.
13. P Knaplund, *Moorings Old and New* (1963), p135.
14. Ibid, p138.
15. Ibid, p140.
16. H Wätjen, *Aus der Frühzeit des Nordatlantikverkehrs: Studien zur Geschichte der deutschen Schiffarhrt und deutschen Auswanderung nach den Vereinigten Staaten bis zum Ende des amerikanischen Bürgerkrieks* (1932), pp122–5.
17. M Walker, *Germany and the Emigration, 1816–1885* (1964), pp87–93.
18. D Hoerder, 'The Traffic of Emigration via Bremen/Bremerhaven: Merchants' Interests, Protective Legislation and Migrants' Experiences', *Journal of American Ethnic History*, 13 (1993), 68–81.
19. E Drechsel, *Norddeutscher Lloyd Bremen, 1857–1970* (1994), pp2–3, 21.
20. H Wätjen, *Aus der Frühzeit des Nordatlantikverkehrs: Studien zur Geschichte der deutschen Schiffarhrt und deutschen Auswanderung nach den Vereinigten Staaten bis zum Ende des amerikanischen Bürgerkrieks* (1932), p118.
21. E A Steiner, *On the Trail of the Emigrant* (1906), p35.
22. N Kent, *Trieste* (2011), pp145–6; G Mellinato, *Cosulich Dinastia Adriatica* (2008), p24.
23. W Prausnitz, *Parere del Professore Prausnitz sulle Condizione Igieniche di Trieste in nesso all' Epidemia di Tifo* (1913).
24. E A Steiner, *On the Trail of the Emigrant* (1906), p35.
25. S L Baily, *Immigrants in the Lands of Promise* (1999), pp32–3.
26. TNA, FO 368/30, letter from Sydney J A Churchill, consul for Sicily, 16 July 1906.
27. Ibid, extract from *Ora*, 16 July 1906.
28. TNA, MT 9/270, Report of Committee on Act respecting Emigration and Ordinance respecting the Transport of Emigrants to Transatlantic Places, 7 October 1886.
29. Ibid, letter from Charles S Dundas, Consul-General Hamburg, to Lord Rosebery, Foreign Secretary, 2 July 1886.
30. TNA, FO 64/489, Memorandum, 1898.
31. Ibid, letter from Castle Line to the Marquess of Salisbury, 29 March 1898.

32. H Allmers, *Marschenbuch: Land- und Volksbilder aus den Marschen der Weser und Elbe* (1858), p210.
33. T Rosati, *Assistenza Sanitaria degli Emigranti e dei Marinai* (1908), p48.
34. United States Immigration Committee, *Reports of the Immigration Committee* (1911), p87.
35. T Rosati, *Assistenza Sanitaria degli Emigranti e dei Marinai* (1908), p47.
36. TNA, MT 9/231, Enquiry into Plymouth Emigration Depot, 1883.
37. Ibid, Letter from Ellen Joyce, published in *Friendly Work*, November 1883,
38. Ibid, F D Bell, Agent General, to Minister of Immigration, 19 December 1883.
39. Ibid, Francis Fox, 1883.
40. Ibid, Report of Commission appointed by the Governor of New Zealand, 29 August 1883.
41. Ibid, F D Bell, Agent General, to Minister of Immigration, 19 December 1883.
42. J H Hillary, *Westland* (1995), pp4–5.
43. TNA, MT 9/231, Letter from Ellen Joyce, published in *Friendly Work*, November 1883.
44. K Baedeker, *Austria–Hungary* (1911), p275.
45. See W Prausnitz, *Parere del Professore Prausnitz sulle Condizione Igieniche di Trieste in nesso all' Epidemia di Tifo* (1913).
46. United States Immigration Committee, *Reports of the Immigration Committee* (1911), p86.
47. M A Jones, *Destination America* (1976), pp45–6.
48. E A Steiner, *On the Trail of the Emigrant* (1906), p35.
49. R J Evans, *Death in Hamburg* (1987), pp279–92, 300–1.
50. H H Groppe and U Wöst, *Via Hamburg to the World* (2007), p21.
51. *Hamburgischer Correspondent*, 14 December 1901.
52. J Norbert, *Mit Lust gelebt: Roman meines Lebens kommentierte,*

illustrierte und wesentlich erweiterte Neuausgabe (2004), p113.
53. H H Groppe and U Wöst, *Via Hamburg to the World* (2007), p39.
54. *Hamburgischer Correspondent*, 14 October 1904.
55. H H Groppe and U Wöst, *Via Hamburg to the World* (2007), p60.
56. F H La Guardia, *The Making of an Insurgent* (1948), pp57–8.
57. B Brandenburg, *Imported Americans* (1904), p171.
58. Ibid, p173.
59. *Illustrated London News*, 6 July 1850.
60. NMM, ZBA4022, H N O'Neil, *The Parting Cheer*, 1861.
61. *Saturday Review*, 11 May 1861.
62. *Illustrated London News*, 6 July 1850.
63. P Knaplund, *Moorings Old and New* (1963), p119.

CHAPTER 3

1. *Morning Chronicle*, 21 December 1850.
2. TNA, HO 45/1467, list of ships surveyed by Lloyds surveyors in the port of Liverpool for the conveyance of emigrants, 26 March–30 April 1846.
3. Report from the Select Committee of the Passengers' Act, 1851, PP 1851, XIX (632), *xviii*.
4. Ibid, Q2889, evidence of Sir George Stephen.
5. *Niles Weekly Register*, 27 September 1834, vol 47, pp55–6.
6. G Mittelberger, *Journey to Pennsylvania in the Year 1750 and Return to Germany in the Year 1754* (1898), p19.
7. Ibid, p22.
8. R Whyte, *The Ocean Plague* (1848), p16.
9. Ibid, *xix–xxx*.
10. W Hancock, *An Emigrant's Five Years in the Free States of America* (1860), pp9–10.
11. *Niles Weekly Register*, 27 September 1834, vol 47, pp55–6.
12. Dr Joseph Morin, quarantine station inspector, quoted in Report

on the Affairs of British North
America from the Earl of Durham,
PP 1839, XVII, (3), Appendix A,
pp86–7.

13. TNA, HO 45/1467, letter from W
Shaw to E Rushton, 31 October
1845.

14. Ibid, report from T F Elliot and
Alexander Wood to James Stephen
on *Robert Isaac*, 5 February 1846.

15. Ibid, letter from Edward Rushton
to Sir J R Graham, 1 January
1846.

16. M A Jones, *Destination America*
(1976), p30.

17. New York Emigration
Commissioners, *Annual Report of
the Commissioners of
Immigration, State of New York*
(1868), p126.

18. A Copy of a Letter addressed to
the Land and Emigration
Commission, PP 1881, LXXXI
(2995), pp3–5.

19. TNA, CO 384/88, Letter from
William Mure to Frederick W
Hart, 29 March 1851

20. TNA, CO 384/88, letter from
William Mure to Lord Palmerston,
4 February 1850.

21. *Congressional Globe*, 50/2 (1860),
1147.

22. G Mittelberger, *Journey to
Pennsylvania in the Year 1750 and
Return to Germany in the Year
1754* (1898), p20.

23. E Abbott (ed), *Immigration: Select
Documents and Case Records*
(1924), p13.

24. W Huskisson, *The Speeches of the
Right Honourable William
Huskisson* (1831), pp234–5.

25. Hansard, *Parliamentary Debates*,
XVIII, 18 March 1828, col 1214.

26. Report on the Affairs of British
North America from the Earl of
Durham, PP 1839, XVII (3),
Appendix A, pp87–8.

27. Ibid.

28. Baking soda.

29. TNA, CO 384/88, Letter from
William Mure to Frederick W
Hart, 29 March 1851

30. B Brandenburg, *Imported
Americans* (1904), p184.

31. Ibid, p190.

32. T Rosati, Medical Inspector of

Emigrant Ships, 1908, cited in A
Nicosia and L Prencipe (ed),
*Museo Nazionale Emigrazione
Italiana* (2009), pp414–5.

33. W Bell, *Hints to Emigrants* (1824),
p26.

34. Report on the Affairs of British
North America from the Earl of
Durham, PP 1839, XVII, (3),
Appendix A, pp87–8.

35. R Whyte, *The Ocean Plague*
(1848), p60.

36. House of Lords, *Papers Relevant
to Emigration to the British
Provinces in North America*
(1848), p14.

37. H Wätjen, *Aus der Frühzeit des
Nordatlantikverkehrs: Studien zur
Geschichte der deutschen
Schiffahrt und deutschen
Auswanderung nach den
Vereinigten Staaten bis zum Ende
des amerikanischen Bürgerkriegs*
(1932), pp138–42.

38. Reports from Committees:
Colonization from Ireland, PP
1847, VI, p86.

39. A Trollope, *The Way We Live
Now* (1995), p334.

40. *New York Herald*, 4 May 1850.

41. *The Times*, 19 April 1850.

42. C Kinealy, *This Great Calamity:
The Irish Famine 1845–52* (1994),
pp158–61.

43. S Fox, *The Ocean Railway* (2003),
p181.

44. *The Times*, 13 May 1854.

45. Ibid, 22 April 1854.

46. Ibid, 13 May 1854.

47. First Report from the Select
Committee on Packet and
Telegraphic Contracts, PP 1860,
XIV, p220.

48. Report from the Select Committee
on Mail Contracts, PP 1868–9, VI,
p129.

49. Report from the Select Committee
on Contract Packet Services, PP
1849, XII, p135.

50. First Report from the Select
Committee on Packet and
Telegraphic Contracts, PP 1860,
XIV, p255.

51. Ibid, p263.

52. Ibid, p255.

53. H Morford, *Over-Sea* (1867), p31.

54. H W Bellows, *The Old World in*

its New Face (1870), p18.

55. *A Report on Emigrant Ships by the Sanitary Commission of the Lancet* (1873), p26.

56. S Amos, 'In The Steerage', *Harper's New Magazine*, 31 (1865), 295.

57. Ibid, p296.

58. Ibid, p297.

59. Ibid, p298.

60. T Rosati, *Assistenza Sanitaria degli Emigranti e dei Marinai* (1908), p91. See also A Nicosia and L Prencipe (ed), *Museo Nazionale Emigrazione Italiana* (2009), p415.

61. TNA, MT 9/340, 'Report of the Lancet Special Sanitary Committee on the British Emigrant Service', 24 November 1888, p1041.

62. Report with Regard to the Accommodation and Treatment of Emigrants, PP 1881, LXXXII (2995), pp3–5.

63. T Rosati, *Assistenza Sanitaria degli Emigranti e dei Marinai* (1908), p91.

64. 'Atlantic Drift: Gathering in the Steerage', *Catholic World*, 16 (1873), 648–58, 837–44.

65. Report of the Investigation into the Treatment and Condition of Steerage Passengers, Senate Document 23, 43 Congress 1 Session (1874), p145.

66. Ibid, pp146–7.

67. C O'Brien, *Pall Mall Gazette*, 6 May 1881.

68. Hansard, *Parliamentary Debates*, CLXI, 30 May 1881 col 1659.

69. TNA, MT 9/340, Extract from Minute of Mr Chamberlain on 'Horrors of an Emigrant Ship', 1888.

70. 'Atlantic Drift: Gathering in the Steerage', *Catholic World*, 16 (1873), 842.

71. T I Wharton, 'Steerage to Liverpool and Return', *Lippincott's Magazine*, 35 (1885), 127–40, 134.

72. Ibid, p129.

73. Ibid, p134.

74. Ibid, p133.

75. *New York Times*, 21 April 1868.

76. S Amos, 'In The Steerage', *Harper's New Magazine*, 31 (1865), 297.

77. H Morford, *Over-Sea* (1867), p352.

78. 'Atlantic Drift: Gathering in the Steerage', *Catholic World*, 16 (1873), 654–5, 843.

79. T I Wharton, 'Steerage to Liverpool and Return', *Lippincott's Magazine*, 35 (1885), 132.

80. Report of the Investigation into the Treatment and Condition of Steerage Passengers, Senate Document 23, 43 Congress 1 Session (1874), p12.

81. T I Wharton, 'Steerage to Liverpool and Return', *Lippincott's Magazine*, 35 (1885), 132.

82. Report by Dr F H Blaxall on the Sanitary Aspects of Emigration and Immigration from and into the United Kingdom, C.3778, 1883, p160.

83. 'Atlantic Drift: Gathering in the Steerage', *Catholic World*, 16 (1873), 652.

84. Report by Dr F H Blaxall on the Sanitary Aspects of Emigration and Immigration from and into the United Kingdom, C.3778, 1883, p149.

85. Cited in T Motta and A Dentoni (ed), *L'America* (2008), p17.

86. United States Immigration Committee, *Reports of the Immigration Committee* (1911), p297.

87. Ibid, p7.

88. *New York Tribune*, 28 September 1904.

89. Ibid, 18 April 1906.

90. Ibid, 27 July 1888.

91. Edward A Steiner, *On the Trail of the Immigrant* (1906), p37.

92. Ibid, p35.

93. J Wilson, *Memories of a Labour Leader* (1910), pp149–50.

94. United States Immigration Committee, *Reports of the Immigration Committee* (1911), p23.

95. E A Steiner, *On the Trail of the Immigrant* (1906), p41.

96. C Dickens, *Martin Chuzzlewit* (1907), p240.

97. S Graham, *With Poor Immigrants*

to America (1914), pp13–14.
98. Ibid, p16.
99. Ibid, p18.
100. P Knaplund, *Moorings Old and New* (1963), p145.
101. S Graham, *With Poor Immigrants to America* (1914), p23.
102. Ibid, p26.

CHAPTER 4

1. John White, surgeon to the First Fleet of convict ships, cited in C Bateson, *The Convict Ships* (1959), p87.
2. BL, Add MS 47966, journal of Arthur Bowes, 1787–9.
3. D R McNeil, 'Medical Care Aboard Australian-bound Convict Ships 1786–1840', *Bulletin of Medical History*, 26 (1952), 117–40.
4. C Bateson, *The Convict Ships* (1959), p153.
5. Ibid, p49; see also E Ford, *The Life and Work of William Redfern* (1953).
6. K Brown, *Poxed and Scurvied* (2011), p142.
7. C Bateson, *The Convict Ships* (1959), p188.
8. Ibid, p205.
9. C Lloyd and J L S Coulter, *Medicine and the Navy* (1963), pp136–7.
10. TNA, ADM 101/254/1D, medical journal of *Hyderabad*, T H Keown, 20 August–24 December 1850.
11. TNA, ADM 101/252/1A, medical journal of *Martin Luther*, Thomas Crawford, 1 June–9 December 1852.
12. TNA, HO 20/13, journal of the ship *Mandarin*, Captain John H Smith, 29 June 1843.
13. Ibid, 3, 15 July 1843.
14. Ibid, 29 June 1843.
15. Ibid, 8 August 1843.
16. Ibid, 15 August 1843.
17. Ibid, 1 September 1843.
18. Ibid, 9 August 1843.
19. Ibid, 6 August 1843.
20. Ibid, 19 September 1843.
21. Ibid, 1 August 1843.
22. G B Wilkinson, *South Australia* (1848), p33.
23. J Willcox, *Practical Hints to Intending Emigrants for Our Australian Colonies* (1858), p24.
24. TNA, MT 9/231, Report of Commission appointed by the Governor of New Zealand to enquire into the case of the emigrant ship *Oxford*, 29 August 1883.
25. J Hood, *Australia and the East* (1843), p5.
26. C Dickens, *Little Dorrit* (1908), p62.
27. TNA, MT 9/86, qualifications of surgeons on emigrant ships, 1874.
28. TNA, MT 9/122, *The Lancet* (13 November 1875), 707.
29. Ibid, 708.
30. TNA, MT 9/612, 'Health of Seamen', 1899.
31. TNA, MT 9/309, Merchant Shipping Act, 1854, section 230.
32. TNA, MT 9/309, Passenger Act, 1855, sections 41–44.
33. TNA, MT 9/309, Merchant Shipping Act, 1867, section 4.
34. TNA, MT 9/103, medical scale for emigrant ships, January 1875; MT 9/221, 'scale of medical comforts per 100 passengers', 1883.
35. TNA, MT 9/340, 'Report of *The Lancet* Special Sanitary Committee on the British Emigrant Service', 24 November 1888, p1039.
36. TNA, MT 9/103, letter from Mississippi and Dominion Steam Ship Company, 22 March 1875.
37. TNA, MT 9/340, 'Report of *The Lancet* Special Sanitary Committee on the British Emigrant Service', 24 November 1888, p1039.
38. TNA, MT 9/322, letter from representatives of Royal Colleges of Physicians and Surgeons and Board of Trade, November 1888.
39. TNA, MT 9/309, Dr Tanner, MP for Mid-Cork, quoted in *The Times*, 13 May 1889.
40. N Fogg, *The Voyages of the Great Britain* (2004), pp97–8.
41. HMSO, *Instructions for Surgeon Superintendents on Government Emigrant Ships* (1866), pp5–6.
42. TNA, CO 201/269, Report of the Board of Enquiry in to the case of the Emigrant Ship *Lady McNaghten*, 7 July 1837, f37.

43. J C Byrne, *Emigrants' Guide to New South Wales Proper* (1848), p10.
44. W Harcus, *Handbook for Emigrants Proceeding to South Australia* (1873), p29.
45. J Hood, *Australia and the East* (1843), pp23–4.
46. J H Hillary, *Westland* (1995), p35.
47. Ibid, p26.
48. Ibid, p20.
49. TNA, HO 20/13, journal of the ship *Mandarin*, Captain John H Smith, 1 August 1843.
50. Ibid, 21 September 1843.
51. J Hood, *Australia and the East* (1843), p20.
52. Ibid, p54.
53. J Hood, *Australia and the East* (1843), p4.
54. Ibid, p57.
55. J E Alexander (ed), *The Albatross: A Voyage from Victoria to England* (1863), p23.
56. TNA, ADM 101/77/9, medical journal of the emigrant ship *Juliana*, surgeon Henry Kelsall, 17 October 1838–21 May 1839.
57. TNA, CO 201/269, Report of the Board of Enquiry in to the case of the Emigrant Ship *Lady McNaghten*, 7 July 1837, f65.
58. G B Wilkinson, *South Australia* (1848), p33.
59. J Willcox, *Practical Hints to Intending Emigrants* (1858), p16.
60. G B Wilkinson, *South Australia* (1848), p30.
61. TNA, CO 201/269, Report of the Board of Enquiry in to the case of the Emigrant Ship *Lady McNaghten*, 7 July 1837, f48.
62. G B Wilkinson, *South Australia* (1848), p21.
63. Ibid, p24.
64. J Hood, *Australia and the East* (1843), p33.
65. TNA, ADM 101/77/7, journal of Hired Ship *James Pattison*, surgeon superintendent G Roberts, 25 October 1839–11 February 1840.
66. TNA, CO 201/269, Report of the Board of Enquiry in to the case of the Emigrant Ship *Lady McNaghten*, 7 July 1837, f38.
67. Ibid, f24.
68. Ibid, f29.
69. Ibid, f65.
70. Ibid, f51.
71. Ibid, f3.
72. TNA, HO 20/13, journal of the ship *Mandarin*, Captain John H Smith, 21 September 1843.
73. Ibid, 20 July 1843.
74. TNA, CO 201/269, Report of the Board of Enquiry in to the case of the Emigrant Ship *Lady McNaghten*, 7 July 1837, f71.
75. J Willcox, *Practical Hints to Intending Emigrants* (1858), p21.
76. TNA, ADM 101/76/3, medical journal of the *Amity* emigrant ship, surgeon and superintendent James McTernan, 5 April–9 July 1825.
77. TNA, CO 201/269, Report of the Board of Enquiry in to the case of the Emigrant Ship *Lady McNaghten*, 7 July 1837, f71.
78. Ibid, f68.
79. Ibid, f67.
80. TNA, HO 20/13, journal of the ship *Mandarin*, Captain John H Smith, 3 July 1843.
81. Ibid, 12 September 1843.
82. J Hood, *Australia and the East* (1843), pp51–2.
83. TNA, HO 20/13, journal of the ship *Mandarin*, Captain John H Smith, 5 August, 9 August 1843.
84. M Crompton, *A Journal of a Honeymoon on the SS Great Britain* (1992), p17.
85. SS *Great Britain* Museum, BRSGB 1997.003, letter to family of William Wheatley, 24 April 1866.
86. Ibid, BRSGB 1997.014, diary of female passenger, 14 October 1865.
87. TNA, ADM 101/76/1, journal of Emigrant Ship *Adam Lodge*, surgeon Alexander Stewart, 9 October 1839–18 February 1840.
88. TNA, ADM 101/78/1, journal of Emigrant Ship *Maitland*, surgeon John Smith, 21 June–5 November 1838.
89. R Haines, *Life and Death in the Age of Sail* (2006), pp29–30.
90. Ibid, pp86–7.
91. Ibid, p110.
92. J Pocock, *Travels of a London Schoolboy 1826–1830* (1996),

p138.

93. M Crompton, *A Journal of a Honeymoon on the SS Great Britain* (1992), p16.

94. J Pocock, *Travels of a London Schoolboy 1826–1830* (1996), p138.

95. D Hastings, *Over the Mountains of the Seas* (2006), p51.

96. J Hood, *Australia and the East* (1843), p4.

97. J Willcox, *Practical Hints to Intending Emigrants* (1858), p27.

98. J Sams, *The Diary of Joseph Sams* (1982), p31.

99. J Pocock, *Travels of a London Schoolboy 1826–1830* (1996), p139.

100. Ibid, p11.

101. Cited in C Deakes and T Stanley, *A Century of Sea Travel* (2010), p30.

102. D Hastings, *Over the Mountains of the Seas* (2006), p47.

103. Ibid, p133.

104. J Sams, *The Diary of Joseph Sams* (1982), pp13–14.

105. J H Hillary, *Westland* (1995), pp82–3.

106. C R Deakes and T Stanley, *A Century of Sea Travel* (2010), pp54–5.

CHAPTER 5

1. F Madox Brown, *The Last of England* (1855), Birmingham Museum and Art Gallery; a copy of the painting made in 1860 is in the Fitzwilliam Museum, Cambridge.

2. Cited in L Parris (ed), *The Pre-Raphaelites* (1984), p124.

3. Cited in D Hastings, *Over the Mountains of the Seas* (2006), p14.

4. J Sams, *The Diary of Joseph Sams* (1982), p9.

5. Ibid, p18.

6. Ibid, p7.

7. J Maxtone-Graham, *The Only Way to Cross* (1972), p18.

8. R W Emerson, *Emerson in His Journals* (1982), p117.

9. T Power, *Impressions of America* (1836), pp19–20.

10. F Marryat, *A Diary in America* (1839), p13.

11. H Martineau, *Retrospect of Western Travel* (1838), vol 1, p26.

12. Ibid, p19.

13. Ibid, p34.

14. C Dickens, *Martin Chuzzlewit* (1907), pp524–5.

15. C Dickens, *American Notes* (1908), p17.

16. Ibid, p18.

17. S Fox, *The Ocean Railway* (2008), pp70–1.

18. *New York Morning Post*, 11 August 1845.

19. M Compton, *A Journal of a Honeymoon Voyage on the SS Great Britain* (1992), p19.

20. W Morris, *Letters Sent Home* (1875), p50.

21. Ibid, p458.

22. Ibid, p464.

23. J Sams, *The Diary of Joseph Sams* (1982), p12.

24. Ibid, p16.

25. Ibid, p33.

26. Ibid, p22.

27. Midshipmen.

28. J Sams, *The Diary of Joseph Sams* (1982), p21.

29. Ibid, p9.

30. Commission for the Investigation of Mediterranean Fever, *Reports of the Commission appointed by the Admiralty, the War Office, and the Civil Government of Malta, for the Investigation of Mediterranean Fever* (1907), part vi, pp70–3.

31. R L Stevenson, *The Amateur Emigrant* (1902), p2.

32. E W Howe, *Travel letters from New Zealand, Australia and Africa* (1913), p445.

33. M A M D Poynter, *Around the Shores of Asia* (1921), p36.

34. Cited in C Deakes and T Stanley, *A Century of Sea Travel* (2010), p87.

35. J Sams, *The Diary of Joseph Sams* (1982), p43.

36. B Hays, *Hull Down* (1927), pp147–50.

37. M Compton, *A Journal of a Honeymoon Voyage on the SS Great Britain* (1992), p23.

38. R L Stevenson, *The Amateur Emigrant* (1902), p28.

39. R A Fletcher, *Travelling Palaces* (1913), p164.

40. T Rosati, *Assistenza Sanitaria degli Emigranti e dei Marinai* (1908),

p72.

41. E A Steiner, *On the Trail of the Immigrant*, (1906), pp40–1.

42. *The Sphere*, 4 May 1912.

43. 97.22 per cent of women in first class survived, 86.02 per cent in second class, but only 46.06 per cent of women and 34.18 per cent of children in third class. W Hall, 'Social Class and Survival on the SS *Titanic*', *Social Science and Medicine*, 22/6 (1986), 687–90.

44. L Beesley, *The Loss of the Titanic* (1912), p14.

45. RMS *Titanic*, 93/0269.

46. RMS *Titanic*, 93/0195.2/2.

47. RMS *Titanic*, 93/0329.01b/14.

48. RMS *Titanic*, 93/0290B.

49. RMS *Titanic*, 93/0298A,B.

50. RMS *Titanic*, 93/0329.01c/14.

51. RMS *Titanic*, 00/0404.

52. J B Geller, *Titanic: Women and Children First* (1998), p51.

53. D A Butler, *Unsinkable* (1998), p201.

54. *Nova Scotia Evening Mail*, 30 April 1912.

55. *The Times*, 30 May 1912.

56. J P Eaton and C A Haas, *Titanic: Triumph and Tragedy* (1994), pp179–80.

57. United States Immigration Committee, *Reports of the Immigration Committee* (1911), p33.

58. Cited in C Deakes and T Stanley, *A Century of Sea Travel* (2010), p47.

59. P Knaplund, *Moorings Old and New* (1963), p261.

60. Minutes of Wannsee Conference, 20 January 1942, R Stackelberg and S A Winkle (ed), *The Nazi Germany Sourcebook* (2002), p347.

61. F R Nicosia and D Scrase (ed), *Jewish Life in Nazi Germany*, (2010), pp211–14.

62. H J Sternberg and J E Shelledy, *We were Merchants* (2009,) pp22–5.

63. G Thomas and M Morgan-Witts, *Voyage of the Damned* (2009), p101.

64. Ibid, p138.

65. M S Balestracci, *Arandora Star, Dall' Oblivion alla Memoria* (2008), pp34–5, 216–9.

66. P L Pelosi and D Evans (ed),

Arandora Star Fund in Wales booklet (2010), p30.

67. M S Balestracci, *Arandora Star, Dall' Oblivion alla Memoria* (2008), pp340–2.

68. Ibid, pp182–5, 176–7.

69. TNA, CAB 66/13/12, *Arandora Star* Enquiry, 14 October 1940.

70. P and L Gillman, *Collar the Lot!* (1980), pp215–16.

71. Ibid, pp244–9.

CHAPTER 6

1. J Lind, *An Essay on Diseases Incidental to Europeans in Hot Climates* (1808), p8.

2. J Hunter, *Observations on Diseases of the Army in Jamaica and on the Best Means of Preserving the Health of Europeans in that Climate* (1788), p24.

3. A M Falconbridge, *A Narrative of Two Voyages to the River Sierra Leone* (1794), pp65–6.

4. TNA, T 1/643/487, sailing lists, 1787.

5. J Clarkson, *Clarkson's Mission to Africa* (1971), p167.

6. A M Falconbridge, *A Narrative of Two Voyages to the River Sierra Leone* (1794), p139.

7. J Clarkson, *Clarkson's Mission to Africa* (1971), p162.

8. Ibid, p166.

9. Ibid, p168.

10. BL, Add MS 41262A, letter from J Clarkson to H Thornton, 4 April 1793.

11. A M Falconbridge, *A Narrative of Two Voyages to the River Sierra Leone* (1794), p125.

12. See also A Falconbridge, *An Account of the Slave Trade on the Coast of Africa* (1788).

13. American Colonization Society, *Address of the Board of Managers of the American Colonization Society, to the Auxiliary Societies and People of the United States* (1820), pp11, 13; G S Stockwell, *The Republic of Liberia: its Geography, Climate, Soil and Productions* (1868), pp57–8.

14. TNA, CO 111/250, 'Africans Brought by Her Majesty's Steam

Ship *Growler*', 11 January 1848.

15. I M Crumpson, 'A Survey of Indian Immigration to British Tropical Colonies to 1910', *Population Studies*, 10 (1956), 158–65.

16. British and Foreign Anti-Slavery Society, *Emigration from India* (1842), p7.

17. Ibid, p33.

18. House of Commons Papers, 1841, vol 16, p60.

19. British and Foreign Anti-Slavery Society, *Emigration from India* (1842), p33.

20. House of Commons Papers, 1841, vol 16, p60.

21. Ibid, p31.

22. TNA, CO 384/107, register of emigrants waiting to board *Golden Fleece*, *British Empire*, *Essex*, *Brechin Castle* and *St James* at Trinidad Depot, 1874.

23. TNA, CO 318/218, Report on Mortality of Emigrant Coolies on the Voyage to the West Indies, 1856–7.

24. TNA, CO 318/261, Report on Mortality among Indian Emigrants Shipped from Calcutta to British Guiana, 15 March 1879.

25. TNA, CO 318/218, Report on Mortality of Emigrant Coolies on the Voyage to the West Indies, 1856–7.

26. H Tinker, *A New System of Slavery* (1974), p141.

27. TNA, CO 295/387, Report of W H Combes, Protector of Migrants, Port-au-Spain, 7 January 1897.

28. TNA, FO 17/873, letter from Mayers to Alcock, 1 November 1866.

29. Ibid, FO 97/101, Chinese Passengers Act, 1855.

30. Ibid, FO 17/877, Foreign Office to Governor of Hong Kong, 14 December 1869.

31. A J Meagher, *The Coolie Trade* (2008), pp105–6.

32. A crimp was originally someone, often a lodging-house master, who coerced, intimidated or tricked sailors into signing on for service on a ship, but the term came to be applied to agents who coerced or kidnapped men to become indentured labourers. The practice was also known as blackbirding or shanghaiing.

33. TNA, FO 881/894, letter from Alcock to Bowring, 12 April 1859.

34. Ibid, FO 97/102A, letter from John Bowring to Lord Clarendon, 27 June 1856.

35. Ibid, FO 97/1023, letter from C A Winchester to J Bowring, 22 July 1855.

36. Ibid, FO 17/882, letter from Robertson to Wade, 23 April 1873.

37. Ibid, FO 881/2445, proclamation against kidnapping, 6 August 1873.

38. TNA, FO 97/102B, letter from Parkes to Hammond, 21 May 1860.

39. R Khan, *Autobiography of an Indian Indentured Labourer* (2005), p83.

40. 'Indian Emigration', *Chambers Journal*, 43 (1866), 395.

41. TNA, CO 318/218, Report on Mortality of Emigrant Coolies on the Voyage to the West Indies, 1856–7.

42. TNA, CO 295/387, Report of W H Combes, Protector of Migrants, Port-au-Spain, 7 January 1897.

43. TNA, CO 318/218, Report on Mortality of Emigrant Coolies on the Voyage to the West Indies, 1856–7.

44. TNA, CO 318/220, letter from J W Murdoch to Herman Merrivale, 22 July 1858.

45. 'Indian Emigration', *Chambers Journal*, 43 (1866), 395–6.

46. TNA, CO 318/165, tender for the conveyance of Indian emigrants to the West Indies, 1845.

47. Captain and Mrs Swinton, *Journal of a Voyage with Coolie Emigrants from Calcutta to Trinidad* (1859), p16.

48. J Conrad, *Typhoon* (2003), p23.

49. D Aldus, *Coolie Traffic and Kidnapping* (1876), p31.

50. A J Meagher, *The Coolie Trade* (2008), p155.

51. TNA, FO 97/101, letter from John Bowring to Lord Clarendon, 15 November 1855.

52. D Aldus, *Coolie Traffic and*

Kidnapping (1876), p36.

53. TNA, CO 318/218, Report on Mortality of Emigrant Coolies on the Voyage to the West Indies, 1856–7.

54. TNA, CO 318/220, letter from J W Murdoch to H Merrivale, 11 August 1858.

55. Captain and Mrs Swinton, *Journal of a Voyage with Coolie Emigrants from Calcutta to Trinidad* (1859), p13.

56. TNA, CO 318/165, Dietary Scale for Emigrants from India to the West Indies, 1845.

57. TNA, CO 318/218, Report on Mortality of Emigrant Coolies on the Voyage to the West Indies, 1856–7.

58. TNA, CO 295/387, Report of W H Combes, Protector of Migrants, Port-au-Spain, 7 January 1897.

59. TNA, FO 881/744, Report to Emigration Commissioners, 10 December 1853.

60. D Aldus, *Coolie Traffic and Kidnapping* (1876), p325.

61. Ibid, p46.

62. W Speer, *The Oldest and the Newest Empire* (1870), p483.

63. G W Cooke, *China and Lower Bengal* (1861), p67.

64. A J Meagher, *The Coolie Trade* (2008), pp176–7.

65. E Holden, 'A Chapter on the Coolie Trade', *Harper's New Monthly Magazine*, 29/169 (June 1864), 7.

66. D Aldus, *Coolie Traffic and Kidnapping* (1876), pp51–2.

67. Captain and Mrs Swinton, *Journal of a Voyage with Coolie Emigrants from Calcutta to Trinidad* (1859), p14.

68. E Holden, 'A Chapter on the Coolie Trade', *Harper's New Monthly Magazine*, 29/169 (June 1864), 5.

69. D Aldus, *Coolie Traffic and Kidnapping* (1876), p156.

70. TNA, CO 318/218, Report on Mortality of Emigrant Coolies on the Voyage to the West Indies, 1856–7.

71. Ibid.

72. Captain and Mrs Swinton, *Journal of a Voyage with Coolie Emigrants from Calcutta to Trinidad* (1859), p14.

73. TNA, CO 318/165, tender for the conveyance of Indian emigrants to the West Indies, 1845.

74. Captain and Mrs Swinton, *Journal of a Voyage with Coolie Emigrants from Calcutta to Trinidad* (1859), p3.

75. Ibid, p4.

76. Ibid, p15.

77. TNA, FO 97/102B, Testimony of Doctor on the Norwegian ship *Norma*, 1860.

78. TNA, CO 318/218, Report on Mortality of Emigrant Coolies on the Voyage to the West Indies, 1856–7.

79. TNA, CO 318/165, tender for the conveyance of Indian emigrants to the West Indies, 1845.

80. Captain and Mrs Swinton, *Journal of a Voyage with Coolie Emigrants from Calcutta to Trinidad* (1859), p12.

81. TNA, CO 101/117/28, dispatch from Lieutenant Governor Cartwright to the Governor of Barbados, 1 June 1861.

82. TNA, CO 318/261, Report on Mortality among Indian Emigrants Shipped from Calcutta to British Guiana, statement of Robert Sinclair, 15 March 1879.

83. Ibid, Lieutenant Governor's Comments, 15 March 1879.

84. TNA, CO 318/218, Report on Mortality of Emigrant Coolies on the Voyage to the West Indies, 1856–7.

85. Ibid.

86. Captain and Mrs Swinton, *Journal of a Voyage with Coolie Emigrants from Calcutta to Trinidad* (1859), p13.

87. D Aldus, *Coolie Traffic and Kidnapping* (1876), p218.

88. TNA, CO 318/220, letter from J W Murdoch, Emigration Office, to Herman Merivale, 22 July 1858.

89. Ibid, letter from J W Murdoch to H Merivale, 11 August 1858.

90. H Polak, *The Indians of South Africa* (1909), p90.

91. Proceedings of a Conference between the Secretary of State for the Colonies and the Premiers of

the Self Governing Colonies, June
and July 1897, C 8596, 1897, p12.
92. D Northrup, *Indentured Labour in
the Age of Imperialism, 1834–
1922* (1995), p145.

CHAPTER 7

1. *Illustrated London News*,
2 September 1848.
2. *United Service Gazette*, 26 August
1848.
3. *Illustrated London News*,
2 September 1848.
4. *United Service Gazette*, 26 August
1848.
5. *Illustrated London News*,
2 September 1848.
6. *New York Herald*, 28 September
1858.
7. *The Times*, 11 October 1858.
8. Ibid, 15 October 1858.
9. *Illustrated London News*,
9 January 1875.
10. *The Times*, 1 January 1875.
11. Ibid, 2 January 1875.
12. Ibid, 4 January 1875.
13. *Illustrated London News*, 8 May
1847.
14. Ibid, 10 March 1849.
15. M A Jones, *Destination America*
(1976), pp34–5.
16. *The Times*, 22 April 1854, 13 May
1854.
17. *The Times*, 29 March 1876.
18. TNA, HO 45/1623, letter from
Lord Aberdeen to Sir Hamilton
Seymour, 27 March 1846.
19. Ibid, letter from J Colquhoun to G
S Syme, 23 March 1846.
20. Ibid, note on *Helen Marie*, 1828.
21. S Smith, *The Settler's New Home*
(1850), p39.
22. J R McCulloch, *A Dictionary,
Practical, Theoretical and
Historical, of Commerce and
Commercial Navigation* (1839),
p92.
23. Report on the Wreck of the
Emigrant Ship *Annie Jane* and
Alleged Grievances of the
Emigrant Passengers on Board, PP,
1854 (296), LX.
24. F R Nixon, *The Cruise of the
Beacon* (1857), pp91–2.
25. *The Times*, 15 May 1841.
26. Chief Justice of the United States

Circuit Court for the Eastern
District of Pennsylvania, *Trial of
Alexander William Holmes, One
of the Crew of the Ship William
Brown, for Manslaughter on the
High Seas* (1842), p16.
27. *The Times*, 20 May 1841.
28. *New York Herald*, 8 April 1873.
29. *The Times*, 3 April 1873.
30. Ibid, 18 May 1855.
31. *The Times*, 24 January 1873.
32. *New York Times*, 18 June 1895.
33. *The Times*, 27 March 1891.
34. *Gibraltar Chronicle*, 20 March
1891.
35. Gibraltar Archives, Enquiry
papers, Inquest, SS *Utopia*,
information of James Thompson,
First Officer, 21 March 1891.
36. *Gibraltar Chronicle*, 18 March
1891.
37. Gibraltar Archives, letter from
Lothian Nicholson, Governor, to
the President of the Board of
Trade, 16 April 1891.
38. Gibraltar Archives, Enquiry
papers, Inquest, SS *Utopia*,
information of William Colburn,
21 March 1891.
39. Gibraltar Archives, 'The Wreck of
Anchor Line SS *Utopia*', 28 March
1891.
40. *Gibraltar Chronicle*, 18 March
1891.
41. Ibid, 21 March 1891.
42. Ibid, 17 April 1891.
43. Ibid, 14 April 1891.
44. Ibid, 28 July 1891.
45. Ibid, 28 March 1891.
46. Gibraltar Archives, Enquiry
papers, Inquest, SS *Utopia*,
statement of Alexander Sellar,
18 March 1891.
47. Ibid, statement of John Adam,
18 March 1891.
48. *New York Times*, 19 March 1891.
49. Ibid, 6 August 1906.
50. *American Marine Engineer*, 1/9
(September 1906), 13.
51. *New York Times*, 8 August 1906.
52. Ibid, 9 August 1906.
53. Ibid, 7 August 1906.
54. Ibid, 22 April 1907.
55. *The Times*, 6 August 1906.
56. Ibid, 14 November 1854.
57. Ibid, 18 May 1855
58. Merchant Shipping Act, 17 & 18

Victoria, c. 104, 10 August 1854.

59. Hansard, *Parliamentary Debates*,
CC, 21 March 1870, col 324.

60. *Journal of the Society of Arts*,
12 August 1887.

61. Merchant Shipping Act, 60 & 61
Victoria, c. 59, 1897.

62. United States Senate, *Hearing
Before a Subcommittee of the
Committee on Commerce, United
States Senate: Sixty-second
Congress, Second Session,
Pursuant to S Res 283, Directing
the Committee on Commerce to
Investigate the Causes Leading to
the Wreck of the White Star Liner
'Titanic'* (1912), p28.

63. Report of a formal investigation
into the circumstances attending
the foundering on 15th April,
1912, of the British steamship
Titanic, Cd 3352, 1912, Q 22961.

64. L Marshall-Green, *Sinking of the
Titanic and Great Sea Disasters as
Told by First Hand Account of
Survivors and Initial Investigations*
(1912), p212.

65. Report of a formal investigation
into the circumstances attending
the foundering on 15th April,
1912, of the British steamship
Titanic, Cd 3352, 1912, Q 4421.

66. Ibid, Q 2960.

67. United States Senate, *Hearing
Before a Subcommittee of the
Committee on Commerce, United
States Senate: Sixty-second
Congress, Second Session,
Pursuant to S Res 283, Directing
the Committee on Commerce to
Investigate the Causes Leading to
the Wreck of the White Star Liner
'Titanic'* (1912), p1148.

68. Report of a formal investigation
into the circumstances attending
the foundering on 15th April,
1912, of the British steamship
Titanic, Cd 3352, 1912, Q 13872.

69. Ibid, Q 14004.

70. Ibid, Q 14007.

71. United States Senate, *Hearing
Before a Subcommittee of the
Committee on Commerce, United
States Senate: Sixty-second
Congress, Second Session,
Pursuant to S Res 283, Directing
the Committee on Commerce to
Investigate the Causes Leading to
the Wreck of the White Star Liner
'Titanic'* (1912), p79.

72. Report of a formal investigation
into the circumstances attending
the foundering on 15th April,
1912, of the British steamship
Titanic, Cd 3352, 1912, Q 9926.

73. Ibid, Q 9887.

74. Ibid, Q 9925.

75. Ibid, Q 10076.

76. B S Frey, D A Savage and B
Torgler, 'Interaction of Natural
Survival Instincts and Internalized
Social Norms: Exploring the
Titanic and Lusitania Disasters',
*Proceedings of the National
Academy of Sciences of the United
States of America* (2010), 1091–
6490.

77. *Denver Post*, 16 April 1912.

78. *Morning Post*, 22 December 1863.

79. R Davenport Hines, *Titanic Lives*
(2012), p290.

80. United States Senate, *Hearing
Before a Subcommittee of the
Committee on Commerce, United
States Senate: Sixty-second
Congress, Second Session,
Pursuant to S Res 283, Directing
the Committee on Commerce to
Investigate the Causes Leading to
the Wreck of the White Star Liner
'Titanic'* (1912), p140.

81. S H Allen, *International Relations*
(1920), p201.

82. M A Jones, *Destination America*
(1976), p35.

CHAPTER 8

1. E Abbott, *Immigration: Select
Documents and Case Records*
(1924), p28.

2. W Smith, *An Emigrant's Narrative*
(1850), p14.

3. Ibid, p17.

4. Ibid, p6.

5. Ibid, pp18–19.

6. Ibid, p20.

7. United States Senate, *Report of the
Select Committee of the United
States Senate on the Sickness and
Mortality On Board Emigrant
Ships* (1854), p4.

8. A P Wilson Philip, *A Treatise on
Fevers* (1820), p165.

9. TNA, ADM 101/77/7, Journal of Hired Ship *James Pattison*, G Roberts, Superintendent Surgeon, 25 October 1839–11 February 1840.

10. K F Kiple, *The Cambridge Historical Dictionary of Disease* (2003), pp352–3.

11. Papers relative to Emigration, PP 1847–8, XLVII (932), p5.

12. R Whyte, *The Ocean Plague* (1848), p45.

13. M Staniforth, 'Diet, Disease and Death at Sea on the Voyage to Australia 1837–1839', *International Journal of Maritime History*, 8/2 (1996), 119–56.

14. TNA, CO 201/269, f51, Report of the Board of Enquiry in to the case of the Emigrant Ship *Lady McNaghten*, 7 July 1837.

15. Ibid, ff51.

16. Ibid, ff37–8; *Sydney Herald*, 14 August 1837.

17. *Melbourne Argus*, 5 November 1852.

18. Ibid, 28 December 1852.

19. Ibid, 31 December 1852.

20. Correspondence Relating to Emigration, New South Wales, PP 1854, XLVI (52), p436.

21. TNA, MT 9/231, Report of the Commission Appointed by the Governor of New Zealand to Enquire into the Case of the Emigrant Ship *Oxford*, 29 August 1883.

22. R Haines, R Shlomowitz and L Brennan, 'Maritime Mortality Revisited', *International Journal of Maritime History*, 8 (1996), 113–24.

23. Papers relative to Emigration, PP 1847–8, XLVII (932), p5.

24. R Whyte, *The Ocean Plague* (1848), p15.

25. TNA, HO 45/1920 report on typhus fever in emigrant ships, 28 April 1847.

26. W Smith, *An Emigrant's Narrative, or A Voice from the Steerage* (1850), pp15–16.

27. R Whyte, *The Ocean Plague* (1848), p51.

28. E Abbott, *Immigration: Select Documents and Case Records* (1924), p43.

29. J F Maguire, *The Irish in America* (1868), p181.

30. K F Kiple, *The Cambridge Historical Dictionary of Disease* (2003), pp76–7.

31. *Liverpool Mercury*, 15 June 1832.

32. *The Times*, 15 June 1832.

33. K F Kiple, *The Cambridge Historical Dictionary of Disease* (2003), pp74–5.

34. United States Senate, *Report of the Select Committee of the United States Senate on the Sickness and Mortality On Board Emigrant Ships* (1854), pp5–6.

35. K F Kiple, *The Cambridge Historical Dictionary of Disease* (2003), p78.

36. ' Ol Ricini 1 oz, ol, cinnamon 6 gutt, tinc Opii 25 gutt. In a wine glassful of brandy'.

37. TNA, HO 45/5428, cure for cholera, 1854.

38. Ibid, 'The Cause and Cure of Asiatic or Malignant Cholera', by John Adamson, 1851.

39. T S Wells, *The Scale of Medicines with which Merchant Vessels are to be Furnished* (1851).

40. TNA, MT 9/309, Dr Tanner, MP for Mid-Cork, quoted in *The Times*, 13 May 1889.

41. TNA, MT 9/316, 'Hospitals on board Ships', 1888.

42. Report by Dr F H Blaxall on the Sanitary Aspects of Emigration and Immigration from and into the United Kingdom, 1883, C.3778, p160.

43. TNA, MT 9/333, letter from Union Line, 15 June 1888.

44. TNA, CO 318/220, letter from J W Murdoch to Herman Merrivale, 22 July 1858.

45. *The Lancet*, 2 (1853), 473.

46. Hansard, *HC Deb* 27 July 1866, vol 184, cc1620.

47. *New York Times*, 4 November 1865.

48. Hansard, *HC Deb* 27 July 1866, vol 184, cc1620.

49. *Queensland Parliamentary Papers, Votes and Proceedings*, 3 (1886), 781.

50. *Harpers Weekly Journal of Civilization*, 17 September 1892.

51. W Smith, *An Emigrant's*

Narrative, or A Voice from the Steerage (1850), p24.

52. Ibid, p25.
53. Ibid, p27.
54. J F Maguire, *The Irish in America* (1868), p145.
55. T Stratton, 'Medical Remarks on Emigrant Ships to North America', *Edinburgh Medical and Surgical Journal*, 73 (1849), 37.
56. R Whyte, *The Ocean Plague* (1848), p87.
57. J F Maguire, *The Irish in America* (1868), p136.
58. Ibid, p77.
59. Ibid, p83.
60. Ibid, p81.
61. Ibid, pp91–2.
62. Ibid, p100.
63. C O Gagnon, *Mandements, Lettres Pastorales et Circulaires des Évêques de Québec* (1888), p512.
64. *Boston Pilot*, 4 December 1847.
65. C O Gagnon, *Mandements, Lettres Pastorales et Circulaires des Évêques de Québec* (1888), p511.
66. United States Public Health Service, *Annual Report of the Surgeon General of the Public Health Service of the United States* (1895), p78. See also C Chartré, *La Désinfection dans le Système Quarantenaire Maritime de Grosse-Île 1832–1937* (1995).
67. Australia Parliament Joint Library Committee, *Historical Records of Australia: Governors Dispatches to and from England* (1922), vol 14, p347.
68. *Queensland Government Gazette*, 7 (1862), 375.
69. F S MacLean, *Challenge for Health* (1964), p224.
70. TNA, HO 45/4766, letter from John Francis Maguire to Sir John Young, Chief Secretary for Ireland, 7 July 1853.
71. Ibid, letter to Lord Palmerston from the Chairman of Queenstown Committee of Health, 6 November 1853.
72. Ibid, letter from J F Maguire to Sir J Young, 7 July 1853.
73. Ibid, letter from James Wilson to H Waddington, 21 July 1853.
74. J Simon, *Eighth Report to the Privy Council (1865) in Privy*

Council, *Reports of the Medical Officer of the Privy Council and Local Government Board* (1875), p55.
75. TNA, MT 9/436, sanitary regulations, 1892; W M Frazer, *History of English Public Health 1834–1939* (1950), pp212–14.
76. G Mittelberger, *Journey to Pennsylvania* (1898), p25.

CHAPTER 9

1. C Dickens, *Martin Chuzzlewit* (1907), pp245–6.
2. 'A Steerage Emigrant's Journal from Bristol to New York', *Chamber's Edinburgh Journal*, 251 (21 October 1848), 265.
3. Letter of Gio Batta Mizzan, 17 March 1878, in E Franzina (ed), *Merika! Merika! Emigrazionee Colonizzazione nel Lettere dei Contadini Veneti e Friulani in America Latina 1870–1902* (1984), p81.
4. 'A Steerage Emigrant's Journal from Bristol to New York', *Chamber's Edinburgh Journal*, 251 (21 October 1848), 266.
5. C A Mitchell, 'Events leading up to and the Establishment of Grosse Île Quarantine Station', *Medical Services Journal Canada*, 23/11 (1967), 1436.
6. A Gifford (ed), *Towards Quebec: Two Mid-Nineteenth Century Emigrants' Journals* (1981), p34.
7. Ibid, p59.
8. J Sams, *The Diary of Joseph Sams* (1982), p58.
9. J H Hillary, *Westland* (1979), p45.
10. Ibid, p48.
11. Ibid, p45.
12. United States Senate, *Report of the Select Committee of the United States Senate on the Sickness and Mortality On Board Emigrant Ships* (1854), p72.
13. New York Emigration Commissioners, *Annual Report of the Commissioners of Immigration, State of New York* (1848), p26.
14. Staten Island Executive Committee, *Facts and Documents bearing upon the Legal and Moral*

Questions connected with the Recent Destruction of the Quarantine Buildings on Staten Island (1858), pp47–8.

15. J Higham, *Strangers in the Land* (1988), pp52, 100.

16. J Jensen, 'Before the Surgeon General: Marine Hospitals in Mid-Nineteenth Century America', *Public Health Reports*, 112 (1997), 525–7.

17. J Parascandola, 'Doctors at the Gate: PHS at Ellis Island', *Public Health Reports*, 113 (1998), 83–4.

18. *New York Times*, 27 February 1874.

19. United States House of Representatives, *Testimony taken by the Select Committee of the House of Representatives to Inquire into the Alleged Violation of the Laws Prohibiting the Importation of Contract Laborers, Paupers, Convicts and Other Classes* (1888), p160.

20. M A Jones, *Destination America* (1976), p54.

21. S Graham, *With Poor Immigrants to America* (1914), pp41–2.

22. V J Cannato, *American Passage* (2009), p299.

23. Ibid, p42.

24. V Safford, *Immigration Problems: Personal Experiences of an Official* (1925), p249.

25. H Markel, 'The Eyes have It: Trachoma, the Perception of Disease, the United States Public Health Service and the American Jewish Immigration Experience, 1897–1924', *Bulletin of Medical History*, 74 (2000), 525–60.

26. A M Kraut, *Silent Travellers* (1994), pp383–4.

27. F J Haskin, *The Immigrant, An Asset and a Liability* (1913), p34.

28. E Abbott (ed), *Immigration: Select Documents and Case Records* (1924), pp313–19.

29. Ibid, p420.

30. Ibid, p383.

31. S Graham, *With Poor Immigrants to America* (1914), p44.

32. Pierina Gasperetti, cited in H Rössler, 'The Time Has Come, We are Going to America', in D Knauf and B Moreno (ed), *Leaving Home*

(2010), p101.

33. United States Industrial Commission, *Report of the Industrial Commission* (1901), p647.

34. F H La Guardia, *Making of an Insurgent* (1948), p66.

35. TNA, FO 372/2230, W McUllagh, Major RAMC, 'Ellis Island', November 1924.

36. G B Scalabrini, cited in A Nicosia and L Prencipe (ed), *Museo Nazionale Emigrazione Italiana* (2009), p418.

37. B Brandenburg, *Imported Americans* (1904), pp213–14.

38. P Knaplund, *Moorings Old and New* (1963), p148.

39. S F Martin, *A Nation of Immigrants* (2011), pp92–6.

40. E Lee and J Yung, *Angel Island* (2010), p11.

41. Ibid, p30.

42. T Rosati, *Assistenza Sanitaria degli Emigranti e dei Marinai* (1908), p154.

43. TNA, CO 318/270, *Birmingham Morning News*, 27 June 1873.

44. Ibid, Notice on British Emigrants to Paraguay, 21 January 1873.

45. A James, *The Australian Migrant's Companion* (1852), p19.

46. D MacKenzie, *Ten Years in Australia* (1851), p155.

47. S Butler, *The Hand-book for Australian Emigrants* (1839), p206.

48. A James, *The Australian Migrant's Companion* (1852), pp18–19.

49. H Roth, *Call it Sleep* (1934), p11.

50. M Antin, *The Promised Land* (1912), p165.

51. Letter of Francesco Costantin, 8 June 1889, in E Franzina (ed), *Merika! Merika! Emigrazione Colonizzazione nel Lettere dei Contadini Veneti e Friulani in America Latina 1870–1902* (1984), p174.

52. F Kapp, *Immigration and the Commissioners of Immigration of the State of New York* (1870), p61.

53. E Abbott (ed), *Immigration: Select Documents and Case Records* (1924), p27.

54. American Social Science Association, *Handbook for*

Immigrants to the United States
(1871), pp14–15, 64, 116.

55. E Abbott (ed), *Immigration: Select Documents and Case Records*
(1924), pp144-7.

56. M Wischnitzer, *To Dwell in Safety: The Story of Jewish Migration Since 1800* (1948), p300.

57. E Abbott (ed), *Immigration: Select Documents and Case Records*
(1924), pp319-32.

58. G B Scalabrini, *Scalabrini* (1987), p366.

59. G B Scalabrini, *For the Love of Immigrants* (2000), p125.

60. *New York Times*, 20 October 1912.

61. Ibid, 28 October 1912.

62. United States Immigration Committee, *Reports of the Immigration Committee* (1911), p167.

63. J Jupp, *Immigration* (1982), pp114–31

64. P Knaplund, *Moorings Old and New* (1963), p249.

Bibliography

Archive Sources

NATIONAL ARCHIVES, KEW

TNA, ADM, Admiralty
TNA, CO, Colonial Office
TNA, FO, Foreign Office
TNA, HO, Home Office
TNA, MH, Ministry of Health
TNA, MT, Board of Trade
TNA, T, Treasury

BRITISH LIBRARY, LONDON

BL, Add MS 41262 A, Papers of John Clarkson, 1791–2
BL, Add MS 47966, Journal of Arthur Bowes, 1787–9

GOVERNMENT OF GIBRALTAR ARCHIVES

Papers relating to the *Utopia*

SS *Great Britain* MUSEUM, BRISTOL

BRSGB 1997.003, Letter to family of William Wheatley, 24 April 1866
BRSGB1997.014, Diary of woman passenger, 1865
BRSGB 1997.020, Diary of Allan Gilmour, 1852

Parliamentary Papers

Report from Select Committee on Emigration from the United
    Kingdom, PP 1826, IV

Report on the Affairs of British North America from the Earl of
Durham, PP 1839, XVII

Reports from Committees: Colonization from Ireland, PP 1847, VI

Papers relative to Emigration, PP 1847–8, XLVII

Report from the Select Committee on Contract Packet Services, PP
1849, XII

A Copy of a Letter addressed to the Land and Emigration Commission,
PP 1851, XL

Report from the Select Committee on the Passengers' Act, 1851, PP
1851, XIX

Report on the Wreck of the Emigrant Ship *Annie Jane* and Alleged
Grievances of the Emigrant Passengers on Board, PP 1854, LX

Correspondence Relating to Emigration, New South Wales, PP 1854,
XLVI

First Report from the Select Committee on Packet and Telegraphic
Contracts, PP 1860, XIV

Report from the Select Committee on Mail Contracts, PP 1868–9, VI

General Report of the Emigration Commissioners, C.768, PP1873,
XVIII

Land and Emigration Commission, PP 1881, LXXXI

Report with regard to the Accommodation and Treatment of
Emigrants, PP 1881, LXXXII

Report by Dr F H Blaxall on the Sanitary Aspects of Emigration
and Immigration from and into the United Kingdom, C.3778,
1883

Papers relating to the Work of the Emigrants' Information Office,
C5078, PP1887, VI

Proceedings of a Conference between the Secretary of State for the
Colonies and the Premiers of the Self Governing Colonies, June
and July 1897, C 8596, 1897

Report of the Departmental Committee appointed to consider Mr
Rider Haggard's Report on Agricultural Settlements in the British
Colonies, Cd 2978, PP1906

Report of a formal investigation into the circumstances attending the
foundering on 15th April, 1912, of the British steamship *Titanic*
of Liverpool, after striking ice in or near latitude 410 46' N,
longitude 500 14' W, North Atlantic, Cd 3352, 1912

Dominions Royal Commission on the Natural Resources, Trade and Legislation of Certain Parts of His Majesty's Dominions, Cd 8458, PP 1917–18, VIII

Acts of Parliament

An Act for the Amendment and better Administration of the Laws relating to the Poor in England and Wales, 4 & 5 William IV, c. 76, 14 August 1834

An Act for the More Effectual Relief of the Destitute Poor in Ireland, 1 & 2 Victoria, c. 56, 31 July 1838

An Act to Amend the Acts for the More Effectual Relief of the Destitute Poor in Ireland, 12 & 13 Victoria, c. 104, 1 August 1849

Merchant Shipping Act, 17 & 18 Victoria, c. 104, 10 August 1854

Merchant Shipping Act, 60 & 61 Victoria, c. 59, 6 August 1897

Congressional Papers

Report of the Investigation into the Treatment and Condition of Steerage Passengers, Senate Document 23, 43 Congress 1 Session, 1874

Primary Printed Sources

Abbott, Edith (ed), *Immigration: Select Documents and Case Records*, Chicago, University of Chicago Press, 1924

Aldus, Don, *Coolie Traffic and Kidnapping*, London, McCorquodale, 1876

Alexander, James E (ed), *The Albatross: A Voyage from Victoria to England*, Stirling, Charles Rogers, 1863

Allen, Stephen Haley, *International Relations*, Princeton, Princeton University Press, 1920

Allmers, Hermann, *Marschenbuch: Land- und Volksbilder aus den Marschen der Weser und Elbe*, Gotha, Scheube Verlag, 1858

American Colonization Society, *Address of the Board of Managers of the American Colonization Society, to the Auxiliary Societies and People of the United States*, Washington, Davis and Force, 1820

American Social Science Association, *Handbook for Immigrants to the United States*, New York, Hurd and Houghton, 1871

Amos, Samuel, 'In The Steerage', *Harper's New Magazine*, 31 (1865), 295–8

Anon, 'A Steerage Emigrant's Journal from Bristol to New York', *Chamber's Edinburgh Journal*, 251 (21 October 1848), 264–6

Anon, 'Atlantic Drift: Gathering in the Steerage', *Catholic World*, 16 (1873), 648–58, 837–44

Antin, Mary, *From Plotzk to Boston*, Boston, W B Clarke, 1899

____, ____, *The Promised Land: The Autobiography of a Russian Immigrant*, Boston, Houghton Mifflin, 1912

Australia Parliament Joint Library Committee, *Historical Records of Australia: Governors Dispatches to and from England*, Canberra, Australia Parliament, 1922

Baedeker, Karl, *Austria–Hungary: with Excursions to Cetinje, Belgrade, and Bucharest: Handbook for Travellers*, Coblenz, K Baedeker, 1911

Barnardo, Syrie Louise Elmslie, and Marchant, James, *Memoirs of the Late Dr Barnardo*, London, Hodder and Stoughton, 1907

Batt, John Herridge, *Dr Barnardo: The Foster Father of Nobody's Children*, London, S W Partridge, 1907

Beesley, Lawrence, *The Loss of the Titanic: Its Story and Its Lessons*, New York, Houghton Mifflin, 1912

Bell, William, *Hints to Emigrants*, Edinburgh, Waugh and Innes, 1824

Bellows, Henry W, *The Old World in its New Face*, New York, Harper, 1870

Booth, W, *In Darkest England and the Way Out*, London, Salvation Army, 1890

Boy Scouts Association, *The Call of Empire*, London, Boy Scouts Association, 1939

Brandenburg, Broughton, *Imported Americans: The Story of the Experiences of a Disguised American and his Wife Studying the Immigration Question*, New York, Frederick A Stokes, 1904

British and Foreign Anti-Slavery Society, *Emigration from India: The Export of Coolies and Other Labourers to Mauritius*, London, Thomas Ward, 1842

Butler, Samuel, *The Hand-book for Australian Emigrants: being a Descriptive History of Australia, and Containing an Account of the Climate, Soil and Natural Productions of New South Wales,*

South Australia, and Swan River Settlement, Glasgow, W R M'Phun, 1839

Byrne, J C, *Emigrants' Guide to New South Wales Proper*, London, Effingham Wilson, 1848

Carpi, Leone, *Delle Colonie e dell' Emigrazione d' Italiani all'Estero sotto l'Aspetto dell' Industria, Commercio, Agricoltura e con Trattazione d'Importanti Questioni Sociali*, Milan, D Salvi, 1874

Chief Justice of the United States Circuit Court for the Eastern District of Pennsylvania, *Trial of Alexander William Holmes, One of the Crew of the Ship William Brown, for Manslaughter on the High Seas*, Philadelphia, Circuit Court for the Eastern District of Pennsylvania, 1842

Clarkson, John, *Clarkson's Mission to Africa 1791–1792*, ed Charles Bruce Fergusson, Halifax, Public Archives of Novia Scotia, 1971

Collins, Wilkie, *The New Magdalen*, White Fish, Massachusetts, Kessinger, 2004

Commission for the Investigation of Mediterranean Fever, *Reports of the Commission appointed by the Admiralty, the War Office, and the Civil Government of Malta, for the Investigation of Mediterranean Fever*, London, Royal Society, 1905–7

Compton, Mary, *A Journal of a Honeymoon Voyage on the SS Great Britain*, Bristol, SS *Great Britain* Trust, 1992

Conrad, Joseph, *Typhoon and Other Stories*, Oxford, Oxford University Press, 2003

Cooke, G W, *China and Lower Bengal: being the Times Correspondent in the Years 1857–58*, London, Routledge, Warne and Routledge, 1861

Dickens, Charles, *David Copperfield*, London, Dent, 1907

———, ———, *Martin Chuzzlewit*, London, Dent, 1907

———, ———, *American Notes and Pictures from Italy*, London, Dent, 1908

———, ———, *Little Dorrit*, London, Dent, 1908

———, ———, 'Home for Homeless Women', *Household Words*, 1/33 (23 April 1853), 169–75

Duden, Gottfried, *Bericht über eine Reise nach den westlichen Staten Nordamerika's*, Elberfeld, E Weber, 1829

Emerson, Ralph Waldo, *Emerson in his Journals*, Cambridge, Mass,

Harvard University Press, 1982

Falconbridge, Alexander, *An Account of the Slave Trade on the Coast of Africa*, London, J Phillips, 1788

Falconbridge, Anna Maria, *A Narrative of Two Voyages to the River Sierra Leone*, privately published, 1794

Fletcher, R A, *Travelling Palaces*, London, Isaac Pitman, 1913

Forster, Stephen Vere, *Work and Wages, or the Penny Emigrant's Guide to the United States and Canada, for Female Servants, Labourers, Mechanics, Farmers &*, London, W and F G Cash, 1855

Franzina, E (ed), *Merika! Merika! Emigrazionee Colonizzazione nel Lettere dei Contadini Veneti e Friulani in America Latina 1870–1902*, Verona, Cierre Edizione, 1984

Gagnon, Charles Octave, *Mandements, Lettres Pastorales et Circulaires des Évêques de Québec*, Quebec, A Coté, 1888

Gaskell, Elizabeth, *Mary Barton: A Tale of Manchester Life*, London, Chapman and Hall, 1850

Gifford, Ann (ed), *Towards Quebec: Two Mid-Nineteenth Century Emigrants' Journals*, London, HMSO, 1981

Graham, Stephen, *With Poor Immigrants to America*, London, Nelson, 1914

Hale, Edward Everett, *Letters on Irish Emigration*, Boston, Phillips, Sampson, 1852

Hancock, William, *An Emigrant's Five Years in the Free States of America*, London, T Cautley Newby, 1860

Harcus, William, *Handbook for Emigrants Proceeding to South Australia*, London, G Street, 1873

Haskin, Frederick Jennings, *The Immigrant: An Asset and a Liability*, New York, Fleming H Revell, 1913

Hays, Bertram, *Hull Down*, London, Cassell, 1927

HMSO, *Instructions for Surgeon Superintendents on Government Emigrant Ships*, London, Eyre and Spottiswoode, 1866

Hillary, John Haddon, *Westland, the Journal of John Hillary, Emigrant to New Zealand*, London, Janus Publishing, 1995

Holden, E, 'A Chapter on the Coolie Trade', *Harper's New Monthly Magazine*, 29/169 (June 1864), 1–11.

Hood, John, *Australia and the East*, London, John Murray, 1843

House of Lords, *Papers Relative to Emigration to the British Provinces in North America*, London, William Clowes, 1848

Howe, Edgar Watson, *Travel Letters from New Zealand, Australia and Africa*, New York, Crane and Co, 1913

Hunter, John, *Observations on Diseases of the Army in Jamaica and on the Best Means of Preserving the Health of Europeans in that Climate*, London, G Nicol, 1788

Huskisson, William, *The Speeches of the Right Honourable William Huskisson*, London, John Murray, 1831

International Labour Office, *Emigration and Immigration Legislation and Treaties*, Geneva, International Labour Office, 1922

James, Anne, *The Australian Migrant's Companion Containing Practical Advice to Intending Emigrants Especially to Those of the Working Class*, London, H Green, 1852

Kapp, Friedrich, *Immigration and the Commissioners of Immigration of the State of New York*, New York, Nation Press, 1870

Khan, Rahman, *Autobiography of an Indian Indentured Labourer*, Delhi, Shipra Publications, 2005

Knaplund, Paul, *Moorings Old and New: Entries in an Immigrant's Log*, Madison, State Historical Society of Wisconsin, 1963

La Guardia, Fiorello H, *The Making of an Insurgent: An Autobiography 1882–1919*, Philadelphia and New York, J B Lippincott, 1948

Lind, James, *An Essay on Diseases Incidental to Europeans in Hot Climates with the Method of Preventing their Consequences*, London, J and J Richardson, 1808

Löffler, A, *Der Entwurf eines Gesetzes betrefend die Auswanderung*, Vienna, Ein Kritik, 1913

McCulloch, John Ramsay, *A Dictionary, Practical, Theoretical and Historical, of Commerce and Commercial Navigation*, London, Longman, Orme, Brown, Green and Longmans, 1839

MacKenzie, David, *Ten Years in Australia*, London, William S Orr, 1851

Maguire, John Francis, *The Irish in America*, London, Longmans, Green, 1868

Marryat, Frederick, *A Diary in America with Remarks on its Institutions*, London, Longman, Orme, Brown, Green and Longmans, 1839

Marshall-Green, Logan, *Sinking of the Titanic and Great Sea Disasters as Told by First Hand Account of Survivors and Initial Investigations*, New York, L T Myers, 1912

Martineau, Harriet, *Retrospect of Western Travel*, London, Saunders and Otley, 1838

Maxtone-Graham, John, *The Only Way to Cross*, London, MacMillan, 1972

Mittelberger, Gottlieb, *Journey to Pennsylvania in the Year 1750 and Return to Germany in the Year 1754*, tr Carl T Eben, Philadelphia, J J McVey, 1898

Morford, Henry, *Over-Sea: England, France and Scotland as Seen by a Live American*, New York, Hilton, 1867

Morris, William, *Letters sent Home: Out and Home Again by Way of Canada and the United States, or, What a Summer's Trip Told me of the People and the Country of the Great West*, London, F Warne, 1875

New York Emigration Commissioners, *Annual Report of the Commissioners of Immigration, State of New York*, New York, New York Emigration Commissioners, 1848

——, ——, ——, ——, *Annual Report of the Commissioners of Immigration, State of New York*, New York, New York Emigration Commissioners, 1868

Nixon, Francis R, *The Cruise of the Beacon, A Narrative of a Visit to the Islands in Bass Strait*, London, Bell and Daldry, 1857

Norbert, Jacques, *Mit Lust gelebt: Roman meines Lebens kommentierte, illustrierte und wesentlich erweiterte Neuausgabe*, St Ingberg, Röhrig Universitätsverlag, 2004

Philip, Robert Kemp, *The Dictionary of Medical and Surgical Knowledge and Complete Practical Guide in Health and Disease for Families, Emigrants and Colonists*, London, Houlston and Wright, 1864

Pocock, John, *Travels of a London Schoolboy 1826–1830: John Pocock's Diary of Life in London and Voyages to Cape Town and the Swan River Settlement*, ed Tom Pocock, London, Historical Publications, 1996

Polak, Henry, *The Indians of South Africa: Helots Within the Empire and How They are Treated*, Madras, G A Natesan, 1909

Power, Tyrone, *Impressions of America*, London, Richard Bentley, 1836

Poynter, Mary Augusta Mason Dickinson, *Around the Shores of Asia: a Diary of Travel from the Golden Horn to the Golden Gate*, London, Allen and Unwin, 1921

Prausnitz, W, *Parere del Professore Prausnitz sulle Condizione Igieniche di Trieste in nesso all' Epidemia di Tifo*, Graz, 1913

Privy Council, *Reports of the Medical Officer of the Privy Council and Local Government Board, Issues 5–8*, London, HMSO, 1875

Rosati, Teodorico, *Assistenza Sanitaria degli Emigranti e dei Marinai*, Milan, Vallardi, 1908

Roth, Henry, *Call it Sleep*, New York, Ballou, 1934

Rynning, Ole, *True Account of America for the Information and Help of Peasant and Commoner*, tr T C Blegen, St Paul, Minnesota Historical Society, 1917

Safford, Victor, *Immigration Problems, Personal Experiences of an Official*, New York, Dodd, Mead, 1925

Salvation Army, *Empire Migration and Settlement*, London, Salvation Army, 1937

Sams, Joseph, *The Diary of Joseph Sams*, London, HMSO, 1982

Sanitary Committee of *The Lancet*, *A Report on Emigrant Ships by the Sanitary Commission of The Lancet*, London, *The Lancet*, 1873

Scalabrini, Giovanni Battista, *Scalabrini, A Living Voice: Excerpts from his Writings*, Oak Park, Illinois Scalabrinian Congregations, 1987

____,____,____, *For the Love of Immigrants: The Migration Writings and Letters of Bishop John Baptist Scalabrini*, New York, The Center for Migration Studies, 2000

Simon, John, *Public Health Reports*, London, Sanitary Institute of Great Britain, 1887

Smith, Sidney, *The Settler's New Home or Whether to Go or Whither*, London, John Kendrick, 1850

Smith, W, *An Emigrant's Narrative, or A Voice from the Steerage*, New York, William Smith, 1850

Speer, W, *The Oldest and the Newest Empire: China and the United States*, Hartford, Connecticut, S S Scranton, 1870

Stackelberg, Roderick, and Winkle, Sally A (ed), *The Nazi Germany*

Sourcebook: An Anthology of Texts, London, Routledge, 2002

Staten Island Executive Committee, *Facts and Documents bearing upon the Legal and Moral Questions connected with the Recent Destruction of the Quarantine Buildings on Staten Island*, New York, W C Bryant, 1858

Steiner, Edward A, *On the Trail of the Immigrant*, New York, Revell, 1906

Stevenson, Robert Louis, *The Amateur Emigrant*, New York, Scribner, 1902

Sternberg, Hans J, and Shelledy, James E, *We were Merchants: the Sternberg Family and the Story of Goudchaux's and Maison Blanche Department Stores*, Baton Rouge, Louisiana State University Press, 2009

Stockwell, G S, *The Republic of Liberia: its Geography, Climate, Soil and Productions, With a History of its Early Settlement*, New York, A S Barnes, 1868

Stratton, Thomas, 'Medical Remarks on Emigrant Ships to North America', *Edinburgh Medical and Surgical Journal*, 73 (1849), 33–49

Swinton, Captain and Mrs, *Journal of a Voyage with Coolie Emigrants from Calcutta to Trinidad*, London, A W Bennett, 1859

Thackeray, William Makepeace, *The Book of Snobs and Sketches and Travels in London*, London, Smith, Elder, 1869

Trollope, Anthony, *The Way We Live Now*, Ware, Wordsworth Editions, 1995

United States House of Representatives, *Testimony taken by the Select Committee of the House of Representatives to Inquire into the Alleged Violation of the Laws Prohibiting the Importation of Contract Laborers, Paupers, Convicts and Other Classes*, Washington DC, United States Government Printing Office, 1888

United States Industrial Commission, *Report of the Industrial Commission*, Washington DC, United States Government Printing Office, 1901

United States Immigration Committee, *Reports of the Immigration Committee*, Washington DC, United States Government Printing Office, 1911

United States Public Health Service, *Annual Report of the Surgeon*

General of the Public Health Service of the United States, Washington DC, United States Government Printing Office, 1895

United States Senate, *Report of the Select Committee of the United States Senate on the Sickness and Mortality On Board Emigrant Ships*, Washington, DC, Beverley Tucker Senate Printer, 1854

——, ——, ——, *Hearing Before a Subcommittee of the Committee on Commerce, United States Senate: Sixty-second Congress, Second Session, Pursuant to S Res 283, Directing the Committee on Commerce to Investigate the Causes Leading to the Wreck of the White Star Liner 'Titanic'*, Washington, DC, US Government Printing Office, 1912

Wakefield, Edward Gibbon, *The Art of Colonisation*, London, J W Parker, 1849

Wells, Thomas Spencer, *The Scale of Medicines with which Merchant Vessels are to be Furnished with Observations on the Means of Preserving Health and Increasing the Comforts of Seamen*, London, Orr, 1851

Whyte, Robert, *The Ocean Plague: or a Voyage to Quebec in an Irish Emigrant Vessel*, Boston, Coolidge and Wiley, 1848

Wharton, Thomas I, 'Steerage to Liverpool and Return', *Lippincott's Magazine*, 35 (1885), 127–40

Willcox, John, *Practical Hints to Intending Emigrants for Our Australian Colonies*, Liverpool, Henry Greenwood, 1858

Wilkinson, George Blakiston, *South Australia: Its Advantages and its Resources*, London, John Murray, 1848

Wilson, John, *Memories of a Labour Leader*, London, Fisher Unwin, 1910

Wilson Philip, A P, *A Treatise on Fevers Including the Various Species of Simple and Eruptive Fevers*, London, Thomas and George Underwood, 1820

Secondary Printed Works

Alexander, June Granatir, *Daily Life in Immigrant America 1870–1920*, Westport, Greenwood Press, 2007

Arnold, Rollo, *The Farthest Promised Land: English Villagers, New Zealand Immigrants of the 1870s*, Wellington, Victoria University

Press and Price Milburn, 1981

Baily, Samuel L, *Immigrants in the Lands of Promise: Italians in Buenos Aires and New York City 1870–1914*, Ithaca, Cornell University Press, 1999

Baker, Mark, 'A Migration of Wiltshire Agricultural Labourers to Australia in 1851', *Journal of the Historical Society of South Australia*, 14 (1986), 67–82

Balestracci, Maria Serena, *Arandora Star, Dall' Oblivion alla Memoria*, Palma, Monte Universitá Palma, 2008

Ball, Adrian, and Wright, Diana, *SS Great Britain*, Newton Abbot, David and Charles, 1981

Bateson, Charles, *The Convict Ships, 1787–1868*, Glasgow, Brown, Son and Ferguson, 1959

Bergquist, James M, *Daily Life in Immigrant America 1820–1870*, Westport, Greenwood Press, 2008

Billigmeier, Robert H, and Picard, Fred A, *The Old Land and the New*, St Paul, University of Minneapolis Press, 1965

Broeze, Frank, 'Private Enterprise and the Peopling of Australasia, 1831–50', *Economic History Review*, 25 (1982), 235–53

Brown, Kevin, *Poxed and Scurvied: The Story of Sickness and Health at Sea*, Barnsley, Seaforth, 2011

Bumstead, J M, *People's Clearance*, Edinburgh, Edinburgh University Press, 1982

Butler, Daniel Allen, *Unsinkable: the Full Story of RMS Titanic*, Mechanicsburg, Pennsylvania, Stackpole Books, 1998

Cannato, Vincent J, *American Passage: The Story of Ellis Island*, New York, Harper Collins, 2009

Chartré, Christine, *La Désinfection dans le Système Quarantenaire Maritime de Grosse-Île 1832–1937*, Quebec, Parks Canada, 1995

Crumpson, I M, 'A Survey of Indian Immigration to British Tropical Colonies to 1910', *Population Studies* 10 (1956), 158–65

Davenport-Hines, Richard, *Titanic Lives, Migrants and Millionaires, Conmen and Crew*, London, Harper Press, 2012

Deakes, Christopher, and Stanley, Tom, *A Century of Sea Travel: Personal Accounts from the Steamship Era*, Barnsley, Seaforth, 2010

Drechsel, Edwin, *Norddeutscher Lloyd Bremen, 1857–1970*,

Vancouver, Cordillera, 1994

Dubrovi, Ervin, *Merika, Iseijavanje ¡z srednje Europe u Ameriku 1880–1914, Emigration from Central Europe to America 1880–1914*, Rijeke, Muzei Grada, 2008

Eaton, John P, and Haas, Charles A, *Titanic: Triumph and Tragedy*, New York, Norton, 1994

Evans, Richard J, *Death in Hamburg: Society and Politics in the Cholera Years 1830–1910*, Oxford, Clarendon Press, 1987

Feys, Torsten, *Maritime Transport and Migration: the Connections between Maritime and Migration Networks*, St Johns, International Maritime Economic History Association, 2007

Fogg, Nicholas, *The Voyages of the Great Britain: Life at Sea in the World's First Liner*, London, Chatham Publishing, 2004

Ford, E, *The Life and Work of William Redfern*, Sydney, Australian Medical Publishing Company, 1953

Fox, Stephen, *The Ocean Railway: Isambard Kingdom Brunel, Samuel Cunard and the Revolutionary World of the Great Atlantic Steamships*, London, Harper Perennial, 2004

Frazer, W M, *History of English Public Health 1834–1939*, London, Bailliere, Tindall and Cox, 1950

Frey, B S, Savage, D A, and Torgler, B, 'Interaction of Natural Survival Instincts and Internalized Social Norms: Exploring the Titanic and Lusitania Disasters', *Proceedings of the National Academy of Sciences of the United States of America* (2010), 1091–6490

Geller, Judith B, *Titanic: Women and Children First*, Sparkford, Patrick Stephens, 1998

Gillman, P and L, *Collar the Lot!*, London, Quartet, 1980

Groppe, Hans Hermann, and Wöst, Ursula, *Via Hamburg to the World: From the Emigrants Halls to BallinStadt,* Hamburg, Ellert and Richter, 2007

Haines, Robin, *Life and Death in the Age of Sail: The Passage to Australia*, London, National Maritime Museum, 2006

——, ——, Shlomowitz, Ralph, and Brennan, L, 'Maritime Mortality Revisited', *International Journal of Maritime History*, 8 (1996), 113–24

Hall, Wayne, 'Social Class and Survival on the SS *Titanic*', *Social*

Science and Medicine, 22/6 (1986), 687–90

Hammerton, A James, *Emigrant Gentlewomen: Genteel Poverty and Female Emigration*, London, Rowman and Littlefield, 1979

Handlin, Oscar, *The Uprooted: The Epic Story of the Great Migrations that made the American People*, Philadelphia, University of Pennsylvania Press, 2002

Harper, M, and Constantine, S, *Migration and Empire*, Oxford, Oxford University Press, 2010

Harris, Jose, *Unemployment and Politics: A Study in English Social Policy 1886–1914*, Oxford, Oxford University Press, 1972

Harrison, Mark, *Disease and the Modern World, 1500 to the Present Day*, Cambridge, Polity Press, 2004

Hastings, David, *Over the Mountains of the Sea: Life on the Migrant Ships 1870–1885*, Auckland, Auckland University Press, 2006

Higham, John, *Strangers in the Land: Patterns of American Nativism 1860–1925*, New Brunswick, Rutgers University Press, 1988

Hitchman, J, *They Carried the Sword: The Barnardo Story*, London, Victor Gollancz, 1966

Hoerder, Dirk, 'The Traffic of Emigration via Bremen/Bremerhaven: Merchants' Interests, Protective Legislation and Migrants' Experiences', *Journal of American Ethnic History*, 13 (1993), 68–81

Jensen, J, 'Before the Surgeon General: Marine Hospitals in Mid-Nineteenth Century America', *Public Health Reports*, 112 (1997), 525–7

Johnson, W R, 'Acquiring Emigrants: The Information Chain in Wales 1860–70s', *Proceedings of the University of Queensland History Research Group* (1992), 6–7

Johnston, H J M, *British Emigration Policy 1815–1830*, Oxford, Clarendon Press, 1972

Jones, Maldwyn A, *Destination America*, New York, Holt, Rinehart and Winston, 1976

—, ——, *American Immigration*, Chicago, University of Chicago Press, 1992

Jupp, James, *Immigration*, Oxford, Oxford University Press, 1998

Kent, Neil, *Trieste: Adriatic Emporium and the Gateway to the Heart of Europe*, London, C Hurst, 2011

Kershaw, Roger, and Sacks, Janet, *New Lives for Old: The Story of Britain's Child Emigrants*, Kew, The National Archives, 2008

Kinealy, Christine, *This Great Calamity: The Irish Famine 1845–52*, Dublin, Gill and McMillan, 1994

Knauf, Diethelm, and Moreno, Barry (ed), *Leaving Home: Migration Yesterday and Today*, Bremen, Temmen, 2010

Kraut, Alan M, *Silent Travellers: Germs, Genes and the Immigrant Menace*, New York, Basic Books, 1994

Lawson, Jack, *Peter Lee*, London, Hodder and Stoughton, 1936.

Lee, Erika, and Yung, Judy, *Angel Island: Immigrant Gateway to America*, Oxford, Oxford University Press, 2010

Lloyd, Christopher, and Coulter, Jack L S, *Medicine and the Navy*, vol 4, Edinburgh and London, E and S Livingstone, 1963

MacLean, Francis Sydney, *Challenge for Health: A History of Public Health in New Zealand*, Wellington, Owen, 1964

McNeil, D R, 'Medical Care Aboard Australian-bound Convict Ships 1786–1840', *Bulletin of Medical History*, 26 (1952), 117–40

McNeill, Mary, *Vere Foster 1819–1900: An Irish Benefactor*, Birmingham, Alabama, University of Alabama Press, 1971

Markel, Howard, 'The Eyes have It: Trachoma, the Perception of Disease, the United States Public Health Service and the American Jewish Immigration Experience, 1897–1924', *Bulletin of Medical History*, 74 (2000), 525–60

Martin, Susan F, *A Nation of Immigrants*, Cambridge, Cambridge University Press, 2011

Meagher, Arnold J, *The Coolie Trade: The Traffic in Chinese Laborers to Latin America 1847–1874*, npl, Xlibris, 2008

Mellinato, Giulio, *Cosulich Dinastia Adriatica*, Milan, Silvana, 2008

Mitchell, C A, 'Events leading up to and the Establishment of Grosse Île Quarantine Station', *Medical Services Journal Canada*, 23/11 (1967), 1436

Motta, Titti, and Dentoni, Anna (ed), *L'America: Da Genova a Ellis Island, il Viaggio per Mare negli Anni dell' Emigrazione Italiani 1892–1914*, Genoa, Sagep Editori, 2008

Nicosia, Alessandro, and Prencipe, Lorenzo (ed), *Museo Nazionale Emigrazione Italiana*, Rome, Gangemi Editori, 2009

Nicosia, Francis R, and Scrase, David (ed), *Jewish Life in Nazi*

Germany: Dilemmas and Responses, New York, Berghan Books, 2010

Northrup, David, Indentured Labour in the Age of Imperialism, 1834–1922, Cambridge, Cambridge University Press, 1995

Parascandola, John, 'Doctors at the Gate: PHS at Ellis Island', Public Health Reports, 113 (1998), 83–4

Parris, Leslie (ed), The Pre-Raphaelites, London, Tate Gallery, 1984

Pelosi, Paulette L, and Evans, David (ed), Arandora Star Fund in Wales booklet, Llanelli, Arandora Star Fund, 2010

Rediker, Marcus, The Slave Ship: A Human History, New York, Viking, 2007

Richards, E, Britannia's Children. London, Continuum International Publishing Group, 2004

Rössler, Horst, 'The Time Has Come, We are Going to America', in D Knauf and B Moreno (ed), Leaving Home: Migration Yesterday and Today (2010), 89–103

Sherrington, Geoffrey, 'A Better Class of Boy: The Big Brother Movement, Youth Migration and Citizenship of Empire', Australian Historical Studies, 120 (2002), 267–85

Staniforth, Mark, 'Diet, Disease and Death at Sea on the Voyage to Australia 1837–1839', International Journal of Maritime History, 8/2 (1996), 119–56

Thomas, Gordon, and Morgan-Witts, Max, Voyage of the Damned, London, JR Books, 2009

Thomas, W I, and Znaniecki, F, Il Contadino Polacco in Europa e in America, Milan, Edizioni di Communitá, 1968

Tinker, Hugh, A New System of Slavery, London, Hansib, 1974

Vecoli, R J (ed), Italian Immigrants in Rural and Small Town America, Essays from the Fourteenth Annual Conference of the American Italian Historical Association, New York, The American Italian Historical Association, 1987

Walker, Mack, Germany and the Emigration, 1816–1885, Cambridge, Massachusetts, Harvard University Press, 1964

Wätjen, Herman, Aus der Frühzeit des Nordatlantikverkehrs: Studien zur Geschichte der deutschen Schiffahrt und deutschen Auswanderung nach den Vereinigten Staaten bis zum Ende des amerikanischen Bürgerkrieks, Leipzig, Felix Meiner, 1932

Wischnitzer, Mark, *To Dwell in Safety: The Story of Jewish Migration Since 1800*, Philadelphia, Jewish Publication Society of America, 1948

Zucchi, J, 'Immigrant Friulani in North America', in *Italian Immigrants in Rural and Small Town America, Essays from the Fourteenth Annual Conference of the American Italian Historical Association*, ed R J Vecoli (1987), 62–71

Index